FOOTBALL

Also by CHUCK KLOSTERMAN

Fiction

Downtown Owl

The Visible Man

Raised in Captivity: Fictional Nonfiction

Nonfiction

Fargo Rock City: A Heavy Metal Odyssey in Rural Nörth Daköta

Sex, Drugs, and Cocoa Puffs: A Low Culture Manifesto

Killing Yourself to Live: 85% of a True Story

Chuck Klosterman IV: A Decade of Curious People and Dangerous Ideas

Eating the Dinosaur

I Wear the Black Hat: Grappling with Villains (Real and Imagined)

But What if We're Wrong?: Thinking About the Present As If It Were the Past

Chuck Klosterman X: A Highly Specific, Defiantly Incomplete History of the Early 21st Century

The Nineties: A Book

FOOTBALL

CHUCK KLOSTERMAN

PENGUIN PRESS | NEW YORK | 2026

PENGUIN PRESS
An imprint of Penguin Random House LLC
1745 Broadway, New York, NY 10019
penguinrandomhouse.com

Copyright © 2026 by Charles Klosterman

Penguin Random House values and supports copyright. Copyright fuels creativity, encourages diverse voices, promotes free speech, and creates a vibrant culture. Thank you for buying an authorized edition of this book and for complying with copyright laws by not reproducing, scanning, or distributing any part of it in any form without permission. You are supporting writers and allowing Penguin Random House to continue to publish books for every reader. Please note that no part of this book may be used or reproduced in any manner for the purpose of training artificial intelligence technologies or systems.

PP colophon is a registered trademark of Penguin Random House LLC.

Designed by Amanda Dewey

ISBN 9780593490648 (hardcover)
ISBN 9780593490655 (ebook)

Printed in the United States of America
1st Printing

The authorized representative in the EU for product safety and compliance is Penguin Random House Ireland, Morrison Chambers, 32 Nassau Street, Dublin D02 YH68, Ireland, https://eu-contact.penguin.ie.

CONTENTS

◀ ▶

Introduction 1

1. It's Not Like That 13
2. Evidence of Meaning 41
3. My Own Prison 51
4. The Semantics of GOAT Herding 91
5. Allegory of the Cave, from the Perspective of the Shadows 127
6. This Is Still Your Father's Oldsmobile 157
7. Drinking Hot Coffee Through a Straw 175
8. The Cottage Life 205
9. The Question 223
10. Nuclear Football 243
11. A Rose by Any Other Name Would Not Impact the Rose Bowl 259

Acknowledgments 275

Index 279

FOOTBALL

T HIS IS A BOOK ABOUT FOOTBALL, WRITTEN FOR PEOPLE WHO don't exist.

I concede that this is not the savviest business decision I've ever made. It's also a bit misleading, as I'm obviously hoping to *sell* this book to people who are very much alive, including (I can only assume) you. Nonexistence is not a prerequisite to enjoying this book. But I must be honest: Living people are not my target market. My target market is the unborn, closely followed by the recently born, closely followed by a handful of present-day adults who likely have no interest in what I'm writing about.

This promotional strategy is not without drawbacks.

Despite my best intentions, I suspect this book will be easier to understand if the reader is currently alive. Consuming these words today will be less complicated than trying to parse them in some unknown tomorrow, and citizens of the future may eventually view this work as proof that citizens of the past were delusional. It's also possible those future citizens will classify reading as a form of witchcraft. These are risks I accept, particularly since I'll be dead before any of this becomes a problem.

Allow me to explain.

Right now—today—football is so ingrained in American society that it's hard to visualize an America without it. In the same way imagining the end of the world is easier than imagining the end of capitalism, it's easier to envision a dystopia where football is omnipresent than a utopia where autumn weekends are filled with nothing except sweaters and pumpkins. Some of this is due to sheer ubiquity: Of the hundred most watched U.S. television telecasts in 2023, ninety-three involved NFL football, and three of the remaining seven were college games. In 2024, the overall number dipped to seventy-six, but only because it was an election year (though the Super Bowl still outpaced the election night results). Viewership during the second quarter of the 2025 Super Bowl peaked at 137.7 million, another statistical record. Yet popularity is only half of the equation. The language and symbolism of American football have infiltrated every dimension of American life, an immersion amplified by the fact that North America is the only continent where the game is played with real seriousness. Football is the clearest projection of how people of the United States think and of what those people value, even (and perhaps especially) when football is something they actively dislike. The role it plays in the shaping of our contemporary reality is both outsized and underrated. And this is going to pose a problem in the future, because football is doomed, and all those people who do not yet exist are going to misunderstand why it once mattered as much as it did.

We are incessantly told that history is written by the victors. That axiom is true about wars but rarely about culture. Cultural history tends to be written by those who see victories as regrettable and unjust, particularly when the victory is otherwise undeniable. This impending reversal

INTRODUCTION

bodes poorly for the future memory of football. As a social force, it has succeeded on the highest possible level, far beyond what anyone could have projected in the 1970s, a decade when football was merely the country's favorite sport. It has sociologically "won" with a dominance that defies logic, expanding its sovereignty throughout an era when the rest of the monoculture was burned to the ground. It thrives in the face of constant criticism, immune to all ideological progressions that emphatically stand against it. It appears that football is indestructible, and I wish that it were.

But it is not.

The world is changing in many ways, some of which are good, some of which are bad, and all of which undermine what football was, is, and always must be. Its hyperpopularity in the present tense won't matter, because past performance is no guarantee of future returns. The game will never *completely* disappear, in the same way you can still hear jazz on NPR and you can still smoke Lucky Strikes inside a casino. It is, however, destined to recede from the epicenter of American life, for disconnected reasons that will all coalesce at the same time (more on this later). Its decay will be gradual for twenty or thirty or forty years, and then it will be sudden and catastrophic. And when that calamity occurs, there'll be an urge to explain why this dead sport once controlled the cultural landscape, explicated by people who barely experienced what it actually was. As a result, all of their analysis will focus on the presumed issues that caused its demise, inevitably framing football as an exploitative blood sport that appealed to the base desires of a populace craving distraction. Football will be described in the same way we currently recall Roman gladiators, an enforced memory that's mostly wrong. Those hoping to contradict that narrative will make arguments that are even worse, glorifying the sport's stupidest features and inadvertently vindicating the same downfall they

FOOTBALL

bemoan. In both cases, it will be well-intentioned people trying to explain something that can't be understood in retrospect.

This book is for those people.

▶

The cultural value of football is something I've consciously contemplated for twenty years and unconsciously pondered for at least forty. My final conclusion was not a landslide: If forced to convert my analysis into math, I'd place the social upside of football at 53 percent and the downside at 47 percent, with a 2 percent margin of error. But that ratio is still a net positive. I believe football is, on balance, a justifiable and enriching human pursuit, more good than bad. Now, for the sake of transparency, I must admit I'd continue watching football even if it did not feel this way, since I don't think things need to be confirmed as socially positive in order to be loved or appreciated. But if I did not believe this, I would not write this book.

Arguments for and against football are not rare, though they're almost always duplicates of old arguments. The claims traditionally used to disparage the sport are (often) moral and (sometimes) rational, so those claims must be confronted and considered. The claims traditionally used in support of the game are (often) silly and (sometimes) disconnected from the real reasons football has merit, so those can be ignored. As such, here is a short list of things this book will *not* be about:

This will not be a book about how football builds character. Because I don't think it necessarily does. I think it certainly can, but it's not intrinsic to the experience and could just as easily be achieved through other means. O. J. Simpson won the Heisman Trophy and was the finest running back of the 1970s, but I wouldn't classify him as a high-character guy.

INTRODUCTION

This will not be a book about toughness and masculinity. There is, undeniably, a relationship between football and those two qualities. That relationship is profound, and it's a central draw for much of its fan base, including myself. But modern people increasingly classify these qualities as toxic and regressive, and any attempt to lionize such virtues would have the opposite effect. Take, for example, the long-standing legend about Ronnie Lott's pinkie finger. In 1985, Lott was playing safety for the San Francisco 49ers and smashed his pinkie during the last game of the regular season. The popular myth is that Lott allowed a 49er trainer to amputate the tip of his finger on the sideline so that he could reenter the game, an anecdote illustrating Lott's unimaginable level of toughness and the masochistic romance of full-tilt football. Traditional sports fans love this story. But of course, nontraditional sports fans (and pretty much all regular people) consider it nauseating and vainglorious, particularly since it didn't even happen the way most people believe. Lott did smash his pinkie, and he did agree to its amputation, but not on the sideline and not during the game. He was given a choice of either surgically inserting a pin in the finger (which would have required him to miss the start of the following season) or having a surgeon lop off the tip (allowing him to skip the rehab process and play immediately). He chose the latter option, a decision he now regrets.

This will not be a book about the pleasure of escapism. It's about the opposite.

This will not be a book about fandom, tribalism, and community. I view these aspects as negative and perverse. To me, those are all arguments *against* football.

This will not be a "love letter to the game." Because that shit is for babies. I love football, but I don't want to take it to prom. I don't care how it feels about *me*. I am not Eric Clapton, football is not George Harrison's wife, and this is not "Layla."

This will not be one of those books that's about something other than the subject it purports to be about. We are all familiar with this technique: Someone writes an essay about staring through a pane glass window on a rainy afternoon, but it's really an essay about homelessness. Someone writes a poem about chopping wood, but it's really a poem about intellectual intimacy. Someone writes a book about a tiger on a canoe, but the tiger is actually God and the canoe is the illusion of human memory. There's almost an inherent expectation that this is how good writing is supposed to operate, and that nothing can be important unless it signifies something larger and more abstract. I'm not criticizing this technique, because it has been the basis for much of my career. But this book will not be like that, unless I do it wrong. *This is a book about football.* There will be pages and pages of content where football won't be mentioned at all, and it will sometimes seem like football is just an excuse to write about whatever random issue I happen to be contemplating on the morning I happen to be typing. In the end, you may conclude that the book you just read was not really about football at all, and that this disclaimer was a form of misdirection, pushed by a narrator trying too hard to be unreliable. And you know, you might be right. Your outside perception might be sharper than my own understanding of my objectives. I often fear no one misunderstands me as much as I misunderstand myself. But that's life. That's how it goes. All I can tell you is my premeditated intention, and my intention is this: to write about football, even when I am not.

I'm not playing to win. I'm playing not to lose. I'm playing a prevent defense, preventing me from winning.

INTRODUCTION

When I was twenty-five, I was certain all criticism was nothing more than veiled autobiography, and I idiotically imagined I was the first person to ever have that insight. I'm now less certain about this, though not to the point where I don't believe it at all. But even if I did, my opposition wouldn't matter: "Veiled autobiography" has become the default way to view any opinion about any topic whatsoever. In a postmodern environment, no idea matters as much as the biographical identity of the person who expresses it. George Will once wrote an excellent book about baseball, but it temporarily hurt the perception of the game; it made it seem like the only people who still cared about baseball wore bow ties and wanted to eliminate the minimum wage. The same thing will happen here. Any statement I make about football will be scrutinized through the lens of my own experience with football, requiring me to explain what that experience was.

This puts me in a terrible position.

Whatever information I provide about my participatory relationship to football will unintentionally warp my credibility; every positive (or negative) point I make about the sport will seem tainted to any reader predisposed to disagreement. If I pretend I was once an elite football player, it will prompt an intelligent person to suspect I'm trying to glorify the significance of my past. If I claim I was an average player who excelled in spite of my limitations, it will suggest this is an exercise in nostalgia and an attempt to rewrite my own history. If I'm too self-deprecating, it will come across as reverse bragging (nothing is faker than fake modesty). If I insist I was terrible or never played at all, the whole endeavor will seem awkward and pathetic, almost as if I were trying to compensate for failures I should have long forgotten. If I sprinkle in too many references to my

FOOTBALL

own personal experience, the book becomes a memoir; if I don't reference my experience at all, an assumed experience will be projected upon me, based on whatever the reader wants to believe.

There is no way to do this without seeming like some variety of sad jackass. Let's just get it over with. One dispassionate paragraph will suffice:

The first football game I can remember was Super Bowl XII in 1978, though my main memory is that my dad ate his dinner on a TV tray in the living room (a rarity in our household). In third grade, I was obsessed with collecting football cards, then retailing for twenty-five cents a pack; I sorted them by team, secured them with rubber bands, and sequenced the rosters in empty Velveeta cheese boxes. Around the same time, I joined something called the NFL SuperPro Club, a league-sponsored mail-order marketing campaign that dramatically increased my knowledge of the sport's history while also providing many adhesive stickers and a subpar Frisbee. We played tackle football at recess in fourth and fifth grade, usually four on four and always with a Nerf ball (we didn't switch to leather until grade six). Organized practices started in junior high. There were twenty-three kids in my class and only five hundred people in the entire town, so my school played in the nine-man*

---

*Nine-man is a version of football primarily played by midwestern high schools with small enrollments. On offense, the two players removed are the offensive tackles, with tight ends inserted in their place. This creates a standard five-man line (two TEs, two guards, and a center), backed by a quarterback, two running backs, and a flanker or wingback. In coaching parlance, this grouping is classified as "22 personnel." Over the past two decades, more teams have started to use two wideouts and only one RB ("12 personnel") from a shotgun set. A nine-man defense can be configured in multiple ways, but the standard orientation is a 3-4 alignment without any cornerbacks (the strong safety lines up over the flanker and the free safety patrols midfield). A 4-2-3 configuration also works well. The nine-man game is strategically identical to the conventional eleven-man variety, although more wide open and high scoring (since there are still five eligible receivers but more space with which to operate). The main difference is that the truncated line of scrimmage makes placekicking more difficult, since the distance for a kick blocker coming off the edge is shorter. Field goal attempts are rare and most teams attempt a two-point conversion instead of kicking a PAT. In states outside the upper Midwest, small-town schools tend to play eight-man (or even six-man) football, which generally requires a slightly smaller field.

INTRODUCTION

division. Practically every boy in school was expected to participate, and anyone halfway decent played both ways. I wasn't as good as I'd always anticipated. I quit the team in eighth grade in protest over the head coach's abusive training methods, a decision I knew was correct but that I still feel deep shame about. I rejoined the team as a freshman and tried to play quarterback. I lacked poise and confidence, though not as much as my arm lacked velocity. I didn't possess the cocksure demeanor of a quarterback. My teammates didn't trust or respect me. I wasn't clutch. My one talent was running the veer option, but we weren't really an option team, minimizing the impact of my lone utility. On the upside, I was incredible at learning the playbook and memorizing the audible system, exceedingly adept at explaining all the plays I couldn't necessarily execute. When I was a sophomore, my school went 12-0 and won the state championship. I didn't play one meaningful down that entire season. As a junior, I was the fourth-string quarterback on a thirty-man roster, though I did cover kickoffs and started a few games on defense as an undersized edge rusher. I liked to hit and I practiced hard, though not as hard as I should have. The summer before my senior year, I finally accepted I would never be a quarterback and transitioned to receiver. It was the right move. I also played outside linebacker and had three sacks in the season opener, inducing me to wonder if I had a shot at breaking the school record (I did not, as it turns out). I became the team's punter out of necessity and wasn't terrible, averaging 42 yards a kick (I'd spent the previous summer practicing by punting over a barn). I was named to the All-Conference team, largely due to the arcane system used by the league's governing body; the school that won the conference title was awarded five automatic roster spots, and we won the conference. So I was the fifth-best player on a successful nine-man team. If I'd grown up in a bigger town or attended a larger school, I might not have played football at all, unless the team was based in Amish country and they needed someone to punt over barns. I should also note that I'm not (to the best of my knowledge) any relation to the longtime NFL and USFL executive Don Klosterman, though many people asked me about this when he died.

FOOTBALL

These achievements do not make me uniquely qualified to write about football, nor do they disqualify me. In fact, I'd argue the amount I've played football is exactly the right amount to make it completely beside the point.

Something you often see in postgame press conferences is a coach or player recoiling at a question from a journalist and dismissing the query by informing the reporter he or she "never played the game." This is a worthless retort, since extending that sentiment to its rational conclusion would mean journalists could only interview other journalists. It is, however, an understandable reaction. Having worked in media for three decades, I'm psychologically invested in journalism, and my nonthinking inclination is to assume that what I read in a newspaper or a magazine is relatively reliable. My life outside the media tells me this assumption is irrational and incorrect. Anytime I've read an article about a subject I legitimately understand, the article has been at least partially wrong, a response that's become increasingly pervasive. Every national story about a localized conflict will seem erroneous to the local population it depicts; any entry-level exposition about a technical problem will seem imprecise to genuine tacticians. It's easy to understand why a professional athlete playing a physical, byzantine sport would be nonplussed by some Ivy League bozo asking a question that implies the underinformed interrogator already knows the answer. Such annoyance is magnified by the insinuation that a journalist's lack of nontheoretical experience is somehow a professional advantage (the title of Howard Cosell's 1985 autobiography was *I Never Played the Game*, expressed as a badge of honor). Such attitudes have swelled with the growth of analytics. Of course, the flip side to this is that most football analysis seen on television is performed by ex-players and ex-coaches, the majority of whom are either excessively generous to their still-employed peers or bombastically critical of whoever happens to warrant condemnation on the day they need to look into the

INTRODUCTION

camera. There's not much middle ground: Football is difficult to understand if you haven't played and difficult to explain if you have. Yet in this one highly specific scenario, I feel confident about my reliability. Yes, I have played football . . . but not really. For multiple years, I wore a helmet and got screamed at for missed assignments and underwent the weekly intensity of a staged reproduction of warfare—but always at the lowest possible level, and without any risk of surrendering my identity. I have an elementary understanding of how football works in a practical capacity, allowing me to assess and appreciate how much of the game I don't understand at all. I'm not a dilettante, though closer to a dilettante than an expert. Most critically, my individual history with the game has generated an unusual psychological paradox: I believe football is positive for society, despite it having a negative effect on me. I sometimes suspect I'd be better off if I had never played football and didn't love it. It's a cognitive dissonance that plays to my advantage. My experience is not a universal experience; my involvement shaped my understanding but not my conclusions. I'm not claiming football is good for everyone because it was good for me, nor is this some attempt at justifying "my truth." This is an expository obituary, published before the subject has died, delivered by someone who wants to explain why the victim mattered so much to so many, despite so much evidence to the contrary.

1.
It's Not Like That

FOOTBALL IS AN ALMOST IMPOSSIBLE GAME TO PLAY. THIS IS not because it requires a unique set of physical skills or mental requirements, nor is it due to any social or political barriers. It's because the game itself is so complicated and overorganized that there's no reasonable way to replicate it recreationally. Any version of football that isn't (in some capacity) "official" is not football. This would seem, on the surface, to work to the sport's detriment: The game is undemocratic. But this is actually a strength, and a big part of what makes it different from so many other seemingly similar pursuits. Football is exclusionary, and that makes it special.

When we think about sports in the abstract, the ease of participation plays a significant factor in how we view the purity of that experience. Soccer is the most popular sport in the world, largely because no team game is easier to play or understand. All that's required is a kickable object and two roughly equal teams to kick that object around. Basketball can be even more spartan—the crux of the game can be pursued and perfected by

FOOTBALL

a single individual playing alone.* A pickup game among ten serious hoopers can feel the same as a coordinated league championship, and half-court 3-on-3 encompasses all the core qualities of the standard full-court variety (screening away from the ball, help-side defense, the give-and-go). Baseball needs eighteen players and a geometrically specialized playing surface, which would normally present an obstruction to amateur competition—except we've already established an ancillary sport as a surrogate: Softball is not the same as baseball, but it's more similar than different, and nine million Americans play it every summer. Hockey requires ice and expensive equipment, but the sport's free-flowing nature makes low-impact amateur versions surprisingly plausible (there are at least three adult hockey leagues in Portland, a midsize market with no professional franchise). Golf can be played by anyone who can afford it. Tennis thrives as a leisure activity, and when its physical demands become too taxing, the participant can transition to pickleball (or even ping-pong). You want to play volleyball? Go to a public beach. You miss your bygone days as a high school wrestler? Have six drinks in a bar and insult a stranger who's had nine. A former prep track star can always go for a run; a former swimming sensation can always find a pool; any novice bowler can reproduce the same perfection as a PBA legend, at least for one frame. Our relationship with most spectator sports is tied to a nebulous understanding of how the sport *feels*. We can replicate the game we see on TV.

But football is not like that.

Tackle football is played by one million people at the high school level, eighty thousand people at the college level, and twenty-seven hundred people at the pro level. That's it. That's the total North American adult football population, equating to .002 percent of the continent as a whole. I

---

*The broadcaster Dick Vitale built an inspirational speech around this quality, brilliantly and melodramatically known as "A boy, a ball, and a dream."

IT'S NOT LIKE THAT

mean—sure: You can always play touch football in the backyard, like the Kennedys on the White House lawn or the cast of *Friends* on Thanksgiving. And yes, 5-on-5 flag football is now an Olympic event, and there's a handful of semipro football leagues scattered across various municipalities.* But tackle football does not work as a hobby. It has no wide-scale participatory component as a recreational activity, and unofficial reconstructions have no meaningful relationship to the sport we collectively understand. Legitimate contact football requires large rosters, thousands of dollars of equipment, and multiple weeks of practice and repetition. It's possible to play without coaches, but not without referees. This is not a situation where participants can police themselves. Football is so multifaceted that it's difficult to visualize how a spontaneous version of the game would even be attempted. Imagine if you and ten of your friends were all given helmets and shoulder pads, and a sizable grassy field was procured as the venue. Let's also imagine seven officials were available for the enforcement of rules, and eleven other people were randomly enlisted to serve as your opponent. How many minutes would it take to figure out what position every person was supposed to fill? How many hours would be needed to work out even twenty-five basic plays? After the first two minutes of full-speed collisions, how many of your friends would need immediate medical attention? It would be easier to stage an amateur production of *Death of a Salesman* than an amateur version of a Raiders-Broncos game. Even if you're not trying to produce an actual competitive game—even if you're just trying to accurately mimic the various actions football players do—the outcome will never feel like football. And this is because every detail of football is divorced from non-football life, in a way that other sports are not.

---

*It's telling that the only newsworthy semipro football player of the past twenty-five years was a man named Odin Lloyd, a member of the Boston Bandits who was murdered by New England Patriot Aaron Hernandez in 2013.

FOOTBALL

If I go to an open gymnasium with a basketball under my arm and shoot jump shots from the top of the key, I am (obviously) not having the same experience as Steph Curry when he takes an open jumper against the Lakers. Those are two different experiences. They are not, however, *unspeakably* different. The way I shoot a basketball when I'm by myself is the same way I'd want to shoot it if I were playing in a serious game, and the way Curry releases his jumper against the Lakers has been modeled on the thousands of hours he's spent shooting baskets in a gym by himself. The mechanics of what we're doing is the same in both scenarios, despite a massive difference in the rate of success. If a father sidearm-rifles a baseball at his teenage son standing 90 feet away, the father is making the same throw he'd make playing second base for the Mets; if that father and son visit a batting cage and juice the pitching machine to 103, the machine can photocopy a Nolan Ryan fastball. A hack golfer at Rancho Park tries to sink a 10-foot putt in the same way Brooks Koepka tries to sink a 10-footer at Augusta (the pressure is different, but the stroke is identical). Most sports allow for these simulations. Most sports allow a layperson to physically imitate how that sport operates at the highest level, performed with lower stakes. But football makes that impossible. Two shirtless dudes throwing a pigskin around the college quad has almost no connection to playing quarterback or wide receiver. For one thing, it's exceedingly rare to throw a football at an uncovered, nonmoving target; for another, completing a pass in an actual game is the end result of reading a defense and making an instinctive decision in less than three seconds; for still another, both the passer and the catcher need to accomplish those acts while other people try to put them in the hospital. It's possible to increase the realism by having your buddy run a predetermined route and asking a third person to play defense, but it's still not remotely close to the true event. Blocking and tackling can't really be mimicked, and full-speed attempts to do so might result in a lawsuit or an arrest. A VR head-

IT'S NOT LIKE THAT

set can project the visual perspective of a quarterback, but it can't make the user feel like they're wearing pads and it can't generate the visceral sensation of a collapsing pocket. Most critically, the actions of football are based on rehearsal: Almost everything that happens in a football game is the orchestrated extension of trials that have been practiced hundreds (if not thousands) of times, obliterating any possibility for a normal person to connect what they see on television with anything they could attempt or undergo.

This chasm between the game and its audience is so vast that most people obsessed with football have no firsthand perspective on the object of their desire. Logic suggests that should limit the sport's potentiality. And it would, if football was like other sports. But football is not.

▸

A person who loves football on its most basic level can express any litany of subjective reasons explaining that love, and a person who thinks football is boring or immoral can invert those same reasons as proof that it sucks. If narrowly considered as one sport among many sports, its intrinsic value is debatable. But that debate misses the point. The outsized role football plays in U.S. culture is not a product of its rules or its players. What makes football distinctly compelling is that it's a purely mediated experience, even when there is no media involved.

I'm going to reiterate the previous sentence, because it's going to come up a lot over the next few pages: *Football is a purely mediated experience, even when there is no media involved.* What this means is that football's significance derives from how it is watched, how it is considered, and the metaphysical power imbuing its animation. This, quite obviously, was not the original intent. None of those elements were pondered when the first football game was played in 1869. They're not often pondered now, in any

FOOTBALL

conscious manner. Yet this subconscious intoxicant is what separates football from all other sports, and it explains why football matters more to American culture than so many other things we'd like to believe have greater value. The reality of football is understood through the unreality of its media depiction, which is the same way we understand most of modern life.

▶

"What was the greatest football game ever played?"

This question, if posed during friendly conversation inside a tavern or a dive bar or a Buffalo Wild Wings, would likely be answered in a highly personal way. Upon considering the query, everyone sitting around the table would nominate the best football game he or she ever witnessed. My reflexive answer is the 1981 playoff between the Chargers and the Dolphins, a game now nicknamed the Epic in Miami. If I kept talking, I might change my answer to the 1984 Orange Bowl (when Nebraska coach Tom Osborne valiantly and unsuccessfully attempted a late two-point conversion, costing the Huskers the national title to Miami) or the 2006 Rose Bowl (when Vince Young and Texas beat USC 41–38). Maybe I'd mention the 2021 AFC Divisional Playoff as a more recent example (a 42–36 overtime shootout between Patrick Mahomes and Josh Allen). If our dialogue continued unabated, I might start nominating perverse alternatives that focus on the weather or a statistical anomaly or an unrelated event happening in my own life. Such a conversation could last hours, with all involved parties referencing any halfway memorable game they halfway remember. If, however, this conversation was *not* friendly and uninhibited—if it was a trivia contest, or if the discussion was being recorded for a podcast—any well-educated person would give the same answer: the 1958 NFL Championship between the Baltimore Colts and the

IT'S NOT LIKE THAT

New York Giants. This is the only irrefutable answer to the question, "What was the greatest football game ever played?" in part because that specific phrase has become the event's designation. That game happened fourteen years before I was born. I've never watched it in its entirety, and I doubt even 10 percent of those who'd classify this contest as "the greatest game ever played" believe that statement to be true. However, I can't remember any point in my life when I was not aware that this was the greatest game in football history. How I came to know this is unclear, though I do know *why* I came to know this, and why so many other people know the same thing: television.

The 1958 Colts-Giants championship was the first overtime game in NFL history. It's sometimes cited as the first example of a quarterback utilizing a two-minute drill to rapidly move his team downfield (a claim that's almost certainly untrue, though the QB in this case—the Colts' Johnny Unitas—was still regularly classified as the greatest quarterback in history until the end of the 1980s). It was a tight game and a meaningful game and a game involving many noteworthy figures. But the reason we continue to venerate this game (above all others) is barely connected to what happened on the field. It's primarily remembered for the 45 million people who watched it on NBC, a then-colossal ratings number achieved without a single viewer from metro New York (where the game was blacked out).

The 1958 NFL title game is the origin of modern football, not as a sport but as an idea that exists for TV. What happened on the field became imperative because it was simultaneously happening everywhere else, with a capacity for detail its live audience in Yankee Stadium completely missed. It's not as if 45 million people watched this game and realized that football was somehow unlike what they'd previously imagined. What they realized is that nothing—*nothing*—had ever been better designed for TV than this particular sport. It was the sudden comprehension of accidental perfection, spawning a relationship that would transform the parameters of what a sport can mean to a society increasingly controlled by a mediacentric view of everything.

▶

Television defined the last half of the twentieth century, outperforming all other mass media combined. This was already understood by the onset of the 1970s, prompting countless network executives to kill themselves in the hope of creating something impeccably suited for sitting in front of an electromagnetic box and remaining there for as long as possible. This typically entailed thoughtful consideration over the *content* of TV: what a program was about, how it was written, and what personalities were involved. But what's even more critical, and far harder to manufacture, is the *form* of the program: the pacing, the visual construction, and the way the watcher experiences whatever they happen to be watching. How a person thinks about television is a manifestation of its content; how a person feels about television is a manifestation of its form. And there's simply never been a TV product more formally successful than televised football. This was an accident. But it turns out you can't design something on purpose that's superior to the way televised football naturally occurs.

I realize I'm making an aesthetic argument many will not accept, particularly if they start from the position that football games are boring, meaningless, or both. The merits of televised football as a formal spectacle are immaterial to someone who hates the thing being televised, in the same way the harmonic simplicity of Miles Davis is immaterial to someone who hates jazz. Appreciating the TV experience of football requires some casual interest in the game itself. But what makes the TV experience of football so remarkable is how "casual interest" is more than enough to generate an illogically deep level of satisfaction. The way football is broad-

IT'S NOT LIKE THAT

cast manages to obliterate any difference between an informal consumer and a face-painting fanatic. This is due to many factors, the most critical being that football is always, always, *always* better on television than it is in person. The televised experience is so superior to the in-person experience that most people watching a football game live are mentally converting what they're seeing into its TV equivalent, without even trying.

The only sport universally understood to be better when watched in person is hockey. In the same way football is always better on TV, hockey is always better live. With almost every other sport, the difference is debatable. Baseball is sometimes better in person, because it's nice to sit outside in the summer (the weather and the park have more influence than the game). Basketball becomes more compelling if you sit close to the court and less compelling if you're in the rafters, though the prime seats in any NBA arena tend to provide ticket holders with the same viewpoint they'd get from a TV broadcast. Live tennis and live golf offer details that can't be captured on television, but there are rules of decorum and big potential for monotony. Soccer is *exclusively* about atmosphere and identity, so the experience of being in the crowd and the experience of the game itself are only nominally associated, in the same way going to see the Grateful Dead in the late 1980s was only nominally about music. Live boxing and live auto racing deliver palpable electricity with subpar sightlines. In all of these non-football examples, the debate boils down to how effectively the televised depiction of an event can translate its in-person actuality, which is why hockey is an outlier (the ambient feeling of bodies colliding with plexiglass is not digitally transferrable). Televised football is an outlier to an even greater extent, and for a much stranger reason: The TV experience doesn't translate the live experience *at all*, in any way. The game happening in the physical world only exists to facilitate the broadcast version of the game, even if the game is not being televised. Here again, it must be reiterated: *Football is a purely mediated experience, even when there is no media involved*. It's not just that you can see a game better when you watch it on television. Television is the only way you can see it at all.

Football fans attend football games for lots of different reasons. However, one of the expressed reasons can never be "A desire to see what's really happening." If that was someone's true desire, they would stay home and watch it on TV. No one inside a football stadium—including the coaches on the sideline and the players on the field—can see the game with the consistent clarity of a person watching remotely. The announcers have the game happening directly in front of them and still watch the action on TV monitors, in part because they want their commentary to match what the home viewer is seeing but mostly because the camera is the perspective that matters.

And even when there is no camera, our minds insert one.

By now, it's difficult to find any football game that isn't being filmed by someone. When CBS broadcast Super Bowl LVIII in 2024, the network utilized 165 cameras. When Super Bowl I was broadcast in 1967 (on two competing networks at the same time), the total number of cameras was eleven. This is now unthinkable. Show up at a random Pop Warner football game in rural Idaho, and you might find twenty-two different parents recording the action on twenty-two different camera phones. When I played high school football in the 1980s, not even the state championship was broadcast by any local station; today, most regular-season high school games in every state can be streamed live, sometimes with a multicamera professionalism on par with the broadcast of Super Bowl I. A camera-free event has become rarer than the alternative. But the mental phenomenon I'm describing has little to do with how videography has expanded. The mentally inserted "camera" is not a machine. It is a way of seeing. It's a type of forced perspective, invented by cameras and normalized through the omnipresence of television. In other realms of existence, such a phenomenon would be bad, since what I'm describing is a kind of psychologi-

IT'S NOT LIKE THAT

cal fascism. It is, technically, a form of mind control. Yet in this one particular instance, it benefits both the sport and the audience. With football, the psychology of fascism works.

Visualize, for a moment, a capacity crowd at Michigan Stadium, the third-largest sports venue on earth. Imagine the Michigan Wolverines are playing the Ohio State Buckeyes, with 107,601 people in the stands. Those 107,601 people are all seeing the event in a unique way, because every individual seat is in a unique location. All 107,601 sight lines are personal. Throughout the game, the ball moves up and down the field, and—every so often—a play will happen directly in front of a handful of fans coincidentally located in the ideal spot to see the action. Perhaps a woman's seat is in the tenth row of section 15, located in the westerly corner of the south end zone: If an Ohio State receiver runs a fade pattern and catches the ball over his shoulder in front of the southwest pylon, that ticket holder will witness the reception with an unmatched lucidity. No one else will experience that extemporaneous moment like the woman in that particular seat. However, this solitary play is probably the only time when that will be true. There will be 179 other plays throughout the game, none of which will unequivocally cater to the singular view of this specific woman in this specific location. And what will happen during those other 179 plays is a bypassing of consciousness: The woman will see a play from her unique vantage point and automatically reframe what she saw into the way it would appear on television. She will watch the play from where she is sitting, but she will process the play from the standard TV perspective of a wide-angle camera stationed in the press box at midfield. What she sees with her eyes will not be what she sees with her mind.

"But that's not true," you say. "That's not how it is for me." And maybe it's not. There are exceptions to everything. Maybe your mind doesn't work like this. Maybe you've attended three football games a week for twenty years without ever owning a television. Maybe your visual relationship with the world is completely authentic and unchanged by technology. I can't crawl inside your skull and prove you wrong. But this is how it works for most people, including most who insist it does not. The visual imprinting of television is more overpowering than the visual imprinting of life; a TV screen presents an enclosed reality inside the preexisting reality of your house, and that manufactured reality overwrites both your memory and your imagination. Think of the primary setting from an old multi-camera sitcom (Jerry's apartment on *Seinfeld*, the living room on *The Big Bang Theory*, the bar from *Cheers*). The standard shot of the set is ingrained in your memory and can be instantly recalled, but try to imagine physically entering that set through a different door and meandering around, without referencing the original image and triangulating where everything is supposed to be. Think of a real place or a historical event you've only experienced through film (the streets of 1950s San Francisco in *Vertigo*, West Baltimore as depicted on *The Wire*, the invasion of Normandy as seen in *Saving Private Ryan*). How difficult is it to now reimagine these places or events in a manner unlike the fake images you've seen only a few times? If you're still skeptical, try this test: Host a party in your home and prop up your smartphone in an inconspicuous corner. Film twenty minutes of the party while you mingle with various guests. Rewatch that footage once a week for a month. At the end of the month, try to mentally reconstruct interactions from the party that aren't anywhere on the recording. Try to visualize how the party looked, but from a different angle. You may be alarmed to realize your own unrecorded memories are locked into the perspective of wherever you placed your phone.

"But that's not how football on TV works at all," you say in response. "Football is seen from multiple angles that constantly shift. A few paragraphs ago, you noted that CBS used 165 different cameras for the Super Bowl. Football is better on TV, but not for the reason you claim. It's better on television *because* there isn't one static view."

IT'S NOT LIKE THAT

That's a valid response, and it might feel true on a moment-to-moment basis. A controversial play might be replayed from seven different angles in the span of thirty seconds. It can even be argued that the standard camera view of a TV football game is the worst camera angle available. During the college football playoffs, ESPN's family of networks will sometimes show the same game on multiple channels, with one channel broadcasting the whole affair from the Skycam camera. This is a remote camera hovering above and behind the line of scrimmage, replicating the perspective one sees in a video game. Coaches call this the "All-22" view, because all 22 players on the field are simultaneously observable. It's the camera angle coordinators use for film study, and—when it's available—it's the way I prefer to watch football. The Skycam allows the viewer to see how the defense is aligned, to follow pass patterns as they develop, and to (almost) see the game the way it's seen by the quarterback. In terms of absorbing what's transpiring, it's vastly superior to the traditional midfield perspective from the press box. Yet even as I'm watching the Skycam view, I can sense what's happening inside my brain: I'm unconsciously converting what I see into the classic sideline sight line, even though that's an inferior shot. I prefer the Skycam, but I *understand* what I'm seeing through the limited perspective of the most traditional camera angle: a master shot that (a) exclusively fixates on the location of the ball, (b) doesn't include every involved player, and (c) provides no sense of depth or spacing. It's an inadequacy that should be a death blow.

But like I keep saying: Football is different. These are the flaws that make the magic.

▸

In 2010, David Biderman of *The Wall Street Journal* published an article that's still referenced (either directly or glancingly) in just about any ill-fated attempt at explaining why football is tedious. After studying four NFL games, *WSJ* researchers concluded that the average three-hour NFL broadcast involves only about 11 minutes of actual football. Described in this manner, it feels like a damning statistic. Baseball, golf, and cricket all involve a lot of inactivity from their participants, but those are games without clocks (so the tedium is part of the allure). Football is the peculiar example of a sport with a running clock that still runs when nothing is happening, while also pausing and regrouping after every play. The *WSJ* graphic accompanying Biderman's original story noted how the average 60-minute football game involves 67 minutes of dudes just standing around, a troubling ratio for an event intended as entertainment; it would be like a prequel to *The Fast and the Furious* that includes 134 minutes of Vin Diesel waiting in line at the DMV. If football did not already exist and was being invented today, there's no way this amount of idle loitering would be included. The elevator pitch would seem like a joke: "Let's create a complicated, violent game where nothing happens during 94 percent of the telecast, shown from a camera perspective that limits the viewer's ability to see what's happening."

There is no way this should be popular, much less the most popular thing available. So how did this happen, and why does it keep succeeding? Why is football, despite its comically defective construction, the best television product ever produced?

I have a theory.

Now, I must warn you: This is not the kind of theory that required a lab coat. I did not pursue a degree in neuroscience in order to write about Tony Romo. I haven't mapped any orangutan brains or run a rat through a maze. But there's something here that's too weird to be ignored. There's something psychologically mysterious about the way football is presented on television. Everything about it contradicts the normal definition of entertainment, and if you examined any of its individual quirks in isolation, you might conclude it succeeds *in spite* of that specific problem. You might find yourself insisting, "Football is fun to watch despite providing only 11 minutes of action within a three-hour window" or "Football is fun to watch despite the limitations of its optic perspective" or "Football is fun to watch despite the viewer's inability to relate to the sensation of how it feels to play." But when all of these quirks are considered together, as a package, the problems suggest something different. What it suggests is that televised football combines a host of qualities we're conditioned to consider undesirable, even though we instinctively prefer how those qualities inform the experience. In other words, we're wrong about ourselves. What we want from television, and what we *think* we want from television, are not the same.

The idea of a three-hour football broadcast containing only 11 minutes of football is the easiest example. As a math equation, it sounds like a waste of time. Sports are action-based entertainment, so the natural assumption is to want as much action as possible. But this doesn't translate, in sports or anything else. Constantly getting the thing you supposedly want makes you lose interest. It's the same with movies: Ask any fan of action movies what they want from a prospective film, and they will unthinkingly say, "As much action as possible." It seems like the reasonable thing to want. But when this wish is granted—as in the Jason Bourne and John Wick films, and perhaps most relentlessly in 2011's *The Raid* and 2015's *Mad Max: Fury Road*—the result is a well-received film that becomes forgettable and interchangeable. Perpetual intensity has a deadening effect, desensitizing its audience and mirroring the sensation of boredom. *Fury Road* is a 120-minute movie where the main character has only 63 lines of dialogue. It features 2,700 cuts, averaging 22.5 visual edits every minute. It's certainly possible to love this kinetic style, and to love this movie in particular—if you only watch it once. You might be able to love it twice, or perhaps even three times, if you're studying its cinematography. But football happens every week for five months, sometimes for 12 consecutive hours, best appreciated by people who've already invested decades of exposure. Providing only 11 minutes of action within the expanse of three hours is not evidence of a failed concept. As it turns out, *11 minutes of action is the ideal amount.* The intermittent moments of nothingness add to the pleasure. You can hold an entire conversation by talking in between plays without losing focus on the game itself. You can think about what you just saw or what might happen next. You can check your phone or drink a beer or daydream about something completely unrelated. Your mind can relax without detaching from engagement.

I know that seems backward. I know it seems like I'm asserting that people don't have the ability to know what they want, or that I've convinced myself that the way things accidentally worked out is accidentally perfect. Like most people, I'd prefer if the overall running time of the average football game was slightly less, which could be accomplished through the elimination of nonsense (I would shorten halftime, eliminate booth reviews, and outlaw commercial breaks after kickoffs). But generally speaking, this alleged 11-minute problem is not a problem at all. The fact that a three-hour football game involves only 11 minutes of true play is essential and brilliant, particularly in combination with the limitations of the camera view and the lack of firsthand experience most viewers have with the sport they're watching. It's a little like what the epistemological author Nassim Nicholas Taleb refers to as "antifragility"—the rare circumstance where something benefits from a combination of its own problems.

▸

When I write, "Football is the best television product ever produced," I'm telling the truth. I am, however, basing my assertion on a metric some might consider dubious, since it's the same metric one uses when arguing that pizza is the finest food ever invented: Football's televisual preeminence is not a reflection of its apex, but of its nadir. An incredible football game is not necessarily better than an incredible Final Four game, the last inning of a tight World Series, or any other sporting event reaching the height of its potential. A transcendent Super Bowl isn't necessarily better than the finest episodes of *Mad Men* or *Lost* or *Succession* or hundreds of other scripted shows I could catalog without much consideration. When competing aesthetics hit their respective peaks, the margin of difference becomes negligible. Differences become more obvious when competing aesthetics fail. The gap between the best AC/DC album, the best Metallica album, and the best Guns N' Roses album is minuscule, and the case for which one is the best of the three can go in any direction. However, the difference between the best AC/DC song and the worst AC/DC song is relatively minor, which can't be said about the other two groups. Its innate form compensates for any failure of function. The reason football is such an amazing television product derives from this *High Voltage* utility; even a mediocre game is eminently watchable. Part of this is because football can't be played at half speed. There's no coasting. The players always have to try, lest they get broken in half. But that's not the only reason.

In 2012, the NFL started airing football games every Thursday night (there had always been a few Thursday games here and there, but 2012 was when it became an entrenched part of the schedule). Since most teams playing on Thursday have only three days to rest and prepare, it's become common to moan about how *Thursday Night Football* is the most deplorable version of the game, poorly played and needlessly punishing. The worst NFL game of 2023 was a *TNF* game between the 2-7 Chicago Bears and the 1-7 Carolina Panthers (the Bears won 16–13). The worst game of 2022 was a *TNF* overtime matchup between the Broncos and the Colts featuring twelve punts, six fumbles, four interceptions, and no touchdowns. On a

FOOTBALL

Thursday night in 2014, the Arizona Cardinals' backup quarterback Ryan Lindley salted away the Los Angeles Rams by completing 4 of 10 passes for 30 yards. But you know what's strange? All three of these games were absorbing and enjoyable (the Colts-Broncos affair was actually more fun than most of the other games airing that weekend). I wasn't personally invested in any of the six teams, and none of the three games include a singularly entertaining moment. Still, the overall experience was more than merely acceptable. It was full-on satisfying. But why? How can bad teams playing bad football engage people for more than three hours?

The antifragility of the broadcast.

There's a tendency to lump all sports entertainment into the broad category of "sports on television." That's what a cable company does when it tries to upsell a special sports package. But this is wrong. There are actually three categories, unknowingly defined by the experience of the viewer.

The first category comprises free-flowing, high-volume, "hypnotic" sports. These are fast-twitch games like soccer, basketball, hockey, auto racing, and boxing. The action is perpetual, but the moment-to-moment stakes are relatively low. Instances of meaning are either hyperconstant (as in boxing) or maddeningly rare (as in soccer). The announcers contextualize the proceedings as they unfold in real time, usually through enthusiasm or self-evident exposition. The adrenalized intensity of hypnotic sports—when performed at their best—is hard to beat. But when the quality is of a lesser vintage, the games adopt a mesmerizing emptiness, akin to staring at the windshield wipers while driving in the rain. A top-flight NBA playoff game still tends to drag in the middle of the second quarter, even if the teams are shooting well and the tempo is brisk.

The second category of sports comprises halting, low-volume, "cerebral" endeavors. These are slow-twitch games like baseball, golf, tennis, bowling, and cricket. In a cerebral sport, the most stimulating moments emerge when *nothing* is happening. The exhilaration comes from the heightening of drama and the depth of consideration over why certain decisions are being made. Cerebral sports tend to be character-driven sports, where familiarity with the involved personalities is more enriching than any knowledge of their skill set. A golfer is faced with a 330-yard dogleg, so he spends 90 seconds staring at the fairway, pondering which club to use. He eventually strikes the ball, which takes all of five seconds. He then walks to wherever the ball has landed while the announcers fill the next 90 seconds with an explanation about the previous shot's efficacy and what the next shot will require. Any single moment within a cerebral sport can be appreciated, but its value is cumulative and futuristic: Anything that happens in the middle of a match is just a prologue for a potential conclusion that *must* be dramatic in order to be watchable at all.

The third category of sports entertainment comprises American football and (as far as I can tell) nothing else.

Football dominates television by amplifying the best aspects of the other two categories while reducing their respective flaws. It is, structurally, a halting and cerebral slow-twitch sport. Most of the time, nothing is happening, which is why there's only 11 minutes of action inside a three-hour investment. But the violence and complexity within those isolated 11 minutes is so over the top that it *feels* like watching something that's too fast-twitch to comprehend. The sheer number of autonomous things happening on a football field within any six-second play from scrimmage is greater than the number of things happening within most 60-second swaths of a free-flowing sport. As a result, football is never hypnotizing. It's anti-hypnotic, because the viewer is constantly forced to stop and intellectualize the meaning of those six anti-intellectual seconds. Football can exist only in the present tense.

Here's what I mean: Let's say Miami has the ball against New England. It's 2nd and 7 from midfield. The previous call on first down had been a tailback dive, which we (watching at home) both saw and did not see. We know it was a running play and we comprehend the three-yard outcome, but we watched from the default camera angle, so we don't fully know why it did (or did not) succeed. We couldn't see the size of the hole the running back ran through, though we know there must have been one, opened by large humans employing blocking techniques that are both unfathomable (because there's no way to simulate the sensation of blocking in normal life) and obvious (since this is, at its core, a physical act of power versus mass). If a football expert is watching with a football novice, the shared entertainment experience is illogically similar. But now it's second down, and the Dolphins line up in the shotgun. We can partially see how the Patriot defense is aligned, but not totally; when the ball is snapped and the Dolphin receivers run their patterns through the Patriot secondary, we lose sight of them. There are high-speed collisions happening all over the field, relentless and frenetic. We hear collisions that can't be seen. In the same moment the Miami quarterback releases a pass, he's driven into the turf, and we temporarily have no idea if he's thrown the ball to an open receiver, a covered receiver, or no one at all. It's a millisecond of mystery, because the downfield receivers are out of the frame. But the camera follows the ball and shows us that it was overthrown and incomplete. From this conclusion, we mentally reconstruct both what we just watched and what we couldn't see, filling in all blanks that were invisible while the action was transpiring. Perhaps we are shown the play again, this time from a different angle, explained by the booth analyst. Now we get to see the open receiver the QB missed and the origin of the blitz that flattened him and the free safety who shaded to the wide side of the field, forcing the receiver to alter his route. The play lasted six seconds, and so much happened in those six seconds that it would be impossible to explain the totality of how it all unspooled, though doing so would also be unnecessary, since (a) we already understand the meaning of what hap-

IT'S NOT LIKE THAT

pened, and (b) it's now 3rd and 7, so the entire mental process must start again.

"Oh, come one. That's not how it is," you tell me with irritation in your voice. "That description actually makes it sound boring as hell. I watch football because *I love football*. I love my team. It's about the game. It's not about semiotics."

Well, sure. Loving anything means loving it without reason, at least at first. There's always a longing to classify love as an emotional response to what something authentically is, as opposed to an involuntary response to how something is presented. But with any mediated experience, presentation matters more than content. Televised football presents itself as a host of contradictions that stimulate the semipassive mind (and when you're engaged in the one-way experience of watching TV, that's how your mind usually is). We often can't get a full picture of what's happening on the field, increasing the creative tension (you'd think we'd want to see everything, but we don't). The fact that the game incessantly starts and stops provides incremental rushes of dopamine, augmented by fleeting bursts of introspection. The intensity and the nothingness work in tandem. The fact that we can't replicate what we see democratizes a fascist experience, placing every variety of viewer the same social distance from hard reality. No one is excluded from pretending to know what's going on.

It was an accidental happening, but it happened nonetheless: Football is perfect for television, and television is perfect for football. It is the best realization of both concepts. And this, I recognize, is where the trickier questions start to emerge.

▸

Maybe you agree with me about football and television. Maybe you don't. Probably you don't. Perhaps you think my argument is wrong and my conclusion is stupid, or perhaps you think my conclusion is right but my explanation is crazy. I know how you feel. I argue with myself, in my own mind, every minute of every day. But even if we discount taste and use only ratings and numbers, football undeniably *performs* like the greatest TV product ever produced, regardless of the underlying reason. And this overwhelming statistical supremacy prompts two questions, similar but not identical.

The first is, "How is that possibly good?"

The second is, "How is this not obviously bad?"

Answering the first query is easy: If one concedes that football has evolved into the best TV product available, its dominance of the television medium is justified and positive. It suggests that mass entertainment is occasionally a meritocracy. The popularity of football on television doesn't prove that football is objectively good, but it does present an objective reflection of what Americans desire (and that achievement alone has virtue). The Academy Awards, a live event with cultural ramifications, was the sixtieth most popular broadcast of 2023. The fifty-ninth most popular broadcast was a football game between the 9-7 Jacksonville Jaguars and the 5-11 Tennessee Titans. Judged in retrospect, the outcome of the Oscar telecast was more consequential than the outcome of the Jags-Titans affair, and there was more next-day interest in which film won Best Picture (*Everything Everywhere All at Once*) than in who won the football game (Tennessee). But as competing live events, future memories matter less than the real-time experience, and the real-time experience of average pro football is more compelling than the real-time experience of celebrities pretending to be happy for their peers. And why is this "good"? Only because we recognize it's a statistical truth about how reality works, and true things need to matter.

Which makes the second query harder.

There's something unsettling about unrestrained popularity, and it doesn't matter what that popular thing is. It's always possible to explain why society makes something huge, until you reach a point where that hugeness becomes its defining feature; after that, the reasoning works in reverse. The hugeness is now required to explain something about society.

Football being the country's biggest televised sport is not inherently noteworthy, because something has to occupy that space. Fractions of the phenomenon, when considered à la carte, can be easily explained. The outsized cultural imprint of *Monday Night Football* throughout the 1970s was not inexplicable, due to the personalities involved and the novelty of the concept. The Super Bowl being the biggest TV spectacle in North America is unsurprising, because the entire event has been organized and orchestrated to operate as an unofficial holiday. The Oscars are less popular than a Jags-Titans game because the audience for sports is more committed than the audience for cinema. These are oddities, but reasonable oddities. Football's all-encompassing tyranny is something different. There are explanations for why it happened, but the explanations are insufficient, especially when considered in total.

One of the few things everyone understands about the entertainment economy is that streaming and on-demand programming has made everything on TV less popular than it was in the past. There are now thousands of options that can be watched at the convenience of the viewer. The exceptions to this are live events with an unknown outcome, making sports the only indispensable content for any network sustained by advertising. Yet liveness alone is not enough. From a ratings perspective, the overall trajectories of the World Series, the NBA Finals, and the Stanley Cup have all gone down. In other countries, sporting events are regularly the most watched broadcast in any given year, mirroring the dominance of the NFL in the United States—though not nearly to the same degree. In the year 2022, the most watched event in the U.K. was a quarterfinal World Cup soccer match between England and France, witnessed by 19.4 million people. Everything about that circumstance was special: It was an elimination game against Britain's most hated historical rival, staged in the biggest tournament in the world, involving the only sport that matters to most Europeans. An audience of 19.4 million people is a huge chunk of a nation with a population of 68 million. Yet British viewership for that game was still significantly smaller than the TV audience for Queen Elizabeth's 2022 funeral, a live event where the outcome was the polar opposite of unknown. Cricket is the dominant sport in India, but 96 of the 100 most watched Indian broadcasts would never be cricket matches. Baseball is the No. 1 sport in Japan, but nowhere close to the exclusion of other Japanese entertainment. Australians love sports with the ferocity of Americans, but the single most watched Aussie sporting event in any given year continually changes (it was women's soccer in 2023, tennis in 2022, Australian Rules football in 2021 and 2020, and rugby in 2019). There's no global equivalent to the way football controls U.S. television, an enigma further underscored by its isolationist quality: American consumers are myopically obsessed with something other countries don't really consume at all.

Does this suggest that American logic has broken? Does it indicate that something has gone horribly wrong, and that perhaps the whole system is rigged? Sometimes I think so. Sometimes I wonder if football organically ascended to the zenith of U.S. interest in the 1960s, but that the game's overpowering TV dominance in the decades thereafter was artificially juiced by the machinations of industrial entertainment, a zero-sum game that operates most effectively in a monoculture. Network television exists only as a means for advertising, and the majority of those advertisements push products that are unnecessary. It could be argued that the elevation of televised football was a business decision, based on the realization that the structure and tempo of football is especially well suited for persuading people to sit through commercial breaks. And once you conclude that this dominance is not natural—if you convince yourself that this is all a construct, and that the desire to watch football has been manufactured by strangers trying to sell stuff you don't need—the premise becomes terrifying. Football becomes the most successful psyop in media history. Making matters worse would be its derivative impact on human nature, since huge sectors of the population would be unknowingly obsessed with something that's exploiting and pacifying them at the same time.

"Sports—that's another crucial example of the indoctrination system," political theorist Noam Chomsky said in a 1992 interview. At the time, Chomsky was promoting *Manufacturing Consent*.

> It offers people something to pay attention to that's of no importance, that keeps them from worrying about things that matter to their lives.... I remember in high school, I suddenly asked myself, why do I care if my high school team wins the football game? I mean, I don't know anybody on the team. They have nothing to do with me, why I am cheering for my team? It doesn't make sense. But the point is, it does make sense: It's a way of building up irrational attitudes of submission to authority, and group cohesion behind leadership elements—in fact, it's training for irrational jingoism.

I don't remember the first time I read that collection of sentences. I know it was long ago, and I know I haven't stopped thinking about those sentences since whenever that was. It's a troubling sentiment, troubling because it's partially true. From my perspective as the guy writing this book, it would be wonderful to belittle Chomsky's quote and end this essay with the line "But football is not like that." It would create the illusion of tying the whole thing together. But I can't do that without lying. His criticisms are reasonable, and classifying football as the finest TV product ever produced strengthens his point. But there is something Chomsky refuses to consider, and it's not a minor point: He believes a sport like football was deliberately designed to distract people from thinking about serious real-world issues, and that this misdirection allows those in power to exert control without most citizens even noticing. In some distant dystopia, Chomsky's claim might become the de facto explanation as to why football was once glorified and ubiquitous for more than half a century. The only problem is that his theory hinges on two components, both of which are wrong. Football was not designed to control people, or even to become popular; that's just how things worked out, mostly due to how it looked on television. And while watching football on TV *is* a form of distraction, the purpose is not to stop people from thinking about important things. Just as often, it allows people to unconsciously consider concepts that would be too hard to otherwise contemplate, particularly for those unwilling (or unable) to ponder such issues in any other way.

"That's a cute thought," you say, "but it's also silly, because it happens so rarely it's irrelevant. Walk into a sports bar on a Sunday in November and show me the people who are watching football while thinking about things that aren't football. They are just being entertained. That's all it is."

What's lost in that response is that being entertained can't be discounted. Chomsky (and those aspiring to hold Chomsky-like thoughts) always want to prioritize competing concepts in the most specific possible context, knowing that specificity plays to their advantage. Did the 1975 Indonesian invasion of East Timor matter more than the Oklahoma Sooners winning their second-straight national title that autumn? Sure. Does the murder rate in Chicago matter more than the effectiveness of Caleb Williams on third down? Of course it does. But this is an impractical, annoying way to think about existence. It's hopeless to view every single thing through the lens of the trolley problem hypothetical, where the only moral endgame is identifying the greater tragedy. There has to be some recognition that things like sports, art, fashion, and all other pleasure-based pursuits are the nonessential notions that make workaday subsis-

IT'S NOT LIKE THAT

tence fulfilling, even if every isolated example seems superficial and dumb. There's no reason to value life if we're not going to value living. Football, and particularly watching football on television, can be dismissed as wasteful and empty. But what that dismissal fails to grasp is that the best version of anything is the way most people find meaning in personhood, and televised football is the best possible version of both the game and the technology. What happens in a hapless Thursday night game between the Colts and the Broncos is not important to the world. It might not be important to the people of Indianapolis and Denver, or even to the players on the two involved teams. But it can still be enriching to a random person watching on TV, and not because of what they see. What they see barely matters. What matters is how they see it.

2.
Evidence of Meaning

THERE'S A DOCUMENTARY SERIES ON THE NFL NETWORK called *America's Game*, partially inspired by Michael MacCambridge's book with the same title. When these entities originally appeared during the first decade of the twenty-first century, the naming choice felt pointed. The implication was that football was now the unequivocal center of American sports culture, something that had been true for thirty years despite baseball's persistent status as "the national pastime." The phrase "America's Game" sounds like an assertion of authority, and perhaps that was the intent. But it's better understood as a description of *why* that power was transferred. The rise of football is the epiphenomenal result of how America works, though not in the way we typically insinuate. Football imitates American society by generating a sensation of chaotic freedom within an environment of near-total control. It's a relationship that contradicts what we are socialized to want from sports, but it works, and it works because what we're socialized to want from sports is only desirable in theory. In practice, control is what we crave—perhaps not for ourselves, but certainly for other people.

FOOTBALL

▶

Dave Hickey's "The Heresy of Zone Defense" ranks among the finest essays ever written about any sport. Using a memorable reverse layup by hoop legend Julius Erving as a proxy, Hickey (an art critic) argues that the rules of basketball (and almost anything else) should not attempt to govern, but to liberate. Hickey believed official regulations and unofficial conventions should always be designed to foster freedom, and that any directive fostering the opposite should be altered. His outlook on basketball intertwines with a larger conviction that what's beautiful and electrifying about any activity is its extemporaneous nature, conveyed through the creativity of its participants. This view, first published in 1995, has become the standard position for basketball essentialists.

"Basketball, unlike football with its prescribed routes, is an improvisational game, similar to jazz," the former NBA coach Phil Jackson wrote in his 2004 memoir, and that's a reasonable way to appreciate the genius of Dr. J or Kobe Bryant or Nikola Jokić. It's an idealization of basketball at its imaginative apex, and it's how most people prefer to think about the aesthetics of sports. We watch a game to watch its players, so the normal wish is to grant those players the maximum amount of freedom. The irony is that the more this thinking has become normative, the more every American sport—with the exception of one aberrant outlier—has evolved away from its central identity, diminishing its symbolic stature.

The aberration is football.

Football flourishes by making freedom impossible.

▶

Every sport involves some level of strategic control, and the more you understand that sport, the more that control becomes visible. Ice hockey

EVIDENCE OF MEANING

appears anarchic and random to a person who rarely watches it, but once that person learns that something called a wheel breakout* exists, he or she can suddenly recognize when it happens in real time. The difference between an informed fan and a casual fan is the ability to see order within disorder; it's nonsensically satisfying to locate the levers of control we're trained to view as suffocating and unfun. What makes football different is that the control is so ingrained and pervasive that we stop thinking about it as control. Instead, we understand it as the game's natural state, and any moment of true improvisation becomes a transfixing exception. This has been true since its earliest days, personified by the influence of Walter Camp, the so-called Father of American Football. A player and coach at Yale near the end of the nineteenth century, Camp was the driving force and central architect behind how the rules of football were constructed. A mainstay at the rule-making meetings for the fledgling Intercollegiate Football Association, he doggedly pushed for a logic-based approach, continually trying to negate any element of chance from how football games were decided. It was Camp who came up with the modern system of downs and the scoring framework, and it was Camp who decided that 11 players per side was the correct number of participants. Camp was so obsessed with the laws of football that the stress eventually killed him; he died in a hotel room in 1925, having traveled to New York to attend yet another rule-related meeting. If Camp were alive today, he'd be delighted by how many of his rules are still relevant to the contemporary version of football. But he'd be even more pleased—and possibly dumbfounded—by the depth to which his scientific approach has infiltrated every facet of the game. Camp's quasi-rationalist philosophy is not merely the foundation for how football is officiated and scored. Camp's philosophy is the spiritual

---

*This is a strategy for clearing the puck out of the defensive end of the ice by "wheeling" (that is, skating) the puck around the back of the net to the opposite side and advancing the puck along the far side boards.

principle for how football is played, how it is understood, and how it is controlled.

Describing how NFL football transpires on a play-by-play basis is like trying to explain the incremental mechanics of a nuclear reactor. The levels of editing are so unlike every other sport that there's a tendency to talk around it, almost as if what's transpiring on the field were somehow a surprise to everyone involved. But there are few surprises in football, and when there are, it usually means someone fucked up. The most elementary of plays—a handoff to the tailback, running between the right tackle and the tight end—is the final manifestation of a decision made by an offensive coordinator sitting in a glass booth hundreds of feet above the field, relayed to the sideline over a landline phone, and transmitted into the wireless headset of the quarterback. The description of the play is converted into a code, decrypted with the assistance of the QB's laminated wristband. The quarterback can then run the play or call an audible, depending on how the defense is aligned (a calculation made by the opposing team's defensive coordinator, generally operating from the sideline but receiving real-time tactical data from a different assistant watching in a different glass booth). Whom each lineman blocks is dictated by the defensive configuration, with every foreseeable scenario rehearsed in practice hundreds of times. The decision to run the tailback off-tackle is an extension of the overall game plan, built from hours of film study and predictive analytics. The play call is rooted in a conceptual philosophy, and the players involved have often been acquired because their skill set matches that philosophy.

Does that sound needlessly convoluted? If so, here's the insane part: My explanation in the previous paragraph is so oversimplified that it doesn't reflect a sliver of how stage-managed the process truly is. It's not that basketball is jazz and football is anti-jazz, or that basketball is jazz and football is prog rock. It's more that basketball aspires to jazz and foot-

EVIDENCE OF MEANING

ball aspires to petroleum engineering. Which, I am fully aware, sounds terrible. Dave Hickey would see this concentration of control as the *worst* thing about football, in terms of its humanity, and that every dehumanizing aspect of football culture originates from this connection to hierarchical control. But if that is indeed the case, there's almost no need to further explain why football is so metaphorically important to society. There is no need to dissect why so many working-class Americans relate to a game built on executive control, or why the institution of football has managed to prosper in an era when public faith in all other forms of institutional power has declined.

Don't see the problem as a problem. See the problem as evidence of meaning.

▸

Do I believe basketball is a better "game" than football? Do I believe basketball is a more satisfying human experience, assuming we remove all symbolic meaning? I do, and that's an inconvenient truth to admit within this specific book. I'm sure part of that feeling is because I was a much better basketball player than I was a football player, and I'm no different from anyone else: I secretly hope my prejudices are universal. I'm not a passionate person, but basketball was the passion of my life for many years. The happiest memories of my adolescence are the hours I spent alone, shooting baskets by myself, and if that sounds sad, you will never understand me. It was never sad. If I could paranormally return to my seventeen-year-old body, the first thing I'd look for is a basketball and a hoop. On the rare occasions I awake from an uplifting dream, it's almost always a dream where I'm still able to play basketball the way I could as a teenager. But even if I'd been born without arms or legs, there are other factors that push me toward this assessment. Basketball is an elegant spectacle and a means of self-expression. The geometric spacing of ten bodies on one half of a 94×50-foot court is ideal, as is the duration of an average offensive possession. Basketball organically balances the tension between teamwork and individualism, and physical limitations can be overcome through dedication to the craft. It's also *fun* to play basketball, in a way that football isn't, and games are supposed to be fun. Basketball is important to me, so I want it to be important in general. But here's the thing: I know it's not, or at least not in the same way that football is. In terms of symbolic significance, the race is an electoral landslide. What matters about basketball is how it makes a person feel; what matters about football is simply what it is, irrespective of its emotional resonance with me or anyone else.

There's a montage from a mid-seventies NFL Films production that describes the sport like this, animated by images of prosaic punt returns:

> Pro football is a mirror of early America, reflecting toughness, courage, and self-denial. The game is not about statistics, but of men who collectively and individually determine victory or defeat.

Voiced by the bottom-heavy baritone of John Facenda, those words now scan as disconcerting for a variety of reasons. The first is the pointed inclusion of the modifier "early" before the word "America," suggesting the country's opinion of itself had already diminished by the bicentennial. The second is that having such a reverent view of "early America" is now considered naive and colonialist. Even more distancing is the way much of Facenda's narration feels antithetical to how we now view pro athletes, particularly the notion that they embrace self-denial and don't care about statistics. Most palpably, it's hard to take this message seriously, since it comes from a production company owned by the league itself. The portrait is propaganda. But there's still something true within the puffery.

EVIDENCE OF MEANING

There really is something about the systemic maneuverings of football that simulate the progress and trajectory of domestic U.S. life.

Around the same time that NFL Films feature was produced, the hot debate within offensive football was a philosophical question over who should be calling the plays. For most of the century, the person responsible for this undertaking had always been the quarterback, the would-be field general. Quarterbacks were expected to call their own plays. It was central to the job description. Around 1950, autocratic Cleveland Browns coach Paul Brown decided he'd call the plays from the sidelines instead of QB Otto Graham, leading to big success for the Browns and mild damage to Graham's otherwise sterling reputation. At the time, Brown was pretty much alone in this way of thinking. The Green Bay Packers dominated the sixties with Bart Starr calling all the plays himself (though it must be noted that Vince Lombardi's 1966 playbook was only forty-five pages in total, with fewer individual plays than most modern high school squads). By the seventies, the NFC's winningest club was the Dallas Cowboys, where all play-calling duties were handled by Coach Tom Landry; in the AFC, the decade's two strongest franchises (Pittsburgh and Oakland) were among the last to still cede play-calling duties to their on-field quarterbacks. By the eighties, the practice of a quarterback calling his own plays had almost entirely disappeared. Bearded gunslinger Dan Fouts shattered passing records with the San Diego Chargers, but the mastermind of the Charger scheme was Coach Don Coryell and the plays were called by offensive coordinator Joe Gibbs. San Francisco won four Super Bowls in the eighties with Joe Montana under center, the catalyst for a West Coast offense that was the most controlled system of its era. Didactic 49er coach Bill Walsh reintroduced the premise of "scripting" the opening drive of every game: Walsh would sequence the first fifteen calls several days before kickoff, an esoteric ritual pioneered by Paul Brown back in the fifties. In the wake of Walsh's success, pregame scripting became common.

The last quarterback to regularly call his own plays was Jim Kelly of the Buffalo Bills, largely because the Bills played an up-tempo, no-huddle style in an era just before the legalization of wireless helmet headsets. Established twenty-first-century megastars like Peyton Manning and Tom Brady routinely changed plays at the line of scrimmage, but the original call always came from somewhere else, and it's unlikely any contemporary coach would even consider allowing a quarterback to fully dictate what is and isn't called. The 2025 version of the 49ers didn't even allow their quarterbacks to audible.

So why did this change?

From a football perspective, it's not a hard question: Every additional stratum of control increased the complexity of the scheme and the efficacy of the outcome. There's no way football could be played as it is today if quarterbacks were still expected to memorize every possible contingency and situationally decide what to call on every down, and there's no way to argue the intellectual density of the sport has not increased due to this shift. But as is so often the case, that collective improvement comes with a cost to the individual. When Paul Brown stripped play-calling duties from Graham in 1950, it was a blow to the quarterback's ego, diminishing Graham's standing as a leader. Among his less generous peers, Graham was seen not as a field general but as a well-paid foot soldier.

Even as Cleveland won championships, a bias against Brown's ideology emerged within his own roster. The way Brown messengered plays to Graham was by shuttling various linemen from the sideline to the huddle, and one of those linemen was the future Steeler head coach Chuck Noll. Noll was heavily influenced by Brown, but he never agreed with the concept of coaches calling plays. "It emasculates the quarterback," said Noll, who gave Steeler QB Terry Bradshaw full autonomy to call whatever he wanted for his entire career (an irony, since the long-standing knock against Bradshaw was that he wasn't particularly smart). If Bradshaw wanted wide receiver John Stallworth to run a slant pattern instead of the predesigned curl route, he'd simply look at Stallworth in the huddle and say, "Run a slant on this instead." That dialogue was the entire equation. Pittsburgh won four Super Bowls with Bradshaw calling the plays, a robust argument for letting players control the action. But when Bradshaw retired in 1983, the concept retired with him, eradicated by a begrudging acceptance that one autonomous mind could never compete with the resources and fail-safes of an organized hierarchy. Mass advancement requires an increase in control. But since every team in the league came to accept this actuality at roughly the same time, the complexity of every offense advanced in the same manner, at roughly the same rate. Every offense improved in the same way. By 1990, there was no competitive advantage to scripting plays or managing the game from the press box, and there still isn't. It's just how things are done. Quarterbacks are better at their job, but the job is not the same.

What happened to quarterbacking is what happened to most of America over the same seventy-five-year span. The overall efficiency of society has increased, the result of an ongoing escalation of corporate and technological control. It's difficult to find industries that have not improved both their speed of production and the volume of what they make, and there are innumerable examples of tasks that once took weeks and now take minutes. But because these improvements are happening to everyone simultaneously, they only feel remarkable the first time we benefit from the improvement. As soon as an advancement becomes normal and expected, it can only underperform. The arc of collective progress degrades the individual experience for all involved, turning every disempowered person into an ineffectual component. This is abundantly clear to any computer user who's ever tried to fix a problem with their home internet by calling customer service on a telephone, or to any restaurant patron who's had a waitress verbally explain that they need to scan a QR code in order to see a menu. Pervasive institutional control, so entrenched that it's become unremarkable, is both the facilitator for society's overall enhancement and the reason so many individuals within that society feel alienated by the very things making their life easier. Everything was upgraded and nothing got better.

The relationship is a mirror. Football improved over time, and those improvements made the game less human. The world improved over time, and those improvements made the world less human. A football game is a construction of control, where players succeed by doing exactly what they're instructed to do; life is a transaction of control, where personal freedom is exchanged for pleasure and prosperity. Football is a chaotic replication of bureaucratic life. Life is a means for watching football (so that our bureaucratic life can be better understood). When I insist that football explains America, it's not a compliment or an insult to either. It means only that both have improved and advanced at the same time, in the same way, in a manner that almost never feels good. Because once something becomes what you want, it can only get worse.

3.
My Own Prison

YOU CAN'T UNDERSTAND A PLACE YOU'VE NEVER BEEN TO. This is an easy assertion to make, and just about everyone will agree in principle. Claiming the opposite seems arrogant and weird. How can any person comprehend an experience they've never experienced? It cannot be done. Yet everyone who agrees with that axiom still does so constantly, without even trying. Most Americans have never visited Russia, North Korea, or West Hollywood, but they still have strong ideas about what those places are like and the mentality of the people who live there. Visiting a different locale provides firsthand insight, and Americans are often told their myopic worldviews result from an unwillingness to travel abroad. But traveling almost makes it worse. A person who thinks they understand the Irish after four hours inside Blarney Castle would be better served by reading Wikipedia. A tourist is always an imbecile; to truly understand a culture, you must *live* that culture. You need to be a native. Except that isn't always true, either. I spent the first eighteen years of my life in rural North Dakota and wrote a novel about a rural North

Dakota community, set during the time period in which I was there. A few years after it came out, I ran into a guy from my hometown in a bar, and he insisted I didn't actually understand the fictional town I invented, a criticism that seemed both totally impossible and partially true. But all of this, in a practical sense, is not a case of conscious duplicity. When reasonable people say they "understand" a certain place, what they're saying is that they understand it *enough*. It's not a claim to total understanding but an expression of psychological security: It means they understand the locality well enough to recognize when an interloper with zero understanding asserts something incorrect, particularly when that person is a reporter from *The New York Times* or Fox News or *This American Life* or any other organization that ceaselessly tries to inform local residents about what they're like and how they think. Still, these media miscategorizations are important. They are more significant than what a place is actually like, because what a place is *actually* like matters only to those who are actually there, and sometimes not even to them.

I've spent my life dreaming of Texas. It's a lucid dream, anchored by the limitations of my imagination and impervious to the fact that I've visited enough to know better. It is a vast, unregulated dreamscape, so vast and unregulated that anything is possible as long as it's unreasonable. The Humane Society claims the number of privately owned pet tigers in Texas is greater than the population of wild tigers in all of India, a nugget of trivia that's either too insane to be true or too insane to be false, though everyone who hears it is barely surprised. I've been to Austin at least a dozen times, and every person I know who lives there tells me Austin isn't really Texas. Every Texan who's not from Austin says the same thing, leading me to believe it must be the only issue they agree on. I've been to Dallas on a few occasions, awestruck by how the entire downtown is made of glass, only to suddenly realize this was what David Berman meant when he sang, "How'd you turn a billion steers into buildings made of mirrors?" Houston is a city I've visited twice (lots of driving, decent food). San Antonio has a miniature diorama of the Alamo that's apparently the actual Alamo, along with a scenic River Walk that offers sightseers an incredible opportunity to sweat like William Hurt in *Body Heat*. I know Texans who live in Texas and I know Texans who've moved away, and I know all the details everyone else knows: Every carbonated beverage is a Coke, pork ribs are for communists, and—most critically—nothing matters more than football. But I would never pretend to "understand" Texas, any more than I understand the surface of Mars. I'm likewise skeptical of the notion that football *explains* Texas, no matter how many times I've been told that it does. More than thirty million people live in Texas, a percentage of whom must resent how every reference to their state insists that caring about football is not optional. "Football is to Texas what religion is to a priest," Tom Landry famously claimed, and Landry was not a man who trafficked in hyperbole. He said this as a point of fact. But nothing can be everything. Exceptions always exist. You can find an atheist anywhere, even in a Vatican City foxhole. There must be thousands of Texans, perhaps millions of Texans, who don't care about football. I've just never met any, except for maybe the Butthole Surfers. I choose to think about Texas the same way Landry did, even if he was wrong. The Texas he describes, rightly or wrongly, is the only Texas I want and the only one I can imagine.

There's this impulse to think of football as an electron lens, and that peering into this lens is a way to see what Texas really is. But this is backward. Football is a lens, but it's the convex lens of a film projector, outwardly casting an unreal version of Texas so vivid and emotive that I could spend the next forty years in Marfa without overriding the illusion of my fantasy, even if that was what I wanted, which I absolutely do not.

FOOTBALL

The Dallas Cowboys' designation as "America's Team" is the most remarkable modifier in all of sport, a disposable marketing term that became a mystery of faith. It's an irony so ironical that describing its ethos feels like the epigraph to a Joseph Heller novel: Everyone accepts it, but no one believes it. All protracted discussions orbiting the Cowboy franchise inevitably involve someone referencing how Dallas is America's Team, only so the speaker can then explain why this status is dubious and wrong. It's a little like how every promising singer-songwriter gets classified as "the New Bob Dylan" solely for the purpose of noting how the comparison is undeserved; in the same way the failure of every new Dylan revalidates the old Dylan, every attempt at invalidating the Cowboys' eminence serves only to fortify their position. The designation never stops being interrogated, proving that the designation is correct. The Cowboys are the most beloved and disliked team in the National Football League. They draw the highest TV ratings and are worth $2 billion more than any other franchise. They're far and away the most familiar team to anyone living in a country where football is exotic, inadvertently giving their nickname a practical function. They are who we say they are.

The Cowboys became "America's Team" in the spring of 1979, when the title was bestowed by NFL Films producer Bob Ryan. Nobody thought it was inappropriate or ridiculous. The only anxiety was over what this designation allegedly signified, a question that's continued to annoy Cowboy Haters for almost fifty years. The straightest answer is the one provided by Ryan in 1979: The Cowboys became the national team by default, a result of their on-field success and persistent presence on national television. At the time, NFL Films used to produce an annual twenty-three-minute highlight reel for every team in the league, each one a cooperative effort with the PR department of the involved franchise. Titling the

MY OWN PRISON

Cowboys' mini-movie *America's Team* was a way to make it seem like Dallas's previous season had been an unmitigated success, despite their loss to Pittsburgh in Super Bowl XIII. The subsequent tenacity of this designation is hard to explain. There are no other examples of a highlight reel becoming the titular identity of a franchise.* These little twenty-three-minute films were not easy to find. They were shown in syndication throughout the doldrums of summer, typically on weekend afternoons, randomly broadcast on networks that didn't carry baseball. Most people familiar with the term "America's Team" have no idea of its genesis and assume it was a nickname the Cowboys gave themselves, which partially explains why they find it so objectionable. But the real problem isn't the source. The real problem is that calling Dallas "America's Team" implies that everyone in the country automatically cares about how they play and what they do. It insinuates that the Cowboys' performance has a meaning separate from the rest of the sport, and that how you view a specific football franchise is indicative of how you view the United States.

These are the irrational assertions Cowboy Haters don't believe. They are, however, assertions that Cowboy Haters still must accept, if only for the purpose of pointing out how they can't possibly be true.

The Cowboys will be America's Team as long as people keep insisting they're not.

▶

Part of Bob Ryan's thinking behind the America's Team designation was his hypothesis that Dallas is the second most popular team in any region

---

*The 1979 highlight reel for the Houston Oilers, for example, was titled *The Oiler Cannonball*. It has amazing footage of rookie running back Earl Campbell (the cannonball in question). But the title was just a title. It carries no meaning at all, and nobody refers to Campbell by that nickname.

FOOTBALL

where the most popular team is dictated by geography. The Cardinals are the most popular team in Arizona and the Titans are the most popular team in Tennessee and the Seahawks are the most popular team in the Pacific Northwest, but the Cowboys would probably be number two on all three of those lists. What makes the football identity of Texas so charming is the conviction that this is true even in Texas itself, where The Cowboys can never matter as much as whoever's playing for the local high school.

There's nothing that can be written about the psychosis of Texas high school football that goes too far. Even if you go too far on purpose, someone from Texas will claim you did not go far enough. There's a masochistic delight in the way Texans describe prep football, imbued with the passion of a recovering drug addict who can't stop rhapsodizing about how amazing it felt to shoot heroin. Every quotation about its greatness simultaneously reflects perversion.

"People in Texas live high school football," said a man named Paul Jones. "People in other states just play high school football."

Jones is now retired, but he used to be the athletic director for Boys Ranch, a nonprofit independent school district near Amarillo, designed as a last resort for at-risk teenagers. His quote comes from the 2010 book *Home Field: Texas High School Football Stadiums from Alice to Zephyr*. Upon reading that quotation, one might wonder if it would actually be preferable if at-risk kids only had to *play* football, without having to surrender their entire lives to an extracurricular activity. Such a person might also think it's odd that the University of Texas Press would publish an academic book about high school football stadiums, or that one of the people quoted in said book would be the athletic director from a high school that experienced only one winning season in thirty-three years,* once losing forty-nine games in a row. But if you thought any of those thoughts, it

---
*The Boys Ranch Roughriders went 6-5 in 2008.

only means you do not spend much time thinking about Texas high school football. It's not merely that the madness is the point. The madness is what other places envy. In the state of Ohio, the most unhinged high school football town is Massillon, home of the Massillon High Tigers. Massillon's population is around 32,000. The football stadium holds 16,600 people. There's a 2001 documentary about the program called *Go Tigers!*, and its most memorable scene is a father placing a tiny football into a crib with a baby less than two days old. The subtext of the whole movie is that this community has lost perspective. Yet when I lived in Ohio and people would try to convince me how much football mattered to Massillon, they'd inevitably say some version of the same deviant compliment: "Those people are nuts. It's almost like being in Texas."

▶

In the summer after fifth grade, I spent a lot of time imagining me and my friends as high school seniors, playing football and winning championships. These daydreams were not just mental visions. They were pages upon pages of handwritten documents. I would first create the roster, placing myself and everyone I knew at various positions, projecting our future heights and future weights. I was always the quarterback and I always wore No. 12. I'd then draw up the entire playbook in painstaking detail, sketching and resketching dozens of plays that only I would see. I'd create a ten-game schedule against all the other schools in my area and fabricate the scores and the statistics, sometimes writing dispassionate newspaper stories about our undefeated season. I'd then move on to something even more impossible: I'd advance my fictional team into a fictional countrywide tournament, where we'd play a series of playoff games against fictional schools from states across the nation. The national championship would always—*always*—involve a matchup with an imaginary school from Texas. I'd take a road atlas, study the map of Texas, find a town with a cool-sounding name, and concoct their whole program. The Texas high school was always heavily favored, as one would expect if the best team from Texas faced the best team from North Dakota, or even if an average team from Texas played the forty best players in all of North Dakota history. To the surprise of no one reading this paragraph, my imaginary school almost always won these title games, usually on a two-point conversion on the final play, though sometimes I'd have us lose so that my 300-yard passing effort might serve as a hollow reminder that statistics don't matter.

When I think about this now, I'm amused that I occasionally fantasized about losing to a school in Texas that wasn't even real, and that I evidently longed for the kind of high-profile emotional pain that can come only from losing at high school sports. But what's even weirder is that I was imagining all this in 1983, before *Friday Night Lights* was even a book proposal.

The role *Friday Night Lights* has played in the collective conception of Texas culture is akin to the role *Jaws* has played in the collective conception of shark attacks. It's the finest book ever written about football sociology, a decent movie that failed to replicate the ambivalence of the book, and a long-running TV show that had little to do with the original story except for the emotion, which it manipulated impeccably. Due to the nature of the medium, the television adaption of *Friday Night Lights* has become its most familiar incarnation, as its lowest-rated season still drew a weekly audience of 3.6 million viewers. But every version succeeded. The book was a major bestseller and the film earned $62 million. Moreover, the three renderings are not intellectually or aesthetically detached, unusual for a story told in three different ways. The three versions of *Friday Night Lights* intuitively intertwine, intensifying a premise that's become its entire understanding. Within the Landry-esque specter of football as a Texas religion, the book serves as the Father, the movie is the Son, and the TV show is the Holy Spirit.

When first released in 1990, *Friday Night Lights* was lauded as a sports book that wasn't about sports, generally the highest literary compliment a sports book can receive. Its author, investigative reporter H. G. "Buzz" Bissinger, was (at the time) among the most respected journalists in America. Bissinger moved his family to Odessa, Texas, where he spent a full year embedded with the Permian High Panthers, one of the state's historically dominant Petro-Dynasties.* Though the on-field action is covered in sharp detail, the crux of the book examines the social complexities exacerbated by the town's single-minded obsession with the team's success: race relations, economic fragility, and an overall sense that life in Odessa is autocratically controlled by an oblong leather ball. It is, on balance, a somewhat damning portrait of the community, and people from Odessa did not appreciate it. The 2004 film adaptation, directed by Peter Berg and starring Billy Bob Thornton, perfunctorily explores the book's sociopolitical issues before evolving into a conventional sports movie, best remembered for its use of music by the Texas post-rock band Explosions in the Sky. Two year after that, Berg (a cousin of Bissinger's) developed *Friday Night Lights* into a weekly show for NBC. The TV version was complete fiction, inventing an entirely new cast of characters and placing them in an imaginary West Texas town called Dillon. Well cast and often funny, the show, with its multiple storylines, sometimes drifted into melodramatic realms better suited for *Days of Our Lives* (there's an inexplicable murder in season 2). But what the show got right was something the

---

*The Petro-Dynasties, as described by historian Rick Sherrod, are the winningest high schools scattered across the Texas oil range. Sherrod separates these schools from the winningest programs in proximity to cities like Houston and Dallas, which he classifies as Metro-Dynasties.

original book had captured with agonizing brilliance: in places like this, every human experience is contextualized through its correlation with football, even (and perhaps especially) if those actions are attempts to create distance from the sport. You can love football or you can hate football, but you can't be disinterested; you can think it's stupid, but it's still something you have to think about. It will shape your life against your will. Equally palpable was the message that playing high school football is the apex of any normal Texas male's life, and that peaking at the age of seventeen is pretty much the goal. That sounds painful and sad, which I'm sure was Bissinger's intent when he baked it into the text. But what's striking is how this sentiment, recognized by everyone as negative, is ceaselessly reinterpreted as the reason Texas high school football represents the standard against which all other states are compared: a level of adolescent commitment that all but guarantees adult depression.

At the end of *Friday Night Lights* (the book), there's an eighteen-page epilogue where Bissinger provides short synopses about what happened to various Permian players once the season was over. The portraits are anticlimactic, but it's the section of the book I think about most, and for that very reason: Every ex-player seems demoralized by the relative normalcy of their new life. The record-breaking Permian quarterback doesn't get recruited, walks-on at Baylor, and never makes the traveling squad. He prefers not to talk about the past, still haunted by the pressure that smothered his final year of high school. The Panthers' valedictorian tight end is accepted at Harvard, but immediately realizes Harvard's football program is less serious than a decent middle school squad in Odessa. He quits the team after the first practice. A religious linebacker gets a DI scholarship to Texas Christian University, but the transition is soulless and robotic, and he finds playing against the likes of Texas A&M less exhilarating than the games he played in high school.

When I first read those synopses, I'd graduated from my own high school the year before, and I could not wrap my mind around how any of this could be genuine. How could playing in the Southwest Conference feel less significant than a handful of games from high school? Why were these kids disenchanted by an experience so rarefied that a Pulitzer Prize–winning writer would move to Texas, just to ask them questions about how it felt? It made me skeptical. But it makes sense to me now.

You can't make something transcendent by insisting, "This is transcendent." It never works, and sometimes it has the opposite effect. The only way to force something into transcendence is to prioritize it so far above everything else that any alternative reality feels pointless in comparison. If it's possible to play high school football and simply move on with the rest of your life—which is how it is for 98 percent of the country—you can't pretend that the outcome of a game is a life-or-death endeavor. Your involvement becomes temporary and personal, an after-school activity that (maybe) prepares you to do something better. But for high school football programs to matter the way they do in certain parts of Texas, participation can't be one step in an ongoing continuum. It needs to be the endgame. There can't be anything better on the horizon, even in theory, and not even if you end up in the NFL. A district playoff game against the crosstown rival can't merely be the biggest moment of your life so far. It must be the biggest moment you will ever have, and you must recognize that while it's happening. You must believe that everyone in the bleachers knows they're witnessing the zenith of your existence, even if you end up living another seventy-five years and die a billionaire. It can't be a personal experience. It must be a universal experience, with one shared feeling. And that, more than anything else, is why the rest of the country imagines Texas high school football as a sick obsession that's also romantic, cathartic, and illogically spiritual. It's the most emotional version of football there is, because the participation fee requires the highest price possible: the relative value of the rest of your life.

FOOTBALL

▶

I haven't watched the pilot episode of *Friday Night Lights* in almost twenty years, but there are two things about it I remember with clarity. The first is that it culminates with the Dillon Panther football team kneeling on the field and praying after the Panthers' star quarterback is paralyzed, a realistic scene so detached from the secular nature of television that I kept waiting for it to be recast in a negative light, which never happens. That, to me, was surprising. But it was another scene, from about twenty minutes earlier, that surprised me more. The Dillon High School team is practicing on a Wednesday afternoon, mentoring a group of Dillon elementary kids who are playing football at the peewee level. The children worship the varsity players and call them sir. One little guy asks the (as yet uninjured) senior quarterback if he wants to eventually play pro football. "I think you should play for the Cowboys," the kid says. "You should be better than Roger Staubach and better than Troy Aikman."

That sentence was all it took. I did not need to hear anything else. That one line, unnecessary to the plot and mildly inexplicable, was enough to make me a fan of the show for life, no matter what did or didn't happen over the next seventy-five episodes. *Friday Night Lights* debuted in 2006, and it takes place in 2006. The kid who asks the question would have been born about ten years earlier, when Troy Aikman was still playing in the NFL. By 2006, Aikman had become the lead analyst for Fox, so it's not odd that a ten-year-old would know who he is. But Roger Staubach retired from the Cowboys in 1980. When *Friday Night Lights* debuted on NBC, he was already sixty-four years old. Is it plausible that a ten-year-old would idolize a man who hadn't thrown a touchdown in twenty-seven years, a private citizen older than his own father? I doubt it. But that reference to Staubach, regardless of its veracity, achieved two things. One was that it vulcanized the belief that in Texas—or at least in the prefab media fantasy of

Texas—the communal memory of football icons is like the communal memory of presidents or popes, and that a child's familiarity with Staubach was natural and normal. The other was the embarrassing realization that *Friday Night Lights*, more than any show ever invented, was intended to appeal to people like me.

I loathe the word "hero" and almost never use it, even when describing heroic acts. It doesn't seem like an adult should look at another adult in a worshipful manner, and there's something sycophantic and insecure about classifying a regular human the same way you'd classify Spider-Man. But you need heroes when you're a child, and whoever is your hero when you're eight is your hero for life, which means Roger Staubach is the only hero I will ever have. And I almost can't believe how fortunate I am that this is how things worked out. I was eight years old and real stupid. I could have picked anyone, for any number of reasons. But I got lucky. I picked the single best man of the twentieth century.

This is not an exaggeration. This is true.

I'm sure it seems suspicious that my own personal hero somehow happens to be the best hero possible, and I'm sure my willingness to make this claim will translate as a laughable manifestation of bias. I don't care. All I can tell you is this: I'm not like that. My entire self-identity is built on depersonalizing every opinion I've ever had. I would never automatically classify my favorite singer as the greatest singer in history, nor do I believe my favorite movie is the best movie ever made, or even among the twenty-five best movies I've ever seen. My objective categorization of almost everything decreases if it happens to match my own subjective taste, since nothing makes a person less rational than emotional investment. This scenario is the lone exception. I can't prove Roger Staubach was the finest citizen of the twentieth century, because the finest citizen would likely be too humble to be famous. I also can't declare Staubach to be the century's most impressive person, because Albert Schweitzer and B. R. Ambedkar put up some huge numbers. But in terms of being a nonfictional character to emulate as a template for how to live, and in terms of being nonnegotiably "good" in the most classic possible context, Roger was untouchable. No other athlete comes close. There's a documentary series on the NFL Network called *A Football Life*, and the episode about Staubach is very much in line with all the other hagiographies in the series, except for one notable difference: About halfway through the story, after running through the litany of Staubach's career highlights, the narrator (Josh Charles) breaks the fourth wall. He admits we have reached the point in the documentary where the subject's skeletons are now supposed to be ripped from the closet, if only so that the story can end with the subject's redemption. The second-act revelations in any biography are supposed to be dark. But with Staubach, they can't do it. They can't find any skeletons, because there aren't any to find. They can't even find old rivals to criticize him in a way that doesn't sound like a compliment. It's not just that the people who hate him still express begrudging respect. The people who hate him still think he's awesome.

My love for Staubach was unconditional and childlike, because I was an unconditioned child. I loved everything about him, including the things I'd later learn I was supposed to find uncool. I loved that he served in the Vietnam War after graduating from the Naval Academy, even though he could have easily gotten out of it. I loved how Catholic he was, and how Catholicism informed every decision he made, even though he almost never spoke of it, except when he joked about beating the Vikings in a playoff game. I loved that he declined the Dodge Charger that came with being named Super Bowl MVP, asking instead for a station wagon better suited for driving his kids to school. I loved that he scrambled and threw deep, that he never avoided contact, and that he used profanity in the huddle in spite of his religiosity. I loved how *everybody* conceded he was clutch, even my relatives who despised the Cowboys. I loved that when my parents let me watch the opening credits to *Dallas* on Friday night, I could see an aerial shot of Texas Stadium for four seconds, because that was where Roger went to work. I desperately wanted a replica of his jersey, but it was too expensive. My mom went to Pamida and found a generic navy blue jersey with the number 12 in white, and she hand stitched S-T- A-U-B-A-C-H in block letters across the shoulders. It didn't look realistic and the older kids made fun of me, but I wore that fake jersey once a week for two years. And what's so goofy about this adoration is that the number of times I saw Staubach play was only slightly more than that fictional kid from the pilot of *Friday Night Lights*. By the time I hit third grade, he'd retired from too many concussions. Staubach belonged to the generation before me; he was already thirty on the day I was born. My relationship was built off magazines, listening to what adults said about him, and fantasizing about games I never watched. I've only the vaguest of memories of Roger in Super Bowl XII, and I don't remember much of his subsequent 1978 season, mostly because I was still more consumed with candy cigarettes and memorizing the names of dinosaurs. I have stronger recall of 1979, though three of the four Cowboy games I still see in my mind were losses: a Monday night game against Philadelphia, a six-point loss to Houston on Thanksgiving, and a playoff defeat to the Rams that became Roger's final game. The only win was the last game of the 1979 regular season, when Dallas faced the Washington Redskins for the East Division title. The Redskins led 34–21 with four minutes remaining before Staubach led a comeback both implausible and predictable, connecting with Tony Hill on a fade route to win 35–34 in the final minute. It was the second game of a CBS doubleheader in mid-December, so the sun had set long before halftime; the only illumination in the house was the glow of the television and the lights around the Christmas tree. My dad was in his chair, still smoking cigarettes because he still hadn't had a stroke. My older brothers were seated on the wood-framed couch, a long way from the TV because we'd rearranged the furniture to place the tree next to the picture window. I was lying on the floor, eighteen inches from the screen, squinting hard. It would still be two years before I'd see an optometrist. My mom and one of my sisters arrived home just after the game was over, having completed some volunteer activity at the church that men in my town were never expected to do. I feverishly told my sister all the details of the game, and she responded with something along the lines of, "Oh." I went up to my bedroom and reenacted the entire affair, throwing passes to myself with a Nerf ball and diving onto the bed, scrawling a scoreboard with my finger on the frosted glass of the uninsulated windows. This happened about forty-five years ago, or maybe it was last night. My throat is closing as I remember this. My eyes are damp and my nose is running. I don't know why. Only sports can do this to me. Only sports.

"They deserve a better fate than to be knocked out of the playoffs," Staubach told postgame reporters when asked about the Redskins. "They're a fine team who played well."

It was a staggeringly dull quote, the kind of banality a brand-conscious athlete now regurgitates after two years of media training. But the difference is that Roger had no brand and was never trained. He was not trying to avoid controversy or provide entertainment. He was naturally expressing the qualities posers attempt to contrive: sincerity, humility, and respect. He was being a generous person in a normal way.

I'm sure it seems like I'm explaining all this as an excuse to write about the only hero I ever had, or that this reminiscence is a calculated performance of male vulnerability. Well, what can I say? That's not how it seems to me. I hate writing this and I hate thinking about it. It humiliates me, makes me feel dumb, makes me morose. Memories are like dreams: Even the good ones are sad. But this memory is the only way I can illustrate something I've always understood: The idea of the Dallas Cowboys being America's Team is really just the idea of Roger Staubach. That's what made it real, and that's what keeps it eternal. It has nothing to do with the star on their helmet or the location of the stadium. It does not reflect any other player. It encapsulates those other players, and it bleeds into everything the franchise has achieved. But the title of "America's Team" means nothing without Staubach, nor would it have been applied to Dallas if he'd been drafted by any other club. He, and he alone, is the source of this perpetual belief. Everything else is a footnote.

There is, and has always been, an unreal projection of what America is and what it represents, endlessly (and justifiably) pilloried by every extension of intellectual thought. It's how the world is now and it's how the world was then. Things sucked in 1979. Gas was expensive. Skylab was falling. Iran had the hostages and the Soviets invaded Afghanistan. It seemed like a bad era, meaning it seemed like a normal era. Yet here, on a shadowy Astroturf field beamed into my pre-Christmas living room, was a real example of an otherwise unreal vision—the one guy who personified a mythology every smart person is conditioned to distrust. It was supernatural and it was inspirational and it would never happen again, but at the time it just felt like football. I wasn't surprised by anything Roger Staubach ever did. Roger was Roger, and it was still possible for a person to be like that.

Life is unfair, but sometimes it's unfair in your favor.

▶

In a coincidence so well timed that it now feels staged, the phrase "America's Team" was mainstreamed to the public at large on September 2, 1979, when CBS play-by-play announcer Pat Summerall referred to the Cowboys in this manner on the season's opening weekend. What this means is that it was possible for someone to watch Team America beat the St. Louis Cardinals that afternoon before heading to a local movie house for a showing of *North Dallas Forty*, a film that damaged the reputation of the Cowboys

FOOTBALL

more than any game they ever lost or any scandal they've ever faced. It must be noted that *North Dallas Forty* is "technically" not about the Dallas Cowboys, in the same way *The Devil Wears Prada* is "technically" not about Anna Wintour. And of course, that technical unreality is what makes the damage so entrenched. When a story is presented as nonfiction, every detail is questioned and mistrusted. One glaring error and all the cards collapse. But when a story is fictionalized, the details don't matter as much as the essence. It only needs the texture of realness. And *North Dallas Forty* feels as real as any sports movie can feel, no matter how many details are wrong.

North Dallas Forty is the most significant football movie ever produced, and you can trust my assessment for one straightforward reason: I hate it. I hate it so much that it *must* be great, because it wouldn't bother me if it was merely good. As a rule, football movies are hard to pull off. There are too many moving parts to make the on-field action realistic, and the hitting can't be simulated without going over the top. *North Dallas Forty* is hampered by both of those problems, but it barely matters. The visual verisimilitude is irrelevant, because the larger theme is that anything we see on a football field is inherently bullshit. The players, however, still care about that bullshit, no matter how fake they understand it to be. It's a mean-spirited film, the cinematic definition of sour grapes. Still, there are ideological properties to *North Dallas Forty* that have never disappeared—adversarial perspectives that increasingly color the way athletes are viewed and how they view themselves. That it was loosely about the Cowboys and emerged precisely as they were being designated as America's Team is a deep synchronicity, solidifying the nickname by complicating its definition. It allowed the term "America's Team" to mean two diametrically different things.

The film version of *North Dallas Forty* was based on a 1973 novel of the same name, written by ex–Cowboy receiver Peter Gent. The popularity of the movie has overridden the book, though the novel is still sometimes referenced as a gridiron equivalent to Jim Bouton's *Ball Four*. Gent was an atypical player in every way. He did not play college football, instead starring for the Michigan State basketball team. Dallas signed him as a free agent, initially projecting him as a defensive back. He evolved into a big offensive target with soft hands. Throughout the Landry era, the Cowboys were obsessed with acquiring athletes who weren't traditional football players. In 1967, they drafted both Rayfield Wright (a small-time basketball player who became a Hall of Fame offensive tackle) and Pat Riley (who stuck with hoops and won eight NBA titles as a player, coach, and executive). The Cowboys once invited a Vietnam vet named Champ Summers to training camp—a guy who'd only played football in high school and eventually spent eleven seasons as a Major League outfielder. They even drafted Carl Lewis before the 1984 Olympics. Gent was an early attempt at this unorthodox philosophy, ultimately proving to be more unorthodox than anyone could have anticipated.

Gent joined the team in 1964, a complicated time to live in the DFW Metroplex. There is a belief, widely noted but impossible to prove, that the national image of Dallas had been irreparably scarred by the 1963 assassination of John F. Kennedy, and that the success and identity of the Cowboys worked as a catalyst for revitalizing the city's reputation over the next twenty years. It's a socially positive view of the franchise, but it was not Gent's view. He saw the Cowboys (and pro football in general) as a pyramid scheme of hypocrisies. In *North Dallas Forty*, the players are treated like insentient commodities, drugged with painkillers but restricted from recreational weed; they are expected to conduct their job with discipline but allowed to behave like ultraviolent sex criminals if their on-field performance is indispensable to winning. Though the entire operation is corporate, the players are never supposed to think about money. The film's most famous line was delivered by John Matuszak, a real-life defensive lineman for the Oakland Raiders and a startlingly naturalistic actor. "Every time I call it a game, you call it a business," he barks at a feckless assistant coach. "But every time I call it a business, you call it a game." Matuszak would die at the age of thirty-eight from an overdose of prescription opioids, the catastrophic embodiment of Gent's belief system.

Certain relationships between the real-life Dallas Cowboys and the fictional North Dallas Bulls are so direct that analysis isn't necessary. The Cowboys and the Bulls play in the same town,* the only town where Gent ever played. Gent's main character, Phil Elliott, is also a wide receiver. Elliott's best friend is the team's quarterback, convincingly portrayed by the country singer Mac Davis. Davis unabashedly impersonates mischievous Cowboy quarterback Don Meredith, Gent's closest teammate with the Cowboys. The North Dallas head coach, B. A. Strothers, is an obvious and unkind† stand-in for Tom Landry, a man whose icy stoicism earned him the nickname Plastic Man. One of the most telling details is the presnap action of the Bull offensive linemen, all of whom briefly stand up in unison before getting into a three-point stance; this was a replication of "the Landry Shift," a strategic principle used only by the Cowboys. These all-too-real connections are what make me hate *North Dallas Forty*. They prompt the casual viewer to accept everything else. But Gent's reliability is always suspect. In the film, Phil Elliott is described as having the best hands in the league, despite the real-life Gent making only sixty-eight total receptions in his entire five-year career. Now, granted, it's his book, and he's the center of the story. I can accept that Gent made himself better

---

*There were always questions about why Gent placed the team in *North* Dallas, an oddly specific location that implies the presence of a rival franchise across town. In a 2002 ESPN interview with Jeff Merron, Gent explained his symbolic reasoning: "I was shocked that in 1964 America, Dallas could have an NFL franchise and the Black players could not live near the practice field in North Dallas."

†Gent's opinion of Landry changed over time. He would eventually describe him as "probably the most brilliant man I ever met," though Landry had been dead for three years when Gent finally said this.

than he was. But I could not, and still cannot, accept the depiction of Art Hartman, the team's backup QB.

Art Hartman is a farcically devout Christian who isn't particularly smart. He works hard and is disliked by the rest of the roster, losing the Bulls' final game by muffing the hold on an extra-point kick. Art Hartman is not, according to Gent, based on Roger Staubach. Their personalities are nothing alike, and the timeline doesn't match (Staubach didn't officially join the team until his military obligation ended in 1969, a year after Gent and Meredith had both retired). Gent, who died in 2011, claimed it wasn't Staubach on multiple occasions, and the Hartman character is barely mentioned in the original book. But anyone seeing this movie in 1979 could only assume it *must* be Roger. It was what I assumed for half my life. And what's galling about this is that I'm certain Gent knew that would happen. Gent, who cowrote the screenplay, realized people would see Hartman as Staubach, expanding the role in the cinematic version for that explicit reason. He also knew he'd bear no responsibility for doing this, since he could easily insist it was unintentional and that he never played with the guy he was allegedly mocking, even though that's exactly what he was doing. It was a purposeful double bind: Staubach could not deny he was Hartman without first claiming that Hartman was him, while the author could reasonably insist it wasn't him at all. It also would have forced Staubach to express offense over Gent's portrayal of him as a Christian workaholic, something Gent knew Staubach would never do.

Perhaps you think I'm being petty for hating a movie I simultaneously classify as excellent, exclusively due to its depiction of a person who's verifiably not the person being depicted. It's as silly as refusing to classify *Debbie Does Dallas* as engaging pornography because its nymphomaniac cheerleading squad was rebranded as the Texas Cowgirls. Maybe you think this is a stupid way to think about art, and if that is what you think, you are correct. I rewatched *North Dallas Forty* two nights ago. I got mad (again) and felt silly (again). It shouldn't have bothered me as a kid and it certainly shouldn't bother me still. There's an especially clever sequence in *North Dallas Forty* when the Landry stand-in (G. D. Spradlin) is lecturing the Gent stand-in (Nick Nolte)[*] and quotes the book of Corinthians: "When I was a child, I thought as a child, I spake as a child, I understood as a child; but when I came to be a man, I put away childish things." When the coach says this to the player in the middle of the movie, he's referring to drugs and partying and countercultural tomfoolery. But at the end of the movie, the player quotes Corinthians back to the coach, and the "childish thing" he's referencing is football itself. And I feel that, from both sides. I realize there's a childishness to my worrying that some anonymous stranger might misinterpret Roger Staubach's personality due to a movie that came out before Ronald Reagan was president. I want to throw these worries into a river, because I know what other people imagine has no bearing on what's actually true. But another part of me understands that this duality is built into everything I believe and everything I distrust, and that I need to stay cognizant of how this process works. *North Dallas Forty* forces me to remember that anything presented as pure is still contaminated, regardless of my own ability to tell the difference. It's also proof that a desire to insist that everything is bullshit is just a lazier form of bullshit, and that those who want to tell you that life is a sham will lie to you just as readily as the people who don't.

▸

There's a lot of money talk in *North Dallas Forty*, discussed in the same way money and football are discussed today. That probably doesn't seem sur-

---

[*]Nolte is terrific in this movie. It was the perfect role for him, because the main thing he needed to do was act exasperated and hungover, his two greatest strengths as a performer.

prising, until you consider that Gent signed with Dallas in 1964, published his novel in 1973, and converted it to film in 1979. From a fiduciary standpoint, comparing those eras to the modern era isn't like comparing apples to oranges; it's more like comparing a dozen Granny Smiths to a Mott's applesauce factory. The average NFL salary in 1964 was $12,000 a year (Gent's biggest contract paid him $22,000). By 1973, it was around $28,000 a season (Joe Namath was the highest-paid player in the league, signing a two-year deal with the New York Jets for $500,000). By 1979, the average annual wage was around $63,000, with all the biggest contracts going to running backs (O. J. Simpson made the most, though it was still considerably less than $1 million). These numbers have no correlation with current salaries, figures that ballooned after the NFL player strikes of 1982 and 1987. When Brock Purdy led the 49ers to the Super Bowl in 2023, it was widely noted that he was (at the time) the lowest-paid starting quarterback in the league. Purdy was making $870,000. That's a fraction of what the opposing QB was making (Patrick Mahomes earned $59 million that season) but still more than what Simpson was making when *North Dallas Forty* was released. Now that college athletes can be compensated, it's not uncommon for "amateur" football players to make more in a season than the total payroll of a pro franchise from the distant past. As a senior at the University of Colorado, Shedeur Sanders's 2024 income from NIL revenue was $6.2 million, an annual paycheck pretty close to what his father, Deion Sanders, was earning as the league's best cornerback in the mid-nineties.

I mention these figures not to highlight some double standard or to minimize Gent's complaints. I mention them only to illustrate how there has never been a time when money wasn't viewed as a problem inherent to football, regardless of how much cash was actually at stake. Every economic grievance currently expressed on ESPN or sports talk radio ("The players only care about themselves," "The players aren't getting their fair share of revenue," "The entire sport is dictated by money") was expressed in the same way, with the same intensity, half a century ago. There's an inherent tension between sports and money, accentuated by how expensive football is. That tension is accentuated further still in Texas, a state delineated by its oil-based wealth. Outside football, new money is the Texas identity. The number of millionaire households in Texas is greater than the entire population of Vermont. Both the University of Texas and Texas A&M are rapidly approaching $1 billion in yearly booster donations, with Texas Tech on the cusp of $500 million. Before the NCAA allowed players to be paid, stories about illegal under-the-table payments to football recruits were as mind-blowing as the on-field exploits of the teams they represented: In 1979, a Texas A&M booster famously gave Eric Dickerson, a senior tailback at Sealy High School, a gold Pontiac Trans Am. Dickerson accepted the car but decided to go to SMU instead, and it wasn't like A&M could call the cops. The boosters just had to eat the cost.

The gratuity of this wealth—and its conspicuous employment within a football context—is part of what makes institutions like the Cowboys and the Longhorns and the Aggies so polarizing among the other forty-nine states. They have every possible advantage, and any history of Texas football inevitably includes an economic component. The Cowboys are owned by Jerry Jones, a charismatic scoundrel who purchased the franchise in 1989 for $140 million, a bargain on par with the Louisiana Purchase. The Cowboys are now worth more than $10 billion. But even the Houston Texans, an organization that didn't exist until 1999, are worth $6 billion, placing them twelfth overall on *Forbes*'s list of the league's most valuable franchises. Part of the reason *North Dallas Forty* still resonates is that its placement in Texas makes it a criticism of football's relationship to good ole boy fossil-fuel avarice that's always easy to demonize. Which is why high school football, and particularly the *Friday Night Lights*–ification of its mythos, is so vital to the production of Texas as a concept: The most treasured extension of the sport must always be the extension where the players don't get paid. It doesn't matter how impressive a school's stadium is or how much of the academic budget is poured into shoulder pads. It doesn't matter if the kids are privileged or poor. High school is still high school. It's romantic by default, particularly when the romance ends at graduation. A lot of Texas football folklore involves guys who are famous for never becoming famous. If you take the word of Harold Ratliff, an Associated Press journalist who covered Texas prep football for forty-eight years, the greatest high school player in state history was someone named J. D. "Boody" Johnson, a kid who played for Waco High in 1922 and died before NASA reached the moon. Around the same time Eric Dickerson was playing for Sealy High, a 155-pound sophomore named Donald Moore averaged 283 yards a game as a running back for tiny Splendora High. Kenneth Hall logged five seasons in the CFL and the AFL, but his legacy is entirely tied to his time with the Sugar Land High Gators (where he ran for 4,045 yards in a single season) and for walking off the Texas A&M roster (Aggie coach Paul "Bear" Bryant had wanted Hall to switch to fullback, a decision Bryant later called the greatest mistake of his career).

Hall became the namesake for the Hall Trophy, a national award that's the high school equivalent of the Heisman Trophy. Whenever the award is presented and Hall is mentioned, a reference is often made to a game he played against Houston Lutheran High from 1953, when Hall somehow ran for 520 yards on 11 carries. He also scored on a punt return and also had a long kickoff return and also had an interception and also kicked all the extra points and also killed a Minotaur with a crucifix made of human bone. There's no video footage of Hall's performance, making those fat stats all the juicier. For pigskin woolgatherers, few things are as satisfying as box scores from high school games where the numerical detritus defies logic. The best-known case is a 1994 semifinal playoff game between undefeated Plano East Senior High and undefeated John Tyler High School. Playing in front of 20,000 fans in the old Texas Stadium, John Tyler established a (seemingly insurmountable) 41–17 lead late in the fourth quarter. Plano East proceeded to score four touchdowns in less than three minutes, a comeback necessitating the recovery of three consecutive onside kicks.* Plano took a 44–41 lead with 24 seconds remaining and finally kicked the ball deep, only to watch a John Tyler senior named Roderick Dunn return it 97 yards, the only touchdown of Dunn's high school career.

John Tyler's 48–44 win is regularly cited as the greatest high school game ever played in Texas (or anywhere else), and the likelihood of that citation being reassigned is only slightly higher than the likelihood of the Carolina Panthers retiring Rae Carruth's jersey. It's more preposterous than any fake game I imagined as a fifth grader. Yet when I fantasize about the hermeneutic weirdness of Texas high school football, this is not a situation I normally think about. What happened between Plano East and John Tyler was insane, but it was a variety of insanity that could happen anywhere. Every state has its own version of a bygone high school epic that will never be reproduced. What makes Texas different is not a manifestation of what happened in any one game or any one season. It's the manifestation of a quasi-antediluvian ethos that makes small-town football a MacGuffin for everything else. It's as if nothing would happen at all, or even exist, if football were removed from the equation.

The smaller the town, the bigger the dream.

---

*That this happened at all verges on mathematical impossibility. Though statistics vary from state to state, the likelihood of converting an onside kick at the high school level (when the opponent is expecting an onside kick) is just under 20 percent. The likelihood of converting three onside kicks in a row is about .8 percent.

MY OWN PRISON

▶

Texas is not the only state that plays six-man football. It's not even the state where six-man was invented (that would be Nebraska). But Texas is the most rural state in the union other than Alaska, and it has more six-man teams than every other state combined. It's also the only state where the abnormality of the six-man game is viewed as positive, and perhaps even desirable. Created for high schools with extremely low enrollment, six-man football is exactly like traditional football, except that it's completely different in every possible way.

Almost every state has some form of reduced football. I played nine-man, and there's roughly a thousand school across the United States playing eight-man. In both the nine-man and the eight-man incarnations of the sport, the unspoken goal is to keep the game as similar as possible to eleven-man football. In a nine-man offense, you remove the two offensive tackles and replace them with two tight ends, duplicating a standard offensive line; in eight-man, you also delete the flanker or the fullback. The elimination of these positions makes the action fast and wide open, but the plays themselves are roughly identical to what's used in standard eleven-man. A dive is still a dive; a screen pass is still a screen pass. The result is a condensed form of vintage football that tends to be dismissed by serious football people, in the same way mathematicians tend to disrespect physicists. But six-man is its own animal, too arcane to be seen as the bastardized version of anything else. It's structured bedlam with jankier rules, most notably that a team needs 15 yards for a first down. Extra-point kicks are worth two points and field goals are worth four (blocking kicks is much easier without the extra linemen). Much like playground football, the player who takes the snap can't cross the line of scrimmage, and everyone on the field is eligible to catch a pass. My father was actually a six-man quarterback in the 1940s, an era when everyone ran the single

FOOTBALL

wing and the quarterback was mainly a blocker. Today, six-man is more like arena football that's played outdoors on an 80-yard field, so the statistics are bonkers. The single-game six-man record for passing yards is 845. The final score of a 2017 game between the towns of Campbell (population 542) and Ladonia (population 597) was 125–122.

I've never attended a six-man Texas football game. I don't need to, because I've imagined an unreal version of the sport that reality could never match. I imagine little towns without stoplights, where grizzled old men drink coffee in the local café and complain about the unpaid volunteer coach. I imagine the gravel and the dust and the security of geographic isolation. I imagine 99-pound freshmen forced to play against seniors because the school couldn't field a roster if they didn't. I imagine the Chevy pickup trucks parked in the end zone on Friday nights, driven by unemployed 23-year-old alcoholics who've already started lying about how good they used to be. I imagine shirtless kids with crew cuts training alone in the summer humidity, running untimed wind sprints in sweat-soaked blue jeans. I imagine the new Wilson football every boy gets at Christmas and the creeping fear of being the seventh-best player on a six-man squad. I imagine everyone in the community caring about only one thing, except when they go to church to be reminded that Jesus was somehow a Republican. And what I am imagining when I do this is not how it is, or even how it was, because I have no experience with either of those realities. What I'm imagining is a way of life we all understand to be lost and can never be recovered, probably because it was never there at all (and eternally unreachable, even if it was). It's the black-and-white world of *The Last Picture Show* and *Hud*, a hard life that still feels desirable as long as it's happening to someone else. It's a portrait of rural America that's beloved in fiction but denigrated in actuality. What's amazing about Texas six-man football is that it *seems* fictional. It seems goofy and outdated, the remnant of a bygone past where going to high school and playing football are so intertwined that the sport *must* be played, even if there aren't enough people to form a team. Six-man football drags the past into the present, reconceptualizing discarded ways of thinking into an acceptable point of view. It's a sincere endeavor that feels like an unrealistic TV show.

Take, for example, the story of Tyler Ethridge. A 5-foot-9 quarterback for Richland Springs (population 244), Ethridge is among the most statistically impressive players in Texas history, a pocket-sized Kenneth Hall. By the time he graduated in 2008, Ethridge had thrown 230 touchdowns, the most by any high schooler ever (though, because the record was achieved at the six-man level, it is not recognized nationally). He passed for more than 10,000 yards, rushed for another 4,536, and added 24 interceptions as a defender. In Ethridge's four years on the varsity, the Richland Springs Coyotes lost only one game. Yet the greatest six-man player who ever lived did not play college football. Ethridge tried out at a Division III school, was switched from quarterback to safety, and quit as a freshman. He started experimenting with drugs, aimlessly driving around Texas until he ran out of money and his truck ran out of gas. He slept under a bridge in El Paso. But then—as is so often the case with these types of stories—Ethridge experienced a moment of metaphysical religiosity: In anger and pain, he screamed at God like a football Job. And much to Ethridge's surprise, God apparently screamed back.

"He said, 'Why are you running?' And when God speaks to you, it's like rivers of water running through every facet of you, and I knew what He meant," Ethridge told Paul Harris of the *San Angelo Standard-Times*. "Here I was thinking I'd been running from marijuana or heartache or depression or suicidal thoughts, but I was actually running from God. I realized I'd been running from God my whole life."

Ethridge moved back to Richland Springs and took a job in the high school cafeteria, humbling himself in front of the same community that once glorified him. Within a year, he would enroll at a Bible college in

Colorado, become a missionary, get married, and have a child. He moved back to Texas and started coaching six-man football with his father. "I'm kind of like a mentor to those that want it," he said at the time. "I'm not forcing my expertise as the six-man football guy to anyone. It's more of a pastoral role." Ethridge was inducted into the Texas Six-Man Hall of Fame at the age of twenty-nine, almost as if he'd lived an entire life before turning thirty, which he more or less did.

Now, if Ethridge's story ended with that HOF induction, it would stand as an enchanted tale of redemption, suitable for a PG-rated biopic to show the kids at Bible camp. This, unfortunately, is not where the story ends. At some point between 2019 and 2021, Ethridge returned to Colorado and began identifying as a Black Robe Christian, a radical branch of Protestant clergy that aspires to make America an exclusively Christian nation through any means necessary. Ethridge was among the insurrectionists who stormed the U.S. Capitol on January 6, climbing the scaffolding just outside the office of Nancy Pelosi. He entered the Capitol and filmed himself inside, posting the footage on social media. Ethridge was unsurprisingly charged with a felony and five misdemeanors, incurring a seven-month prison sentence. He was released in 2025 when the newly reelected president, Donald Trump, pardoned all participants in the January 6 insurgency.

"I don't regret anything," he later told a Texas website, though he did lose his job as a youth minister. "People who weren't there don't understand the moment."

It's an allegory without a consistent message: Our protagonist comes from a town so small every resident could board the same 747 and nobody would need a middle seat. Our protagonist shatters records and becomes a fairy-tale superstar, only to be washed up before he's old enough to drink. It is the dream and nightmare of every small-town hero, a romance that collapses into tragedy by necessity. Our protagonist loses everything, until he finds God. He is redeemed. But with redemption comes ideology, and it's the kind of ideology that compels him to attack the U.S. government. Which—to a certain kind of person—is simply another level of redemption, despite seeming nonsensical to almost everyone else. So does the ending of the story overturn everything else, or is it the most predictable conclusion? Is it the essential conclusion? I can't tell if the narrative is happy or sad, which is why I classify it as a "narrative" instead of a "life." It seems to exist only for the purpose of metaphor. I'd be lying if I claimed to care about Ethridge as a person. I don't care about his thoughts or his feelings or his future. I've seen his photo dozens of times and already forgotten his face. Yet I *do* care about him in another way: I care about him as a six-man football player who matches the melodrama of my imagination. I care about him as an undersized quarterback who did incredible things, dominating a weird game in an empty town. Because that's what this story is. It is not a story about a man. It's a story about six-man football that *involves* a man, where the concept and the setting matter more than the characters or the conclusion. The script deviated from the premise, but not by much, and the plot still works, because the premise was always more important than the moral.

▶

The Dallas Cowboys and the Detroit Lions both host home games every Thanksgiving. The Lions started playing on Thanksgiving in 1934, so their involvement is accepted as a historical institution. Dallas didn't start playing on Thanksgiving until 1966, a scant six years after the franchise was founded, so the Cowboys' annual involvement is sometimes criticized. It's seen as a self-perpetuating extension of their popularity, a vestige of their "America's Team" idolatry, and a slight competitive advantage (though there are now football games on every Thursday of the season, diluting whatever advantage there once might have been). Throughout the past six decades, there have been many memorable Turkey Day performances in Texas Stadium, and we're reminded of those moments whenever the current Turkey Day game is being promoted. However, the single most memorable performance is typically not mentioned at all, mostly (but not entirely) because it has almost nothing to do with football.

During the Cowboys' 2001 Thanksgiving game against Denver, the band Creed performed at halftime, enigmatically surrounded by aerial acrobats wearing massive wind-powered angel wings. The Cowboy cheerleaders were involved, as were a collection of red-clad dancers representing the Salvation Army, a Black gospel choir, and several faceless men in spandex Morphsuits undulating beneath a massive American flag. Creed, a commercial juggernaut who'd established themselves as Florida's more religious Nickelback, were obviously lip-synching. All of this, apparently, was a tribute to the victims of 9/11, which is why a little blond girl released a dove at the conclusion of the third song. The Cowboys, forced to start future felon Ryan Leaf at quarterback, went on to lose the game 26–24, though the outcome remains a footnote to the entertainment.

Reaction to Creed's Thanksgiving spectacle was unsurprising, much in line with how all pop culture operated at the turn of the century. The sixty-five thousand people who watched it live in the stadium went bananas. Everyone else (and especially every blogger who wrote about it) saw it as an atrocity on par with the tragedy it commemorated. But then, as years passed and Creed receded from public attention, the memory of the event reversed. Ironists will now insist it was the greatest halftime show ever produced, inadvertently representing the stupidest and most unabashedly *American* seven minutes in football history. And there is, I suppose, some truth to that. Creed was a megapopular group best known for being unpopular. The aerial acrobats were doing something both impressive and ridiculous, and they were all so bald and shirtless that the whole thing became unintentionally gay. It was multicultural and inclusive, but quietly conservative and loudly patriotic. Nobody could explain what any of this had to do with the terrorist attacks on the World Trade Center, even though the relationship was undeniable and obvious. The show was "American" in the way that term is defined by *The Simpsons* or *Idiocracy* or Louis C. K., a self-deprecating acknowledgment of how bloated and tasteless mainstream culture tends to be. Yet what put this performance over-the-top was not the set but the setting: It happened in Texas Stadium. Had it happened at halftime of Detroit's 2001 Thanksgiving game against the Packers, it would have been nothing more than a kooky idea. It would have been forgotten by Friday morning. But because it happened in Dallas, and because Creed's singer, Scott Stapp, wore a Dallas Cowboy jersey while pretending to sing, the debacle absorbed the legacy of the Cowboy franchise. It absorbed the Cowboys' outsized space in society, regurgitating that history back upon the public with extreme prejudice. Had it happened in Detroit, it would have been something that happened in Detroit. But because it happened in Dallas, it happened everywhere, including all the places where no one watched and no one cared. This was not because of Creed. This was because of the stadium where it happened.

Sadly, it must be said again: The Cowboys will be America's Team as long as people keep insisting they're not.

▶

When Stapp performed that Thanksgiving, the Cowboy jersey he wore was No. 11. Almost twenty years later, on a podcast hosted by a former cast member from MTV's *The Real World*, Stapp said he picked No. 11 because the second and third Creed albums both hit No. 1 on the *Billboard* sales charts, meaning "11" represented the number "1" twice in a row. This is idiotic and mildly confusing, but also a relief. Prior to that podcast, I'd always assumed Stapp must have been a huge fan of Danny White, complicating my view of Creed. But now that I know his selection of "11" had nothing to do with White, I don't have to feel any ambivalence toward Creed. I can simply remain ambivalent about the Dallas Cowboys, the defining ambivalence of my life.

I would guess 50 percent of the people reading this essay assume I love the Cowboys, 30 percent suspect I secretly dislike them, and 20 percent believe I see them only as a concept well suited for essay writing. All of these people are correct. My feelings about the Cowboys make no sense, to me or to anyone who knows me. They are technically my favorite team, though I am not, by any normal definition, a fan. I find myself involuntarily rooting for them to win, an unintentional desire that's hard to kill. On the rare occasions they wear their blue jerseys (as opposed to their classic white jerseys), I inevitably have a bad day, the only superstition I accept. I follow everything they do and I know everything about their history, but I never allow myself to care. Instead, I force myself to feel nothing. I watch every game like I'm watching a medical procedure. This is due to many things, though Danny White is near the top of the list.

White took over as the Cowboys quarterback when Roger Staubach retired, a challenging task widely viewed as totally impossible. White had attended Arizona State on a baseball scholarship, moonlighting with the football team as a kicking specialist until he took over as quarterback and threw for almost 7,000 yards. The Cowboys drafted him in 1974 but only as a punter, prompting him to jump to the short-lived World Football League. When the WFL folded, White joined the Cowboys as the punter and Staubach's unassuming backup. There was no competition between the two, no hot controversy. People like to claim the most popular guy in any football town is the backup quarterback, but that wasn't the case in late-seventies Dallas. Staubach wore 12 and White wore 11. It was a numeric difference emblematic of the relationship: White could only hope to be 92 percent of Staubach. But Roger loved Danny and supported him unequivocally. Roger insisted Danny was going to be great, so I loved Danny, too. Danny White could never be Roger Staubach, but Roger wouldn't be Roger if such replication were possible. It was an arranged marriage, but I was committed.

White was quite good in that first season after Roger's departure. He threw a lot of interceptions but the Cowboys went 12-4, falling to a superior Philadelphia squad in a frigid NFC title game. I was sad but optimistic. It was White's first chance at running the show, and he would only get better. The following year, Tony Dorsett established himself as the league's best runner. The defense added Everson Walls, an undrafted cornerback who led the league in interceptions as a rookie. The only other team on the Cowboys' level was San Francisco, a club who trounced Dallas in October and finished with a record of 13-3. Still, I did not take the 49ers seriously. The season before, they'd gone 6-10. How legitimate could they possibly be? My dad told me their quarterback was from Notre Dame and was good in close games, but my dad had questionable opinions about lots of things. I wasn't worried about Joe Montana. I didn't care how much chicken soup he drank during the 1979 Cotton Bowl. I trusted Danny White.

Now, we all know what's going to happen here. You already know how this story will end, even if you have no memory or knowledge of the 1980s. I wouldn't be telling this story if the ending was happy. Dallas is going to lose to San Francisco in the NFC championship, and I will be crushed. But what remains a mystery, even to myself, is who I was before that game. I know I was in fourth grade and I know I loved the Cowboys, but everything else is a guess or a projection. I cannot access the thoughts and feelings I had prior to watching that playoff game. Was I confident? Was I agitated? No idea. Did I think Dallas *deserved* to win, or that I deserved to experience them winning? No clue. Whoever I was before kickoff is not a person I understand. That person is gone, literally and figuratively, and I

FOOTBALL

hate that. But the person I became when that game ended is still the person I am today, and I hate that more.

The 1981 NFC Championship lasted longer than *The Human Condition*. It was a back-and-forth affair, an epic crusade, a truly horrible way to spend a winter afternoon. I was nine when it started and twenty-nine by the end of the third quarter. I chewed all ten of my fingernails until they bled, a histrionic cliché I'd never done before and have never done since. I had to push my hands into my pants pockets to keep the blood off the carpet. My anxiety was cartoonish and grotesque. I wanted it so bad, and it felt awful to want anything so much. There was nothing good about it.

What's most remembered about this game is "The Catch," an image that's been chiseled into a statue outside the Niners' stadium in Santa Clara. Trailing 27–21 in the final minute, a backpedaling Montana chucked the rock high to the corner of the end zone, where steadfast receiver Dwight Clark skied over Walls and pulled the ball to earth. It was the cover of *Sports Illustrated*, the greatest moment in 49er history, and the most memorable NFL play of the eighties. What is sometimes forgotten, however, is that there were still 51 seconds on the clock after Clark scored. White was not Staubach, but he'd led playoff comebacks before, and Dallas had an excellent kicker. They also had Drew Pearson, the receiver who'd caught the first recognized Hail Mary in history against the Vikings in 1975. I did not believe the game was over. My commitment did not waver. The Niners kicked off with a 28–27 lead. Dallas took over on their own 25. On the first play from scrimmage, Pearson ran a deep post against SF cornerback Eric Wright. Danny drilled Pearson at midfield, his finest throw of the afternoon, a Staubach-level connection. As Pearson tried to break away, Wright desperately grabbed the back of Drew's shirt, pulling him down at the 44. If the year had been 1978, Pearson would have been wearing a tear-away jersey and busted Wright's tackle; if the same scenario happened today, Wright would be flagged for a horse-collar penalty and the ball would advance to the 29. But it wasn't 1978 and it wasn't today. It was January 1982, which meant Dallas still needed ten more yards to realistically attempt a kick. They had enough time. I still believed in Danny White. But when White dropped back on the next play, he was sacked at midfield and the ball was stripped free. San Francisco recovered the fumble. I pulled my bloody hands from my pockets, pushed myself off the floor, and wordlessly climbed the stairs to my bedroom. I lay on my face in the darkness, crying as quietly as I could manage. I cried like I was at a funeral for someone I'd known forever but didn't understand, which was appropriate, because the dead person was me.

After about ten minutes of low-decibel sobbing, my dad came up to my room to comfort me, the only instance I can ever remember him doing that. Later that night, my older brother and I played catch in the kitchen with a tennis ball, and he told me how he had cried when the Vikings lost the Super Bowl in 1970, a revelation so shocking I almost didn't believe him. The next day, my sister's college boyfriend called me on the telephone to ask how I was doing, the first time our family phone had ever rung and the call was for me. My mom must have told my sister about my condition. All of these events were unusual, making me wonder how broken I must have appeared.

I want to say I eventually got over it, but I don't think you'd believe me.

▸

The 49ers went on to defeat the Bengals in Super Bowl XVI, a game I watched without pleasure. Dallas went back to the NFC championship the following season and lost for the third year in a row, though this time I'd pre-convinced myself they never had a chance. Danny White lost his starting job to Gary Hogeboom (a guy who'd later appear on *Survivor*) but eventually won it back, throwing for nearly 4,000 yards in 1983 and retiring with a 40-yard punting average. He remains underrated, a tragic figure whose tragedy was replacing the greatest American of the twentieth century and only making the Pro Bowl once.

The Cowboys declined over the last half of the 1980s, in the worst way possible: steadily and obviously. Early in 1989, the team was sold to Jerry Jones. Jones immediately fired Tom Landry, the only head coach the franchise had ever employed. I hated the decision, but I didn't let it bother me. Jones replaced Landry with Jimmy Johnson, the head coach of the Miami Hurricanes who'd been Jones's college teammate when they'd played football for Arkansas. Johnson deconstructed the roster, traded their only asset (Herschel Walker) for a slew of draft picks, and built a new dynasty. The Cowboys won three Super Bowls in the 1990s. I was pleased by this, though nowhere near ecstatic. They wore the same uniforms and still played in Texas, but the reinvention had been so all-encompassing that even the similarities felt different, a ship of Theseus without the paradox. A Super Bowl loss to the Buffalo Bills would have inflicted no pain, in the same way the wins delivered no joy. To some, this confession will prove I was never really a Cowboy fan at all, and that my ongoing fixation with the franchise is the meager residue of my boyhood obsession with one particular player. I'd counter that accusation by admitting my psychological concern: I sometimes fear I'm experiencing the most bottomless version of fandom, where I love a team I don't even like, emotionally betrothed against my will. Both possibilities seem credible. Both conditions are inescapable. I will always stargaze about the Cowboys. I can keep asking myself why I do this, and I can keep interrogating my own contradictory thoughts, and I can accept that it makes very little sense to love a football team without caring if they win or lose. It won't matter. I still need to do it. I still need to daydream about the Cowboys, in the same way I still need to look up statistics for six-man football teams in panhandle towns I will never visit. I still need to buy T-shirts that promote the Cotton Bowl, and I

MY OWN PRISON

still need the Longhorns to beat the Sooners in the Red River Shootout, and I still need to insist the Southwest Conference should have never disbanded. I still need to wonder what happened to Eric Dickerson's gold Trans Am. I still need to remember the unrealized glory of Kenneth Hall and Tyler Ethridge. I still need to worry about Roger Staubach dying, even though he's eighty-three years old and any actuary would tell me he'll likely be dead before this book is published. I still need to do all these things, and I can't stop. Because the moment I stop, it all goes away. The dream will dissolve and Texas will no longer exist, except in reality.

4.

The Semantics of GOAT Herding

IF YOU BELIEVE, AS I DO, THAT THE BEATLES ARE THE GREATEST pop band of all time, and someone asks you to explain why that is your belief, there's an impulse to say it's because they made the best songs. It feels like the answer one is supposed to give. But that's a flawed argument, even if it's true.

In the span of eight years, the Beatles recorded 213 songs, 188 of which they wrote themselves. Around 80 of those 213 songs fall somewhere between "very good" and "beyond exceptional," an astonishing explosion of brilliance within a small window of time. Yet the sheer number of good songs they released is not what makes the Beatles unrivaled. Greatness is not a numbers game. It's not cumulative or mathematical. Greatness is about the creation of archetypes. It's entirely possible a modern pop artist could have a career similar to the Beatles that lasts five times longer, potentially generating twice as many tracks that surpass the "very good" classification. And if that were to happen, it would still not make this hypothetical artist greater than the Beatles, unless she invented some new kind of previously unimagined music that altered the definition of what pop music is. If she did not, it would mean she was still fundamentally functioning within the same idiom the Beatles established, and her bank vault of anthems would mainly reflect craft, longevity, and the capacity to access and unpack the thousands of familiar songs amassed in the Beatles' shadow. So if you believe, as I do, that the Beatles are the greatest pop band of all time, and you are asked to explain why that is your belief, a better argument would be this: "Though the Beatles did not invent rock 'n' roll, the songs they composed and recorded represent the enduring understanding of rock and pop and psychedelia, and anything still relevant about those musical categories can be traced back to their 213-song catalog, meaning no later artist working in those categories can surpass their greatness, regardless of the quality or quantity of the work they produce."

This reasoning can be applied to many arguments concerning the absolute greatness of many contentious subjects: film (where the answer is *Citizen Kane*), modernist literature (where the answer is *Ulysses*), and carbonated soft drinks (where the answer is Coca-Cola). It does not mean the "greatest" version of something is automatically the first version of something, because the first version of something often has no connection to whatever it spawns. Being first is not enough. To be the greatest [whatever] of all time, something needs to be the *first elite rendering* of an entity *still containing the core characteristics* of its most state-of-the-art version. In other words, it's the earliest incarnation of greatness still intimately related to all subsequent examples of greatness following in its aftermath. The GOAT is the GOAT because it's the model for what greatness is.

There are, certainly, a few exceptions to this, as there always must be (Wayne Gretzky, *Peanuts*, Genghis Khan). No rule is airtight, particularly if that rule was invented by me. But exceptions only complicate a truth.

THE SEMANTICS OF GOAT HERDING

They can't really refute it. The sky can be any color imaginable, yet there's only one reasonable answer to the question, "What color is the sky?"

▸

What follows is a list of the greatest football players of all time, in chronological order of when that term would have been applied (or misapplied) to their career. There have been hundreds of players who've been labeled the greatest of all time for ephemeral moments, but these are the eight where the classification was so common that a subjective opinion became the objective consensus, at least temporarily.

William "Pudge" Heffelfinger (1888–1912): A Jack Reacher–like character from Minneapolis who played for Yale under Walter Camp, Heffelfinger was 6 foot 3 and almost 200 pounds, at a time when the average American male was 5 foot 7. He is, technically, the first man to ever make money playing football. But Heffelfinger's brutal dominion happened when football was still a three-down sport, when only five yards were required for a fresh set of downs. It was a rugby scrum with little strategy and almost no passing, unrecognizable from its present-day form. It's also hard to take the level of competition from this period too seriously. Yale outscored their opponents 694–0 during Heffelfinger's initial season with the program.

Jim Thorpe (1913–1925): Born in 1887 and orphaned as a teenager, Thorpe dominated the 1912 Stockholm Olympics, winning both the decathlon and the pentathlon. He also played major-league baseball, won a national ballroom dancing competition, and was supposedly a genius at billiards. We obviously have no proof of his pool prowess since we don't even have proof of his football prowess. The only existing film of Thorpe playing NFL football is a three-second clip of him punting during warm-ups. A member of the Sac and Fox Nation, Thorpe was a college star

FOOTBALL

at the Carlisle Indian Industrial School. He did not enter pro football until he was in his early thirties and participated in just fifty-two games, but he served as the NFL's first league president and was the best player in every game he ever played. Before Jim Thorpe, the concept of classifying someone as the world's greatest football player was not an issue of public concern, in the same way no one worried about who was the world's greatest escape artist before Harry Houdini.

Red Grange (1926–1942): Born when Thorpe was already a teenager, Grange allegedly scored 531 touchdowns over the course of his lifetime (high school, college, and pro). Grange differed from Thorpe in that he became a one-sport specialist upon his collegiate enrollment at Illinois, exclusively tying his fame to football. He was the most elusive player of the Jazz Age, emerging in an era when the pro game was still considered inferior to the college version. Grange is credited with validating the pro game by signing with the Chicago Bears and going on a barnstorming tour, once playing eight games in eleven days. The first footballer to appear on a box of Wheaties, Grange was willfully marketed as a superstar and nicknamed The Galloping Ghost by overheated sportswriter Grantland Rice, making Grange the first football legend to have a reputation exceeding his accomplishments. He was also the first "greatest player" accused of being overrated, as some experts of the era (including Rice) believed Grange's teammate, Canadian American fullback Bronko Nagurski, was a better all-around talent.

Sammy Baugh (1943–1959): Baugh was a semi-modern quarterback in a premodern age, playing with a ball that was larger in circumference and harder to spiral, albeit slightly easier to kick. He was history's first elite deep passer, the best defensive back of the period, and (still to this day) the finest punter who ever lived.

Jim Brown (1960–1990): During his nine years in Cleveland, Brown won three MVP awards and led the NFL in rushing eight times, failing to do so only in one injury-plagued season where he still ran for 996 yards and gained another 517 receiving. In 1963, he rushed for 1,863 yards in fourteen games. But statistics can't reflect the true universality of Brown's standing. He was regarded as the league's best player by the widest possible margin, even in the years he was not named Most Valuable Player, much in the way Michael Jordan was still considered the world's best basketball player when he was playing baseball. When Brown's single-season rushing record was broken by O. J. Simpson in 1973 and his career mark was passed by Walter Payton in 1984, it did not have the expected impact of erasing Brown's legacy; instead, his eminence was reaffirmed. Any attempt at canceling Brown's standing as the game's greatest runner was met with a scoff, along with an extraneous reminder that Brown was also the greatest college lacrosse player of all time, though that theory was mostly perpetuated by the sportswriter Dick Schaap (who'd played goalie against him when Brown was at Syracuse and Schaap was at Cornell).

Joe Montana (1991–1994): Having won four Super Bowls without a loss, Montana was, for a short stretch in the early nineties, widely considered the greatest ever, in part because the position of quarterback had become so much more important than every other position on the field. He was, and probably still is, the quintessence of composure under pressure. But when he was traded from San Francisco to Kansas City late in his career, his 49er replacement (Steve Young) performed just as well and won the Niners a fifth title. By the time Montana retired in 1995, there were a handful of other quarterbacks (John Elway, Dan Marino, Brett Favre) who were equally exceptional, even if they could never match his postseason win totals.

Jim Brown, again (1995–2009): The soft deflation of Montana reestablished Brown as the argument's simplest solution, imbued with a newfound sense that maybe this would remain the answer forever. Here again, the greatness of other running backs paradoxically improved Brown's reputation. It looked like Barry Sanders of the Detroit Lions was destined to shatter every possible rushing record, gaining more than 15,000 yards in ten seasons. But Sanders retired unexpectedly early, a move reminiscent of the way Brown had quit while still in his prime. When Emmitt Smith of the Cowboys eventually broke Payton's all-time rushing record in 2002, it was taken as evidence that football had changed, and that lesser players could now compile bigger statistics through sheer longevity. Brown, the only runner to average more than 100 yards per game for his entire career, remained the standard.

Jerry Rice (2010–2021): This decade is unusual. In 2010, the 100 greatest players in league history were compiled and ranked by a panel of coaches, executives, ex-players, and media members. The panel was put together by the NFL Network and the list was converted into a TV series. Nearly everyone assumed Brown would end up No. 1, which had been the result of a similar poll conducted by *The Sporting News* in 1999. But instead, the final conclusion was wide receiver Jerry Rice, a potentially controversial choice that generated no controversy at all. The shift was not unreasonable: Rice played for twenty years, retiring with the most career receptions, the most career receiving yards, and the most total touchdowns. Passing records are habitually broken, but Rice's receiving marks will be hard to overcome. His virtuosity was invulnerable to time or circumstance. The years he spent playing in San Francisco with Young were as good as his years playing in San Francisco with Montana. As a forty-year-old with the Raiders, he still made the Pro Bowl. Rice's coronation was the rare example of a decision intended to be provocative that ended up feeling correct.

Tom Brady (2020–present): In what has become an almost non-negotiable designation, Tom Brady is now viewed as history's greatest football player, even among those who despise him. After advancing to nine Super Bowls with the Patriots and winning six, his ascension felt inevitable; when he left the Pats to play with Tampa and won a seventh title as a forty-three-year-old, debate became unnecessary. Brady played for twenty-three seasons. If those twenty-three seasons were trifurcated into three separate careers, all three might qualify for the Hall of Fame. He is the winningest player, the man who played the longest at an elite level, and the automatic answer to this particular question, particularly among people who don't follow football.

Heffelfinger is the only lineman on this list, and there will never be another. The "greatest player of all time" cannot be a lineman, for reasons both illogical and obvious. The illogical part is that everyone believes a football team can't succeed without dominant linemen. The obvious part is that linemen don't touch the ball and work as a unit, making any team's most critical offensive lineman whoever happens to be their worst offensive lineman (a wall is only as strong as its weakest point). It's a lineman's job to facilitate the success of the skill players, elevating backs and receivers into a position of superiority; it's also how football is considered and discussed, rightly or wrongly. If every club in the NFL named its greatest player in franchise history, the only team who could confidently pick a lineman is the Cincinnati Bengals, who'd select left tackle Anthony Muñoz. The Cardinals could make a case for longtime tackle Dan Dierdorf, though not a persuasive one; there was a time when the Patriots might have nominated left guard John Hannah, but never in the post-Brady realm.

The first four players on the GOAT list played both offense and defense, a practice that (mostly) disappeared in the 1950s. As a thought experiment, it's fun to bicker over what football player would be most valuable if he were somehow cloned forty times and forced to play every position on the field. In this hypothetical scenario, identical versions of the same individual would play all eleven position on both sides of the ball, along with handling all special teams duties. This "Total Football" approach, modeled after how the Dutch play soccer, rewards the kind of hyperphysical Renaissance man who excels at all facets of the game, playing to the advantage of someone like Walter Payton. However, if extended to its logical extreme, the best player of all time ends up being Cam Newton, a conclusion that nullifies the value of the test. Specialization has become too integral to discount. Once the NFL moved to the platoon system, it became difficult for a defensive player to win league MVP and impossible for a defender to be seen as the greatest ever. When comparing players from disparate eras, statistical analysis becomes unavoidable, and defensive stats like sacks and interceptions are less meaningful than yards and points. The only guy who circumvents that obstacle is Lawrence Taylor, an outside linebacker so palpably dominant throughout the 1980s that multiple teams redesigned their offense in hopes of stopping him from murdering their quarterback. If someone were to suggest Taylor deserves inclusion among those other eight players, or that he was actually better than Brady or Rice or Montana, the suggestion would not be insane. I would listen to the argument.

But here's the thing: The greatest football player of all time is Jim Thorpe.

It is *still* Jim Thorpe. He is still the color of the sky. And I don't mean this metaphorically or spiritually or politically. I mean this literally, and for reasons specific to this sport.

The greatest football player of all time is Jim Thorpe. The second greatest is Jim Brown. And after that, the gap gets vast.

▶

Before I explicate an argument no one agrees with (except for maybe Sally Jenkins and Leonard Peltier), allow me to set the parameters. Brady and

THE SEMANTICS OF GOAT HERDING

Rice are the most *accomplished* football players of all time, and that's how greatness is measured in most professional contexts. But in athletics, the question is considered differently. In athletics, greatness is (or should be) measured the way it's evaluated on a playground: We're about to play football. Who gets picked first?

"Certainly not Jim Thorpe," you say. Thorpe was 6 foot 1, 202 pounds, and rarely lifted weights. At the 1912 Olympics, he ran the 100-meter dash in 11.2 seconds. In 2024, that wouldn't place him among the ten fastest high school students in Oregon. If someone had tossed Thorpe into a time machine and transported his outmoded 1920 body to the present day, he might be able to make it as a walk-on nickelback for South Dakota State. Put Derrick Henry into the same machine and send him back to the 1920 Canton Bulldogs, and he probably scores the first ten times he touches the ball. They would think he was Godzilla. This, however, is an idiotic way to consider the question, and not just because time travel is impossible. Greatness, like all subjective constructs, is relative. Isaac Newton, the inventor of calculus, would be flummoxed by any upper-level calculus class at present-day MIT. He might not be able to pass the course. But what must be likewise accepted is that many top math students currently at MIT, if born into the seventeenth century and forced to live a Newtonian existence, might never learn to count past the number ten. Time travel is a two-way street that fails in both directions. When comparing individuals from different periods, the comparison must reflect the totality of the experience for every involved detail—the person, but also the circumstance. One of the best-known stories about Thorpe's Olympic triumph is that someone stole his shoes on the first day of the decathlon competition, forcing him to borrow one shoe from an opponent and to rummage through the garbage in order to find another. The cleats were different sizes, and one was so large that he had to wear two pairs of socks to make it fit. He was wearing those random shoes when he ran his 11.2 in the 100 meters, on a track made of cinders and before the legalization of starting blocks. This prompts any reasonable analyst to project his true time in the 100 as much faster, perhaps by a full second. But what's more instructive about the anecdote is how it shows what the world was like in 1912: A world-class athlete (who traveled to Sweden by boat) could show up at the Olympics with only one pair of running shoes. When the shoes were stolen, he did not file a grievance or complain to the officials, and if he'd been unable to fabricate a mismatched pair from the rubbish, he likely would have competed in dress shoes or run barefoot. In 1912, the world's premier sporting event was more slapdash and informal than any middle school track meet from 1982. And those Olympic Games are not an isolated example: This was true for *all* things related to sports, and for most of everyday life. When evaluating someone like Jim Thorpe against someone like Travis Hunter, it's not enough to estimate how much Thorpe might benefit from modern nutrition or how much Hunter might suffer if forced to grow up in rural Oklahoma before the invention of breakfast cereal. One must also consider how those differing environments would cause them to understand almost every aspect of the material world in totally different ways, a contrast that becomes especially apparent when applied to football. And this is not only true when the time disparity is a century. It can be seen just as easily within a single generation.

Passing, at every level of football, has improved dramatically over the past twenty-five years. College football began in 1869, but a list of the 250 most accurate passers in NCAA history includes just 30 quarterbacks who started playing before the year 2000. Dan Marino was the only NFL player to achieve a 5,000-yard passing season in the entire twentieth century, a feat that's been accomplished fourteen times in the twenty-first. The easiest conclusion to draw is that quarterbacks and receivers have evidently improved (stronger, faster, more accurate, etc.). We always assume players are physically advancing, based on advancements in their production. But why would the physical difference be this extreme? What do we now know about speed training and weight lifting that we didn't know in 1995, and why would offensive players improve so much more noticeably than the defensive players trying to stop them? A more plausible explanation is the advent of 7-on-7 passing camps that have become compulsory for aspirant high school quarterbacks. The Manning Passing Academy opened in 1996. The Texas State 7-on-7 Championship started in 1998. There are now hundreds of similar high school passing camps across the nation, all sharing one key characteristic: 7-on-7 is a noncontact version of football, allowing quarterbacks and receivers to master the most complicated aspects of the passing game without any fear of getting hit. By removing the pads and the collisions, novice skill-position players can engage with sophisticated passing schemes at a younger age, fortified by a familiarity with NFL playbooks that were poured into video games around the same time 7-on-7 camps became popular. By the time a capable seventeen-year-old quarterback graduates from high school, he's already been exposed to more high-concept passing stratagems than a 1990 Big Ten quarterback entering the NFL draft. The reason rookie quarterbacks are now expected to become immediate starters is not necessarily that they're more physically prepared than rookie quarterbacks of the past. Sometimes they're less physically prepared. What's different is that a twenty-one-year-old is now justifiably expected to understand what used to be expected of a twenty-six-year-old.

No one is denying that athletes are constantly improving and exceeding previous frontiers. They unambiguously are, and that process is relentless. Re-insert any average football player (from any era) into the same situation from twenty years prior and they instantly become a superstar. That, however, has less to do with physiology and more to do with everything around them. Just before the 2024 Paris Olympics, two reporters from *The Washington Post* published a fascinating article about the limits of human performance, a story contradicting many assumptions about the evolution of speed. Is there a difference between sprinters from the past and the sprinters of today? Yes—but the difference is negligible and mainly due to secondary factors. The sports-science writer David Epstein has argued (quite convincingly) that if Jesse Owens had raced Usain Bolt under identical circumstances with identical technology, Bolt would have been only one stride faster over 100 meters. The law of diminishing returns cannot be overstated. Humans have been running for two million years, making the possibility of any major biomechanic improvements during the most recent two centuries pretty specious. The improvements we see have more to do with culture. The *Post* story quotes an athlete who was already talking about this in 1940. "I'll tell you why men are running 100 yards faster today than they did years ago," said the man. "It's not that one body is more perfect than the other. It is the outside factors."

The man who said this was Jim Thorpe.

My point with all this is not to claim Thorpe was faster than Darrell Green or Chris Johnson or Tyreek Hill, because I'm sure he wasn't. Put them in a footrace and Thorpe places fourth. My point is that such one-to-one comparisons are a bad metric to study when trying to define greatness, unless you're willing to concede that "the greatest player of all time" is always going to be whoever happens to be the best player right now. Doing otherwise would be no different than trying to identify history's most commercially popular movie without adjusting for the inflation of ticket prices. The worst NFL quarterback in 2026 would be a legend if he played in 1956, or even in 1986. Classifying someone as the greatest of all time means significantly less if the selection criteria guarantee that the answer will change every twenty years. A better metric is measuring the gap between the best player from an era against everyone else who was playing at the same time, with an emphasis on their physical abilities (relative to their peers) and their skill set (relative to how much those skills

THE SEMANTICS OF GOAT HERDING

were dependent on the opportunity to develop them). Jim Thorpe was the best athlete among early twentieth-century football players, by an extraordinarily large margin. We know this because he was the best athlete among every early twentieth-century person who was alive at the time, during an era when playing football was not a particularly popular thing to do.

This, I concede, is still an imperfect criterion. The same rationale can be reversed to prove the opposite point: Tom Brady is lionized *because* his physical abilities were underwhelming, forcing him to overcome those limitations through intelligence and practice. Quarterbacking is a craft, and crafts require dedication and repetition. But that, in my view, is a different version of greatness, and not the version I'm interested in. I'm more interested in a kind of "natural greatness" that's harder to quantify. It's a version of greatness that borders on the unknowable. I do, however, know this: It's hard to be naturally great in an increasingly unnatural world, and that plays to Thorpe's advantage.

▸

The main problem with arguing for the greatness of Jim Thorpe is that no one currently alive has ever watched him play football, including me. There's no film of Thorpe running the ball on YouTube, unless you count a grainy, mislabeled eight-second clip that resembles animation and is actually footage of Red Grange. Statistics from the period are sparse, and newspaper accounts of his abilities read closer to creative writing than journalism. By now, even firsthand stories are outdated.

"My memory goes back to Jim Thorpe. He never practiced in his life, and he could do anything better than any other football player I ever saw," recalled one of his former opponents. That former opponent was Dwight D. Eisenhower, speaking fifty years after Thorpe's Carlisle Indians defeated Army 27–6. Because it came from an ex-president, it's the most repeated quotation about Thorpe, though the part about him being better than any other football player doesn't intrigue me as much as the part about how he never needed to practice. That part triggers my own memory of the greatest natural football player I saw with my own eyes: Randy Moss.

Now, I'm not suggesting that Randy Moss didn't practice. He trained maniacally. I'm also not suggesting he's history's greatest wide receiver, because that person (as noted earlier) is Jerry Rice. This is about the experience of watching Moss play and his idealized personification of "natural greatness." Moss was a competitive monster who spent half his career presenting himself as someone who didn't care. He was expelled from high school and forced to leave both Notre Dame and Florida State without playing a game at either college. He was once fined $1,200 for purposefully hitting a female traffic officer with his Lexus, and his most infamous declaration was something he said to Sid Hartman of the Minneapolis *Star Tribune* in 2001: "I play when I want to play."

Moss was not misquoted when he said that, though he did insist the quotation was taken out of context, which is always what you insist when something precariously true is taken at face value. The quotation predates Allen Iverson's more famous "We in here talkin' about practice" rant by six months, and the Moss sentiment was actually more provocative; while Iverson implied he cared only about his performance in games, Moss implied he didn't even care about that. I'm sure Moss regrets that he said this. It was an inaccurate reflection of who he was, and some fans in Minnesota never forgave him. But this misinterpreted claim made Moss even scarier than he was. It validated the fear that Randy Moss could arbitrarily show up in street clothes and annihilate whoever tried to cover him, and that the only thing that could stop him was his own disinterest.

Rice will always be elevated above Moss due to his production over time. Moss managed only eight touchdowns after his thirty-third birthday

THE SEMANTICS OF GOAT HERDING

and was out of the league by the age of thirty-six. Rice still made two Pro Bowls after turning thirty-six. Moss broke the 1,500-yard barrier once. Rice did it four times and was one reception away in two other seasons. Rice had more elite seasons and performed better in the postseason. His peak lasted almost as long as Moss's entire career. Yet at their *highest* peaks—in their most rarefied moments of maximum excellence—Moss was better. If you had to pick one guy for one play, Moss is the better choice. Moss could run the wrong route and still succeed. And that, somewhat irrationally, was the key to his greatness: Moss was so gifted that his mistakes were still unstoppable.

"He was like Mike Tyson," his ex-teammate Robert Smith once said. "He'd beat you before you even faced him. I've never heard defensive players talk the way they talked about him."

There was a freakishness to Moss—a physical disconnection that terrified his foes. Particularly during his college days at Marshall University and his early years with the Vikings, there were many situations where his genetic advantage made the rest of the game irrelevant. One long-standing coaching cliché is that perfection is indefensible: If a receiver runs a perfect route and the quarterback throws a perfect pass from a perfect pocket, there's no defensive maneuver that can stop it from working. When Rice played with Montana and Young, such scenarios happened quite often. What made Moss different was how perfection became unnecessary. He was the fastest guy on the field (by a lot) and the best leaper (by a lot). He needed only one hand to make almost any catch and his wingspan was seventy-eight inches. Even when shadowed by the entire secondary on a predictable pattern, he could still create separation and rip the ball from the sky. He was physicality untethered from the rest of the sport. During his 1998 rookie season in Minnesota, the Viking quarterbacks realized Moss presented such an overwhelming somatic advantage that they could win by underthrowing deep balls on purpose; since smaller cornerbacks were always trailing him from behind, Moss would jackknife back toward the underthrown ball, colliding with the defender and drawing a pass interference penalty. These purposefully underthrown bombs were designed to be uncatchable, so a penalty should not have been enforced. Pass interference can be called only if a pass can be caught. But Moss made these throws look catchable, so the refs had to make the call. It was probable that no one else on earth could catch those underthrows, yet still possible that *one* person could, and Moss was that person. What young Moss possessed, more than other players of his age, was the visual manifestation of natural greatness. It was a schoolyard greatness, where his rudimentary ability to run and jump and catch was slightly beyond every other player he faced. The only person who could have realistically covered him was himself.

Critics of Moss like to focus on the fact that he never won a championship, though he came close twice.* In 1998, the Vikings went 15-1 during the regular season before losing the NFC championship in overtime to the Atlanta Falcons. In 2007, Moss scored 23 touchdowns and was the nuclear warhead for a New England Patriots team that entered the Super Bowl undefeated, finally losing to the New York Giants 17–14. In both of those losses, Moss played well but was held to less than 100 yards receiving. In the loss to the Giants, his natural greatness was perceptible only once, on a play that didn't work: Trapped at their own 16-yard line with 19 seconds on the clock, the Pats' final hope was to have the double-covered Moss run as fast and far as possible, and for Tom Brady to chuck the ball as deep as he could manage, which turned out to be 67 yards. It was a chaos play, devoid of stratagem or scheme. Everyone in the stadium knew it was com-

---

*Three times, if you include his very brief stint as a backup with the 49ers at the end of his career.

THE SEMANTICS OF GOAT HERDING

ing, and it still almost worked—the most thrilling incompletion in NFL history. It was also an uncommonly *pure* football experience, in that the most basic skills of all involved parties were on clear-cut display. What I remember most about this moment when it happened live was something a woman in the room said immediately after Moss nearly made the catch: "Why didn't they try that on every play?"

Her statement made a few jerks at the party chuckle, but it was not a stupid question, particularly coming from someone who watched only one football game a year. Football is based on power and speed, so there's a logic in trying to exploit physical disparities through the most obvious means possible. That's what the Patriots tried when they'd run out of all other options. It's a base mentality that can work for one play, and Randy Moss was engineered for one-play scenarios. But it's a mentality that can't work all the time, or even most of the time, even if you had the original Randy Moss and cloned three more identical copies. The trajectory of football has spent the past hundred years evolving *away* from the hegemony of natural greatness, constantly mitigating physical differences through unnatural means. It obfuscates the advantage of horsepower by amplifying the importance of everything else (strategy, technique, play design, deception, technology, control). This ever-increasing obfuscation is what makes the debate over football's GOAT so tricky: The assignment is not merely to isolate the player with the most natural greatness. The assignment is to isolate the player with the most natural greatness, relative to (a) the disparity between that player and all those he played against and (b) the *value* of that natural greatness within the period when that player was active. It's a measure of a player's skill and ability, multiplied by the benefit those abilities provided within the era he played. Being a superfast 6-foot-4 octopus with a 47-inch vertical made Moss the best specimen I'd ever seen, but that happened in 1999. It happened late in the historical timeline, when the gap between greatness and goodness was smaller, in an era when the potential for one superman to dominate had already been whittled away by an exponential increase in complexity.

So what does that mean?

It means it's impossible for a modern football player to become the greatest of all time, simply because "greatness" has come to matter less.

▶

As a West Virginia high schooler, Moss played basketball with future NBA point guard Jason "White Chocolate" Williams. Moss was still the best player on the team. He averaged 30 points and 13 rebounds a night and was twice named West Virginia player of the year. But more relevant to his future in football was his performance in track. Moss competed for only one high school season, as a fifteen-year-old sophomore. He won both the 100 and 200 meters at the West Virginia state meet, and then he quit the team. Four years later, as a sophomore at Marshall University, he capriciously decided to see what would happen if he ran at the Southern Conference indoor track meet. He won both the 60 and the 200 sprints and then, again, decided to quit. Why Moss would only run track whenever he was a sophomore remains unclear, as are his motives for quitting. He likely viewed track as boring, a common opinion across most of American society. During college, I briefly had a work-study job with my university's sports information department, and I asked our laconic SID why the local newspaper never covered track meets.

"Track has a problem," he said. "The fastest guy always wins."

Every four years, the United States dominates track and field at the Olympics. For two weeks, it's on TV for six hours a day, followed by a four-year period when almost no one in the country cares about track at all. There's always been befuddlement over why this happens, particularly since (a) track is a popular spectator sport in Europe, even in non-Olympic years, and (b) Americans traditionally love things that Americans are good at. But Americans don't need to care about track, because we have football. Football is applied track and field. Football *is* track, but with purpose and drama and an unreliable narrator disguised as an oblong leather spheroid.

The relationship between track and football is like the relationship between pencil sketching and figure painting: dissimilar activities with foundational roots. In both realms, explosive acceleration and straight-line speed are imperative. In the days before youth specialization, it was common for a high school football coach to moonlight as the track coach, often demanding that anyone hoping to play football in the fall needed to run track in the spring. The classic illustration was Jim Thorpe, first noticed by Carlisle football coach Pop Warner after Thorpe nonchalantly broke the school's high jump record without any training or technique, wearing overalls and a twill-cotton work shirt. A second example was always "Bullet" Bob Hayes, the 1964 Olympic gold medalist who later had a fantastic career with the Dallas Cowboys. Hayes was an unpolished receiver from a third-tier college, but he had one preternatural talent: He was the first human to ever run 100 meters in 10 seconds. That raw rapidity was enough to make him the league's most dangerous deep threat throughout the late sixties. Hayes proved that world-class speed could translate into All-Pro practicality. There are, however, aspects to his career that detract from this success. One is the image of Hayes running half-hearted pass patterns in the 1967 championship against Green Bay (the infamous Ice Bowl, where the wind chill was -48°F) with both hands jammed into his pants, forever cementing the stereotype that track guys were soft. The other is that Hayes is really the last track specialist who was transformed into a brilliant football player.

There are, certainly, myriad examples of fast football players who excelled at track as a hobby—Cliff Branch in the seventies, Herschel Walker in the eighties, Michael Bates in the nineties. Such crossovers were not exclusive to the sprints. Terry Bradshaw broke the national high school record in the javelin, only to skip the 1968 Olympic trials. James Lofton won a 1978 NCAA title in the long jump for Stanford before gaining 14,000 yards as an NFL receiver. Michael Carter, an All-Pro nose tackle for the 49ers, medaled in the shot put at the 1984 Olympics while on a SMU football scholarship. J. J. Watt broke high school records in the shot and the discus. Track and football will always have a connection. But what's disappeared in the post-Hayes era are track specialists who converted to football and crushed any competitor who was merely faster than average.

Renaldo Nehemiah was the world record holder in the 110-meter hurdles when he signed with San Francisco in 1982, appearing on the cover of *Sports Illustrated* and drawing periodic comparison to Hayes. He snagged only 43 receptions in an anemic 40-game career. Another world-class hurdler, Willie Gault, fared better than Nehemiah and won a Super Bowl with the Chicago Bears, but Gault never broke the 1,000-yard barrier in any one season. In 1984, Ron Brown won Olympic gold on the 4x100 relay team before joining the L.A. Rams, where he became a top-flight kick returner and a replacement-level pass catcher. All of these guys were the fastest players on their respective teams, if not the entire NFL. But by the time they joined pro football, the utility of the greyhound had declined. Speed was still important, but it was no longer enough to *only* be fast. Too many anti-speed defensive concepts had emerged. Bump-and-run pass coverage, popularized by the AFL's Oakland Raiders, abused speedy receivers who lacked toughness. The variety and sophistication of zone "shells" increased, conceived* to diminish the vertical passing attack. The onus for

---

*The language used to describe zone defenses shows the evolution of the various zone concepts: "Cover 2" is a zone where two deep safeties split the field in half. "Cover 3" places three safeties across the top. "Cover 4" is a prevent coverage that aligns both safeties and both cornerbacks

THE SEMANTICS OF GOAT HERDING

weaponizing speed shifted to the horizontal creativity of the offensive coordinator. Instead of finding the fastest guy possible, the key was designing a formation and a play that isolated a nominally fast player against a slightly slower defender. It was now a matchup equation, reminiscent of the old joke about two men on a camping trip who hear a grizzly bear growling outside their tent. One of the men starts putting on his sneakers.

"What are you doing?" asks the first man. "You can't outrun a grizzly bear."

"I don't need to outrun the bear," replies the second. "I only need to outrun you."

▸

Because football has intellectually advanced, an unprocessed quality like speed (or strength or agility or endurance) matters less than it did a hundred years ago. The inclination is to see this as proof that modern players must be greater than players from the past; philosophically, a player who dominates through speed or force should not be stationed above a player forced to sublimate those qualities and work within the nuance of the sport. Football, as a whole, has improved, meaning the average player has improved along with it. But I'm not interested in "the average player." I'm interested in the *greatest* player. I'm interested in the skills that can't be taught. Jerry Rice ran better routes than Randy Moss. Rice played for better coaches and with better quarterbacks. He was fearless, took better care of himself, and was hysterically competitive. He had a better career. But Moss had the body, and that's what can't be learned. No matter how much

---

deep. "Tampa 2," popularized by Tony Dungy when he coached with the Buccaneers, is a version of Cover 2 that drops the middle linebacker to the top of the secondary, making it easier for the two safeties to take away the sidelines. The consequence of these advances is that throwing the ball deep became increasingly difficult with each iteration.

we want to reward smarts and work ethic and intangibles, the body is what turns the water into wine.

The NFL holds a draft combine in Indianapolis every winter. It's hard to understand why they still do this, unless you view it exclusively as the made-for-TV event it has become. All the participants have just completed a year of college football, and every college game is readily accessible on tape. All their strengths and weaknesses should already be known. It seems odd that a running back who played twelve games in the SEC would still need to prove he can run a decent 40 or bench-press 225 pounds an acceptable number of reps. One would assume his performance throughout the previous season would be a better illustration of who he is and what he has to offer, as opposed to measuring his broad jump or how fast he can maneuver through a series of traffic cones. The measurements are not that telling. What's the real difference between a free safety who runs the 40 in 4.55 seconds and another who runs a 4.59? It almost seems silly to care. But that's not the purpose of the draft combine. It's not a matter of verifying small differences between mediocrities, even if that's how it appears 99 percent of the time. The dream is to stumble across an unexpected example of *natural* greatness—an unrealized physical transcendence* that's beyond our understanding, relative to a world we pretend to understand completely. What makes this dream hilarious is that the most famous performance in the history of the NFL combine is an example of why it's useless.

In February 2000, Michigan graduate Tom Brady showed up in Indianapolis and ran the 40 in 5.28 seconds. As a means of comparison, 366-pound defensive lineman T'Vondre Sweat ran a 5.27 in 2024. Brady's

---

*This is the reason someone like Anthony Richardson, an inaccurate passer who went 6-7 as a starter for Florida, was still taken fourth overall in the 2023 draft: He unleashed the most impressive combine workout anyone had ever witnessed by a QB. The Colts grabbed him early, started him immediately, and benched him before his twenty-third birthday.

THE SEMANTICS OF GOAT HERDING

vertical jump was less than 25 inches and he didn't attempt the bench press at all. His score on the Wonderlic test, similar to an IQ examination, was 33 out of 50 (higher than average, but not by much). What's most memorable is a photo of a shirtless Brady looking like a normal nobody, an image that recirculates online whenever someone wants to prove that athleticism is overrated.

The aftermath of the 2000 combine is now a parable. Brady was not selected until the sixth round of the draft, a humiliation he never forgot. He attempted only three passes as a rookie, helplessly watching his Patriots finish the year 5-11. In 2001, an injury to starting quarterback Drew Bledsoe forced Brady into the lineup, and history began. Five months later, the Patriots won the Super Bowl, the first of six they'd win over the next eighteen years. When Brady left New England in 2020 to sign with Tampa Bay, the Bucs immediately won a championship of their own, making it (almost) impossible to see him as anything except the greatest player of all time.

Brady won the league MVP three times and the Super Bowl MVP five times. He retired with every major passing record and overcame a litany of career adversities, some of which were normal (a serious 2008 knee injury) and some that were bizarre (a 2015 controversy over the illegal deflation of footballs, leading to a four-game suspension). He had a complicated relationship with his coach that ended in estrangement and a high-profile marriage that ended in divorce. He threw 90 touchdowns to a tight end who redefined the position and another 18 touchdowns to a tight end who went to prison for murder. He made at least one of his slot receivers sexually famous. There's a notion that Brady is a timeless figure, and that his mind and dedication would have made him just as magnificent in any era. That might be true. Perhaps Brady could have been dropped into any decade and had the same career. It's an impossible thing to know. But we do know this: In terms of his mentality and lifestyle, Brady was the most modern quarterback of the modern age, and that makes it hard to separate the natural greatness of his body from the synthetic greatness of the world he was born into.

When Joe Montana threw the pass that became "The Catch" in the 1981 NFC Championship, Brady was watching from the stands at Candlestick Park. He was four years old. He already knew what he wanted to become. This, of course, is not rare. Every little kid has an idol. When Montana was growing up in western Pennsylvania, his hero was a quarterback named Terry Hanratty, a local standout who won a national title for Notre Dame in 1966, inspiring Montana to follow him to South Bend in 1974. But loving a player in the sixties was very different from loving a player in the eighties. Brady was able to model himself on Montana (the fact that Brady grew up in San Mateo, California, where the 49ers were the local franchise and constantly on TV, is a not-insignificant coincidence). Brady's college career at Michigan was checkered. He redshirted as a freshman and began his collegiate career seventh on the Wolverine depth chart. Even as he matured, he remained in competition with Drew Henson, a more highly recruited prospect from nearby Brighton, Michigan. But Brady benefited from a method of training that was specific to the late 1990s.

"There used to be college programs. Now there are college teams," he noted upon his retirement, a differentiation reflecting the mercenary nature of post-portal, post-NIL college athletics. "You're no longer learning a program. Now you're learning a playbook. At Michigan, for me, that was a pro-style program." Brady spent five years developing functional professional skills, within the last window of time where player development was still a priority for college football coaching staffs. When Brady entered the NFL, he was more sophisticated than rookie QBs from earlier eras and more traditionally trained than the rookie QBs who'd come later. The timing was ideal. Landing in New England expanded those qualities by matching him with Bill Belichick, a man who'd already been coaching twenty-five years by the time he met Brady. A like-minded, detail-obsessed workaholic, Belichick poured his understanding of football into Brady's brain, chiefly through their shared obsession with watching game film.

The entire practice of film study is an easy example of how technology advances football in an unseen way. Belichick has claimed the strategic value of watching a football game live on the sideline is "less than one percent," meaning the other 99 percent must be learned through the repetitive study of film. This is something football coaches have been doing for more than a hundred years (Bert Bell is credited with pioneering the pastime in the 1920s at Penn). We think of this ritual as static and traditional. But consider how difficult this process was before the advent of the VCR and the ubiquity of cheap videotape. For most of the twentieth century, game films were shot from only one angle, if at all. Film canisters were bulky and hard to load, and physically cutting up a 16-millimeter celluloid reel to focus on specialized situations was an arcane skill that took time to learn and master. Prior to 1980, it was a necessary hassle with limited utility. But VHS tape and digital technology changed everything. Game footage became easy to shoot, easy to edit, and much more portable. Game video could now be watched at home (or, with an iPad, on an airplane or in a hotel room). The amount of video a player could study was limited only by their willingness to sit in a dark room, and Brady's capacity for this was extreme. According to teammates, Brady spent around forty hours a week watching game footage. Even in retirement, he claims to sometimes watch five hours of film a day, an experience he classifies as "soothing." As a retired player, Brady still watches more film in a month than someone like Johnny Unitas watched in a year. This is a testament to Brady's excellence: He cared more, he was more committed, and he absorbed the most information. It made him both the smartest person on the field and the most confident, because he knew as much about the tendencies of his opponents as they knew about themselves. This, more than anything else, made him great. But that is *learned* greatness. It's an *acquired* greatness. It's not a natural greatness. And I know that a greatness that's earned is supposed to matter more than a greatness that simply exists. I know the tortoise is supposed to be more admirable than the hare, because the tortoise has more integrity. But I'm not obsessed with how integrity informs greatness. I'm obsessed with the integrity of greatness itself.

▶

Part of what made Brady so singularly futuristic was his relationship to Alex Guerrero, a nutritionist and alternative medicine practitioner who became Brady's personal trainer. There's also a contradiction in this, since much of what Guerrero advocated was technically ancient. Born in Argentina, Guerrero became the equivalent of a spiritual shaman, even acting as the godfather for Brady's son Ben. Over time, Brady's commitment to Guerrero damaged the relationship between Brady and Belichick, prompting the coach to limit Guerrero's access to the Patriots' practice facilities.

Some sports fans—perhaps most sports fans—marginalize Guerrero as a quack and a huckster. He sells a lot of untested herbal products that are supposed to cure cancer and was barred from referring to himself as a doctor by the Federal Trade Commission. He has a degree from a California college I've never heard of, and the school's name includes a word I'm pretty sure I'm not supposed to say in public (the Samra University of Oriental Medicine). Still, there's one thing about Guerrero's methodology that's indisputable: It benefited Brady immensely. Whether this was tangible or psychological is immaterial. When he was forty-five, Brady looked and moved like a man ten years younger. Guerrero's emphasis was on muscle pliability, pursued through deep tissue massage and the use of resistance bands (as opposed to traditional free weights). His wider philosophy was holistic. Under Guerrero's tutelage, Brady changed everything about his life. He adhered to a high-protein, plant-based diet that avoided dairy, bread, caffeine, alcohol, tomatoes, soy, and sugar. He drank a stupid amount of water, supposedly thirty-seven glasses a day. During football season, Brady would go to bed at 8:30 p.m. and wake at dawn. Part of what made Brady great, it seems, was a willingness to pursue an objectively dismal life.

"There was a mindset of a champion I took to work every day," he'd later recall, responding to the implication that he sometimes made the sport tedious for his less dedicated teammates. "This wasn't daycare. If I wanted to have fun, I was going to Disneyland with my kids."

What's fascinating about Brady's ascetic regime was how it often mirrored the early life of Jim Thorpe, albeit for different reasons. Like Brady, the adolescent Thorpe went to sleep at 8:30 and awoke at daybreak. He had no choice in this. Rural electricity didn't exist until the 1930s. Thorpe went to bed early because it was dark. He also avoided processed foods, unless you classify drying venison into jerky and grinding wheat into flour as a form of processing. The typical Thorpe breakfast was six eggs. Thorpe didn't lift a lot of weights, either, though instead of using resistance bands, he spent his teenage years doing farm labor. Jim Thorpe didn't need to find new ways to make his life miserable. That's how nineteenth-century life was. His mom died during childbirth and his dad died from gangrene. Thorpe smoked unfiltered cigarettes his entire career, perhaps under the illusion that the smoke would make his lungs stronger. I highly doubt Thorpe ever drank thirty-seven glasses of water in a day, since no one of that era thought hydration was particularly necessary. He did, however, drink everything else (whiskey, beer, champagne, and a bottle of cheap wine hours before he died).

When he was six years old, Thorpe would sometimes go on hunting trips that required him to walk twenty or thirty miles in a day. If he misbehaved, his dad beat the snot out of him, an unremarkable punishment in the late nineteenth century (Brady, by contrast, classifies his father as his personal hero). Reading about the day-to-day conditions experienced by Thorpe is the best argument against comparing players from different eras through the thought experiment of a time machine. If a sixteen-year-old version of Thorpe were magically transported to the present day, he'd be a fine athlete, though not automatically elite and possibly too distracted by technology to care about sports. He'd be an unfrozen caveman tailback. But transporting any modern-day high school football star to turn-of-the-century Oklahoma would be way more punishing. His 40 time and his bench press would not matter. The kid would quite possibly die, and if he didn't, he'd want to kill himself.

"But now you're breaking your own rules," you say in response. "If every human experience is relative, you can't transport *any* fully conscious teenager forward or backward in time. You can't transport people who've already been socialized by their time period." And that's a valid point. A modern teenager exiled to the past would want to kill himself only because he knows what he's missing. To make this work, we need to fill our time machine with babies. We need to transport a *newborn* Thorpe to 1987, and we need to exchange him with a Hall of Fame–caliber baby born in that same calendar year. We need to send a genetically gifted infant back to the rustic wilderness of 1887. Thorpe and his modern-day rival must swap their entire lives so that both view their respective experiences as normal.

What would be the result of this diabolical madness? It's obviously impossible to know. But two things are indisputable. The first is that Jim Thorpe would be a significantly better player than whatever he was in 1920, assuming he still cared about football. He'd be faster, stronger, healthier, and more intelligent about the game itself. The second is that whoever was sent back to replace him would not only be inferior to the player we're currently familiar with but also considerably less motivated. He would be susceptible to never playing at all, regardless of his personality. And that matters a lot.

Wearing those ill-fitted shoes on an inhospitable Swedish track, Thorpe ran 100 meters in 11.2 seconds. When he died in 1953, *The New York Times* listed his single-best time at 100 yards as 10.0, equating to 10.94 over 100 meters. The world record at that distance in 1912 was 10.6, a full second slower than it is today. It does not seem implausible that Thorpe could shave a similar amount from his effort, placing him in the category of world-class. It's also plausible he could achieve that speed at a weight heavier* than his actual 202 pounds, especially if those extra pounds were muscle and he was trained by someone who understood things like running mechanics and recovery time. The result of moving a person backward in time is harder to gauge, because it's more psychologically difficult to erase existing qualities than it is to add and project improvements. It's hard to accurately forecast the nineteenth-century version of Justin Jefferson or Micah Parsons, for manifold cultural and physiological reasons. What's easy to understand, however, is how much less they'd be compelled to play. In 1920, Thorpe was the highest-paid player in pro football, rumored to be earning around $250 a game. It was a sum considered so generous that many feared it would bankrupt the Canton franchise. Adjusted for inflation, that's about $3,800. In 2024, the average NFL player made $164,000 a game. That was the average. While still on his rookie contract, Parsons made around $250,000 a game as a defensive end. Justin Jefferson makes more than $2 million a game and plays with diamonds inserted onto his teeth like orthodontic braces. Now, this doesn't mean

---

*Curtis Dickey, a certified world-class sprinter rostered by the Colts and the Browns in the 1980s, played running back at 213 pounds. Herschel Walker was 225 pounds. Bo Jackson was 230. All three of those guys were 6 foot 1, the same height as Thorpe.

FOOTBALL

Jefferson plays nine thousand times harder than Thorpe because his salary is nine thousand times greater. That's not how money works. But an intense motivational difference comes from the *social potential* Jefferson (or anyone of his caliber) always realized was part of NFL stardom. Before Jefferson entered middle school, he knew football was a way to change his life and the lives of everyone around him. It wasn't something he had to figure out. He just knew it, because everyone knows it.

Here's what I mean: Let's say the salary of every public school teacher was tripled overnight. A third-grade teacher making $45,000 a year on Monday is now making $135,000 a year on Tuesday. In the short term, that change would make little difference on how well third graders are educated. A teacher doesn't become a different person just because their paycheck changes. But the long-term impact this would have on education would be seismic. The realization that becoming a public school educator was now a six-figure profession would change the type of person who decides to pursue teaching as a vocation. It would be a better job with more prestige. Someone who once would have gone to college to become a pharmacist might now elect to become a chemistry teacher; someone who loves literature might decide to teach eleventh-grade English instead of going to graduate school in hopes of becoming a novelist or an adjunct professor. Instead of a nationwide shortage of teaching candidates, the field would become large and competitive, and majoring in education would become more rigorous. Triple the average U.S. teaching salary and the public education system is reinvented within ten or twenty years, for reasons simple to understand. So now try to imagine what would happen if teacher salaries went up *65,000 percent* over the span of a single century. Imagine a kindergarten teacher earning way more than a thoracic surgeon. Imagine a shop teacher in Kansas City dating Taylor Swift because he mentioned her on a podcast. Imagine lower-class parents imploring their children to complete their homework in a desperate hope that those kids might one

THE SEMANTICS OF GOAT HERDING

day fulfill the fantastical dream of becoming an assistant high school principal. In this alternative universe, every aspect of society would be different. Every member of society would live a life conditioned to believe that becoming a public school teacher was a rarefied human experience, reserved for the elite and worth whatever sacrifice was necessary in exchange.

That is what happened with football.

Jefferson's salary is not a reflection of personal greed. It's a reflection of what's become the realistic expectation for what the NFL's best receiver is worth, something Jefferson has abstractly understood all his life. Everyone in North America knows that excelling at pro sports involves economic and social rewards bordering on the incomprehensible. It's impressive that Tom Brady watched forty hours of game film a week, and doing so helped him become more successful than his peers. But Brady's motives can't be exclusively credited to his own internal drive, even if that's how it consciously feels to him. His greatness was rewarded with $530 million and a marriage to a supermodel. His desire to win and dominate was (at least partially) informed by a lifelong immersion in a society that places football excellence on the highest possible tier. These are external motives for greatness, dictated by the time in which we live. That's not Brady's fault, in any way. He can't control being born in 1977 any more than Jim Thorpe could control being born in 1887. But if we're thinking about *natural* greatness, it must be acknowledged that any outside motives driving Thorpe—while not nonexistent—were minuscule, at least when compared with what he'd have experienced had he been born a century later. We can't know what Thorpe felt about football, but the source of whatever that feeling was could have only come from himself.

Does this matter? Should this matter? I ask myself these questions a lot. Perhaps I find the concept of "greatness" more vexing than necessary. The consensus around Brady's GOAT status is straightforward and sensible, and it would be easier for me to just accept it and move on. But I can't do that. I increasingly suspect the reasoning is wrong, and not just due to recency bias. The larger problem is this widespread social conviction that humanity is always improving, and that any greatness we see or experience must therefore represent the highest order of those qualities. I think that's backward. The *origin* of modern greatness should be prioritized above whatever that original model eventually evolves into. In realms outside sports, this is common. I've never heard any living artist described as greater than Leonardo da Vinci, nor can I recall a contemporary playwright casually classified as greater than William Shakespeare. Mathematics is improving as a field, but the greatest mathematician is either Carl Friedrich Gauss (who died in 1855) or Euclid (who died before the invention of paper). No modern president can be a greater leader than George Washington or Abe Lincoln. These categorizations seem obvious, in part because we accept that the designations are subjective. Football feels more quantifiable because of statistics and physical evolution and the televised experience of watching the game improve in real time. But this argument is no less subjective than any of the others. I'm not analyzing achievements. I'm analyzing the *nature* of what was achieved, within the context of when the achievement occurred. And that's what makes Jim Thorpe the greatest football player who ever lived.

▶

Among the many sad details about Thorpe's life is that he had a twin brother, Charles, who died from typhoid fever at the age of nine. The boys were exceptionally close (as twins so often are), and their boyish roughhousing was the earliest training for the athlete Jim would become. They had the same genetics and the same domestic origin. They faced the same obstacles and the same potentialities. Had Charles lived, he might have spent his whole life with Jim, doing all the same things and sharing the

THE SEMANTICS OF GOAT HERDING

same competitive desires. Is it possible Charles would have been as awesome as his brother? Is it possible he might have been better? Is it possible the greatest football player of all time never played football at all, dying before he reached puberty? The only viable reply to such questions is, "Probably not." Still, the notion of a Two-Thorpe Reality is fun to consider, if only for how twisted it would make our already twisted sense of speculative history.

When I was a little boy, alone in my little bedroom on the second floor of our little house, I would read little books about the history of football. In almost every book, there'd be a chapter about Jim Thorpe, always focusing on how he was Native American. Now that I'm a not-so-little guy in a not-so-little house, the books I read about the history of football are more scholarly, but similar in emphasis. The best Thorpe biography is David Maraniss's *Path Lit by Lightning*, taking its title from a translation of Thorpe's original Sac and Fox name. *The Real All Americans* is a book about the ignored historic consequence of the Carlisle Indians. *Native American Son* is a book about the hardships and prejudice Thorpe faced as an American Indian. All of that attention is warranted, particularly considering the larger erasure of Native American culture, even within discussions specifically about oppression. No minority group's suffering has been discounted quite as much as that of the Native American. However, the downside to Thorpe's exaltation as a social justice icon is that it sometimes feels as if Thorpe is *mostly* famous because he happened to be Native American, and that his identity is the only important thing about him. That's wrong. The most important thing about Thorpe is that he played football more than a hundred years ago, but he's still around today. He died in 1953, but we still see the animation of his spirit, on Sundays and Saturdays and every Friday night.

A few thousand words ago, I noted the natural greatness of Randy Moss, a guy who retired in 2012. In the year 2023, on the playground of my kid's elementary school, the boys (and a few girls) played football at recess, and when somebody caught a long pass, the kid who scored would taunt his opponent by saying he "mossed" him. One boy even wrote the word "mossed" on a Post-it note and attached it to his own forehead so that he could lift his bangs and mock his rival without speaking. What fascinated me about this was that these children were born in 2014 and appeared to have no idea who Randy Moss was or is. I asked them and got no response. When I mentioned his first name, it did not resonate. They knew only the term and its meaning, and that indicates two things. The first is that "mossed" has entered that uncanny class of modern idioms like "stan" and "bucket list" and "catfish," where many people using the phrase don't know (or never consider) how the phrase originates. The other is that Randy Moss infused something into the game of football that transcends his own involvement. He has become the proper noun for something that has always been. Since the inception of the forward pass, there have been instances of receivers outrunning and outleaping their adversaries in a humiliating manner. It is not something Moss invented. But the Moss version was so distinct and overpowering that his action became expository. "Mossing" is now something young receivers aspire to do, even if they don't know who Moss is. They don't need to know. Knowing isn't necessary, because what he did has been absorbed into the sport's DNA. Which is something that can be said about Jim Thorpe's entire being.

We don't have video footage of Thorpe running the football. It's not available to anyone. Yet we know he was the greatest ballcarrier of his era, and we know this era was when football (as we still understand it) came into being. It was an 11-on-11, full-impact sport. There were four downs and a touchdown was six points. There was passing. There was play-to-play strategy. A game from 1920 would not look the way a game looks today,* but its similarities outweigh the differences. And within that similar, primitive world, Thorpe was the T-Rex. He was the strongest runner, the most punishing tackler, and the best kicker anyone had ever seen. He's the model for how football was supposed to be played, materializing at a time when no previous model had been cast. He was the prototype for what a football player was supposed to be, the first exemplar other players tried to emulate. He was football's Babe Ruth. We don't need footage of Jim Thorpe in order to see "Jim Thorpe." We see him whenever we see anyone run with a football, at any level.

Try to recall the most exhilarating open-field run you've ever witnessed (and if you love football, the task won't be difficult). I'd pick the 2005 incarnation of Reggie Bush running against Fresno State, though there are thousands of others just as good: The Marshawn Lynch "Beast Quake" in the 2010 playoffs. O. J. Simpson's 1975 scamper against the Bengals on *MNF* (where he slips on the turf). Marcus Allen's full-field reversal in Super Bowl XVIII. Steve Young's 49-yard stumble against the Vikings. The classic Johnny Rodgers punt return from 1971. Dozens of runs by Adrian Peterson throughout the 2012 season. Saquon Barkley hurdling a Jaguar defender backward, LSU's Billy Cannon on Halloween night, a ridiculous one-yard (!) gain by Walter Payton versus the Cowboys in 1976, and/or every carry of Barry Sanders's career. They're all eligible. And whatever you're seeing on that video screen inside your mind is the atomic

---

*This was the hardest part of my analysis and the one detail that worries me most. It can be argued that the way football was played in the 1920s is simply too unlike contemporary football to qualify as comparable, and that the modern era of football didn't become recognizable until the 1950s, when players started wearing face masks and quit playing both ways. Under those parameters, Jim Brown is the first elite rendering of a player sharing the core characteristics of modern-day football players. But because Jim Thorpe excelled at the most eternal elements of the game—running, tackling, and kicking—his skills still connect to the present. It's also worth noting that the most innovative offense for Carlisle in the 1920s was the unbalanced single wing, a formation still employed today (though now rebranded as the Wildcat).

structure of what football is—speed, power, agility, and instinct. You're seeing eleven men trying to stop one man, and the eleven men are failing. The man with the ball has more speed and more power. His agility and instincts make it impossible to get him on the ground. The way the ball is carried and the way the runner moves is both unique and familiar, and if one could remove the logos from the helmets and the colors from the uniforms and the numbers from every player's back, it could be happening in any decade. It could be happening in 1920. It is eternal and it is natural, and it's always Jim Thorpe.

He is not the beginning. He is the reason the beginning began.

5.
Allegory of the Cave, from the Perspective of the Shadows

I TOOK MY KIDS TO DISNEYLAND AND I TOOK MY KIDS TO UNIVERsal Studios. These are evidently normal things to do, and I will never get used to that. Until I got to college, I'd never met a single person who'd gone to Disneyland. I assumed the whole concept was a narrative device for sitcom plotlines—an unreachable place that children on television mentioned when discussing impossible dreams. Disneyland was for child actors and the Make-A-Wish Foundation. When the New York Giants won the Super Bowl in 1987, Phil Simms became the first quarterback to declare "I'm going to Disneyland" upon being named MVP. It sounded dumb and obviously contrived, and the implausibility of an NFL quarterback feigning excitement over a humanoid mouse furthered my suspicion that this was something no one actually did. But now I live in a place where vacations are ordinary and expected, where half the parents I know haul their kids to Disneyland (or Disney World) at some point in their young lives. Every suburban child is aware that this is something they're supposed to want, ingrained in their psyche more deeply than a belief in Santa Claus or God or McDonald's. So I took my family to Disneyland and I took my family to Universal Studios and we all had an awesome time, or at least a good time, or at least an expensive time that my kids understood to be amazing and memorable, until they got home and immediately forgot 70 percent of what we did. It was a positive experience. I ate a lot of corn dogs. There was, however, one continually uncomfortable realization about how the modern world operates, impossible to ignore and improbably connected to football's grasp on the public consciousness.

Because these theme parks have been around for so long, there's a clear demarcation between the attractions that are new and the attractions that are old, with the newer attractions serving as the draw and the older attractions serving as stuff to do when lines for the more popular attractions grow excessive. At Universal Studios, the marquee ride is called the Forbidden Journey, themed around the Harry Potter series. At Disneyland, it's a *Star Wars* ride called Rise of the Resistance, an eighteen-minute immersive excursion that has replaced Space Mountain as the park's premier feature. Both of these rides are marvels of engineering, and both are so complicated it's often difficult to understand how the experience is being generated. And this, weirdly, is the discomfiting detail: Most of what I experienced was *generated*, meaning it wasn't really "experienced" at all. The most mind-blowing aspect to both the Forbidden Journey and Rise of the Resistance is the degree to which they're straightforward simulations, palpably intense but devoid of risk. If you stripped away everything from the ride except the industrial mechanics, it would be like driving around a parking lot in a golf cart or riding a ski lift that never ascends. There's a sense of speed, but it's the illusion of speed. The visuals are disorienting, but only because the images around the viewer shift while the viewer remains stationary. There's a sensation of being dropped down an elevator

ALLEGORY OF THE CAVE

shaft, though I'm not sure if that actually happened. You're moving through a terrestrial plane, but it's closer to a movie than it is to a roller coaster. Somewhat amusingly, the passengers on these rides are constantly reminded of numerous safety precautions and activities they're never supposed to do while the car is in motion. The pedantic warnings inadvertently accentuate how safe the guest always is. These types of rides also place an intellectual expectation on the rider; to fully appreciate the story built into Rise of the Resistance, one must recall rudimentary plot points from the third *Star Wars* trilogy. For the simulation to succeed, the ticket buyer needs to know details about an experience they aren't actually experiencing. All this stands in stark contrast to an analog ride like Space Mountain (where the speed and disorientation are real) and old-school carnival contraptions like the Octopus or the Roll-o-Plane (where danger is both central to the appeal and too plausible to contemplate).

What's crazy, of course, is that what I'm criticizing is actually my preference. I enjoyed dangerous experiences when I was a kid, but I don't enjoy them now. Like many parents, I want my children to *want* dangerous experiences, but I don't want them to do anything that could realistically hurt them. As a rule, I like simulations more than I like actualities: Albums are better than concerts, the Sphere in Las Vegas impresses me more than the Nevada desert, and eating psilocybin is more edifying than boarding an airplane. When technology reaches the point where it's possible to upload and transfer human consciousness onto a computer system, I'll insist the process is sick and dystopian, and then I will do it. That Rise of the Resistance requires me to know *Star Wars* lore plays to my advantage—it's perhaps the only way I can utilize all the useless lore I've pointlessly acquired. These hypermodern rides are designed for people like me, precisely *because* they're unreal, and my discomfort only comes from my own self-awareness of how such desires are inhuman. What I want most is an unreality that allows me to ignore that awareness: I want a simulation that's warm and alive, separate and indistinguishable from the nonnegotiable reality I prefer to avoid.

But then I remember: I already have that.

In fact, I have several.

▸

There are risks in taking something widely accepted as real and claiming it's actually a simulation, most notably that people really fucking hate this. It is, in my experience, the easiest way to convince someone to stop reading whatever it is you're writing. Part of that has to do with the difficulty in making a reasonable pro-simulation claim. Another part is that any detractor can respond to that claim by threatening to bash your simulated skull with a simulated hammer in order to test the simulated authenticity of your simulated thesis. Suggesting that an existing object doesn't exist presents the opposite of Pascal's Wager, since being wrong makes the argument a waste of time and being correct makes *everything* a waste of time. But the most pressing issue is that people simply don't want to think this way, about football or anything else. It's complicated, a little nihilistic, more than a little goofy, and inevitably followed by unanswerable follow-up questions like "Even if this were somehow true, what difference would it make?" and "Even if this were somehow true, how could it be proven?" and "Even if this were somehow true, what am I supposed to do with that truth?" There's an inescapable human sensation that life *feels* too real to be fake, and that this sensation is too nuanced and personal to be wholly fabricated. It's telling that Nick Bostrom, the existential philosopher who invented the simulation hypothesis, is only willing to place the mathematical probability of all existence being a simulation at around 20 percent, even though the logic of his argument puts that likelihood closer to 99.99

percent. His own analytics can't convince him; if Bostrom were a football coach facing 4th and 2 from his own 45, he'd still punt. And in my own way, I'm also punting. I'm not insisting that football doesn't exist, nor am I claiming that football is a small simulation built inside a larger simulation. My focus is on simulations more akin to that *Stars Wars* ride at Disneyland—something that technically *is* real, but mainly as a projection of what we know, what we expect, and a desire for conflict that won't actually hurt.

These simulations operate on three levels: the active, the passive, and the symbolic.

▶

The *active* level of football simulation is the simplest to understand: video games. Every variety of video game is an active simulation ("active" in the sense that a human is directly controlling whatever's being simulated). In most cases, virtual scenarios are fun because they're unlike anything experienced in our ordinary, everyday world. *Tetris* simulates the assembly of a geometric puzzle under the stress of incessant gravity. *Grand Theft Auto* simulates driving around a city and committing felonies without consequence. *Fortnite* simulates being air-dropped into a war zone and trying to kill ninety-nine adversaries. The majority of video games allow people to attempt tasks they could never perform, or even visualize, in their real life. What's distinctive about sports-related video games—and football games in particular—is that the fun comes not from the details that are fantastical but from the details that are banal.

It's been bizarre, although not surprising, to witness how much video games have come to inform the way modern audiences think about football. They often serve as a kid's *first* exposure to the sport, sometimes before the child has even touched a leather ball on living grass. This has

FOOTBALL

been true for longer than it seems. The way gaming is presented in mainstream media is a lagging indicator of where the mainstream actually is. As recently as the nineties, showing an adult male playing video games in a movie (such as 1996's *Swingers*) was a shorthand way to illustrate a character's immaturity. That kind of visual coding no longer makes sense, replaced by the implication that gaming has become a reasonable way to develop real-life skills (which was the entire plot of the 2023 biopic *Gran Turismo*). It's still possible to criticize an adult who plays video games as lazy and unserious, but not in a manner any more damning than criticizing an adult who rides a Segway or plays golf three times a week.

The history of video game football is a succession of technological jumps, incrementally pursuing the eternal goal of a game that credibly resembles how football actually operates. It's an obvious ambition, but it wasn't at first. The earliest video games were merely *themed* around football, working from the premise that the gamer was playing an electronic emulation only because they had no serious interest in the real thing. Two of the earliest progenitors were handheld games released by Mattel in 1977 and Coleco in 1978. The objective was to move a blinking light (the ballcarrier) through a maze of other lights (the defense) on a tiny LCD screen decorated to resemble a gridiron, though if you didn't know it was a football game you'd have never guessed the connection. The 1983 arcade game *10-Yard Fight* was a significant advancement, in that the game had recognizable football avatars and stadium sound effects. However, key elements to *10-Yard Fight* were wacky: The most effective move was to throw a long lateral to the wingback, who'd then throw deep to a receiver. Since almost every play was a double pass, the quarterback became superfluous. In 1989, the arcade game *Tecmo Bowl* was adapted for the Nintendo Entertainment System and (temporarily) became the best and most popular football game anyone had ever imagined. The visual perspective in *Tecmo Bowl* was delivered from the sideline (similar to the standard TV camera) and

ALLEGORY OF THE CAVE

played horizontally across the screen. Each team had a playbook of only four plays. But *Tecmo Bowl* managed to do something that completely altered the way people thought about video football: It secured a licensing agreement with the NFL Players Association. *Tecmo Bowl* didn't have a licensing agreement with the league itself, so it couldn't use real NFL teams or logos. It could, however, use the names of actual pro players. One of those players was Bo Jackson, a simulated game changer that changed simulated games.

The historical memory of Bo Jackson is unorthodox, destined to grow even more convoluted in the years to come. His career was short and his achievements were limited. He won the Heisman Trophy for Auburn in 1985 but was unhappy with being drafted by the Tampa Bay Buccaneers, choosing to play Major League Baseball instead. His career batting average was .250, and many of his most memorable moments were unrelated to winning at baseball. When he returned to play football for the Raiders as a "hobby" in 1987, he appeared in only thirty-eight games over four seasons and gained 3,134 yards from scrimmage. He will not make the Hall of Fame in either sport, and historians fixate more on his Nike advertising campaigns than his athletic prowess. His biography is limited. But those biographical details stand in contrast to those who watched Jackson throughout the late 1980s and consider him the greatest athlete who ever lived. Jackson was among the last celebrities to exist as an anecdotal legend, where any fleeting glimpse of his raw ability seemed to validate all the impossible claims that were never filmed or verified. One of these claims is that Jackson, as a 230-pound college senior, casually ran a 40-yard dash in 4.13 seconds. There's no footage of this, and Jackson didn't attend the NFL combine. To anyone who never saw Bo firsthand, it's a story that demands skepticism. But to those who lived through his reign—including the designers of *Tecmo Bowl*—the 4.13 story was plausible, which is why Jackson's avatar in *Tecmo Bowl* was several tiers faster than every other player. By running Jackson in a zigzag pattern, a savvy *Tecmo* competitor could score on every play, rendering any matchup against Jackson's team patently unfair. And this, for the first time, forced people to confront the "reality" of unreal football. Prior to Bo, an unstoppable video game character would have been considered a glitch in the engineering. But because Bo Jackson was a real person, and because his avatar's preternatural speed was intentional, it made the game absurd. Somehow, the *Tecmo* creators managed to overrate the finest athlete on the planet. By exaggerating actual life, *Tecmo Bowl* became aesthetically inauthentic, creating a new problem that had never been previously considered and was now the crux of the entire industry.

By 1996, *Tecmo Bowl* (and its more sophisticated sequel, *Tecmo Super Bowl*) had been pummeled into extinction by *Madden NFL*, the most famous football simulation ever produced. Built by a division of Electronic Arts, the original plan for *Madden* was to make a product with just enough credibility to convince former Oakland Raiders coach John Madden to endorse it with his name; at the time, Madden was the lead CBS color commentator with an outsized personality. To the surprise of EA, Madden would agree to the endorsement only if he had editorial control over the game itself, and realism was all he cared about. EA's founder, Trip Hawkins, wanted to draw *Madden* as a 7-on-7 matchup, deleting the guards and tackles to reduce stress on the computer's memory. Madden demanded that *Madden* operate as an 11-on-11 game with legal formations, providing EA with an old Raiders playbook to better design lifelike pass routes and blocking schemes. Its verisimilitude has only increased over time. All players in the league are meticulously ranked across fifty categories, and younger players care about their *Madden* ranking more than any compliment or criticism from traditional journalists. The annual release of every new *Madden* edition is accompanied by "news stories" about what players were graded as 99 overall, followed by debates on podcasts regarding the accuracy of those scores. The closest *Madden* has come to replicating the Bo Jackson *Tecmo* fiasco was its 2004 version, when QB Michael Vick of the Atlanta Falcons was rated 95 for speed, 95 for agility, and 97 for arm strength.

Madden NFL sells about five million copies a year. I've played *Madden* somewhere in the vicinity of twenty total hours, which (in the world of gaming) is less than nothing. There is, however, an NCAA version of *Madden* titled *EA Sports College Football*, which I have played (ahem) "somewhat more frequently." I can't verify how many hours I played *College Football* between 2004 and 2015.* I've tried to calculate a reasonable estimate, but the number of hours I keep hitting is 2,800, which I've convinced myself is impossible. This figure is even stranger when one considers I never play against the computer and have faced only one human opponent, meaning I've played the same person roughly 3,000 times. But for the purpose of analyzing the quality of a simulation, exclusively playing the same guy is ideal; no matter how much the game improves, we stay the same.

Here, in short, is how this happened: I was working at *Spin* magazine, and someone from the business department was laid off (I can't recall her name, but I know she was cool and somewhat tall). We had a party for her the evening before her final day, and one of the last things she drunkenly told us was that she had ten promotional Sony PlayStations sitting in her office closet. I don't know why Sony sent her ten PlayStations, though I could make an educated guess—rock magazines were only slightly less corrupt than Enron. She probably wasn't supposed to tell us this and I'm sure she wasn't supposed to tell us exactly where they were or how easily

---

*EA Sports could not produce a college football video game from 2015 to 2024. This was a legal and licensing issue related to the likenesses of real players being used in the game. The game didn't use the players' given names, but it often used the same jersey numbers and physical characteristics. It was easy to figure out who was who. Production of the game was subsequently suspended due to lawsuits, and the players are now paid.

FOOTBALL

they could be procured, but as Hyman Roth explained in *The Godfather Part II*, "This is the business we've chosen." The next day, I returned to my apartment across from the United Nations and showed my roommates why I loved my job. I'd never owned an Atari or a Nintendo and wasn't familiar with the contemporary state of gaming, so I walked a few blocks to GameStop and purchased the only title that looked good: *EA College Football*. USC's Carson Palmer was on the cover. Me and one of my roommates (whom I shall call Michael, since that is his name) started playing that same night, and we never stopped. When there was nothing else to do, it was the only thing we did. The game became the vortex of our camaraderie, distilling our friendship into a gelatinous ooze of perpetual competition. I moved out in 2006, but the rivalry continued unabated. It is, perhaps sadly, one of the greatest things that has ever happened to me. It's also proof of how valuable a digital simulation can be, in terms of understanding how real football evolves.

From a game-play perspective, *EA College Football* is roughly identical to *Madden NFL*, except there are more than 130 different schools (instead of only 32 franchises) and the play selection is far more diverse (everything from the Flexbone to the Air Raid, depending on which playbook you select). Michael wins slightly more often than I do, if an 85 percent margin can be classified as "slight." This is due to four factors. The most imperative is that Michael is better at operating the game controllers and would likely beat me at whatever video game we happened to be playing. His fingers are more dexterous than my fingers. A second factor is that I always choke in the red zone, constantly throwing picks off play-action passes when I'm inside the 10. A third component is that Michael cares about winning much, *much* more than I do, allowing me to recline on the infuriating moral high ground of mild indifference. But it's the fourth factor that throws the game into emotional chaos:

ALLEGORY OF THE CAVE

Michael is mainly interested in the outcome, while I mainly care about the realism.

When I play *EA College Football*, there are things I do that would motivate most legitimate gamers to jam a gun down my throat. I always adjust the weather to make it more inclement. I prefer to use teams with imperfect rosters (Pitt, Air Force, any team from the MAC). If our fictional game involves Oklahoma State playing in Boone Pickens Stadium, I imagine (and sometimes discuss) how the 52,202 computer-generated fans in attendance will exit the stadium upon the game's conclusion and pursue their 52,202 fictional lives in an alternative dreamscape of Stillwater, Oklahoma. I love throwing to the fullback for a four-yard gain. I love settling for field goals. My favorite call on 3rd and long is a draw. The habit that irritates Michael most is the way I behave at the end of the first half: If I take possession of the ball late in the second quarter, and if I'm deep in my own territory, I will have my quarterback kneel down twice in a row to run out the clock and head to the locker room. I'll do this even if I'm trailing by two touchdowns.

To Michael, this is so stupid that it shocks him every time, no matter how often he's watched me do it. "This is a fucking video game," he'll say. "We can do *whatever we want*. There are no repercussions. Why wouldn't you throw long, just to see what happens?" But I don't like doing that. It seems unserious. My style is a 1990s style, or maybe even a 1970s style. In my view, what Michael suggests is not what would happen in a real game. Which is, somewhat unironically, something I'm increasingly wrong about. There are now many offensive coordinators who would, if faced with 80 yards of real estate and only 25 seconds on the clock, attempt to move into field goal range. In other words, there are now real collegiate coordinators who call plays the same way a thirteen-year-old kid in 1999 would have called plays in a video game. This is the hidden value of an active simulation: As years pass and times change, things that regularly happen only inside games eventually start happening in life.

Michael's complaint with my *EA* approach is that I play so conservatively it makes things boring for both of us. My complaint with his approach is that his success is built on inauthenticity. He passes constantly and will use the same play over and over again, operating from the belief that calling five consecutive screen passes is reasonable if I can't figure out how to properly control my outside linebacker. If he has an elite running back, he will move that running back into the slot and throw to him whenever he needs a first down (the computer has a hard time reconciling how certain skills don't translate between positions). If he trails by more than two scores, he'll run a pass play called Four Verticals on every down, and I generally can't stop it. Most annoyingly, he'll allow his quarterback to make throws I consider physically impossible. He will roll his right-handed QB to the left and then sidearm the ball across the opposite side of the field. If his quarterback has a high enough accuracy rating and his receiver has a high enough awareness rating, he'll throw into triple coverage on purpose. For years, I pointed to these moments as evidence that Michael's wins were fake, dependent on skills that could only exist in a virtual world. But then something happened: Patrick Mahomes became a non-virtual adult. Mahomes took over as the Kansas City Chiefs' starting quarterback in 2018 and immediately started completing passes that had once existed only in video games. By 2021, there were multiple college guys (and even a few high school kids) who'd regularly make throws previously classified as deranged. Intelligent quarterbacks who predated Mahomes changed their perception of what constituted a pass too risky to attempt. It suddenly seemed conceivable that these types of throws were something that had *always* been possible, but QBs had not been allowed to try, entirely due to coaches who thought like me. My circa-2005 criticisms of Michael's *EA* style were retroactively expunged. He had been ahead of

ALLEGORY OF THE CAVE

the curve, and I was still trapped behind it. An entire sport evolved faster than the aptitude of my mind, a miscalculation made all the more mortifying by the 2,800 hours I'd invested in preparing for the shift. I played an active simulation for more than ten years, fully aware that active simulations foretell the future. But I was erroneously seeing the game as a *passive* simulation, and passive simulations care only about the past.

▶

I started playing fantasy football in the fall of 1990, an era when the math had to be computed by hand and the only way to score was through touchdowns, field goals, and PATs. Yardage wasn't tracked and receptions didn't matter. It was a weird pastime, designed for weirdos who couldn't accept that rotisserie baseball ended in September. This was also an era when sports gambling was still reserved for degenerates. Pete Rose had been banned from baseball for life, and betting lines were never discussed on television. People did not think about fantasy football and football gambling in the same way. The two pursuits did not seem connected, despite some readily apparent similarities. But it now feels obvious that the former activity was indoctrinating fans toward an embrace of the latter. Fantasy football has become the most ordinary hobby any football fan can have, and gambling on sports is more mainstream than Skoal Bandits or pornography. The relationship between fantasy football and football gambling is now visible, largely because they're different versions of the same thing: They're passive simulations, where the person involved is engaged with every aspect of the simulation *except* the event itself.

Fantasy football is basic; it's a video game with no controller and better graphics. You draft a team, the players play, and the sum of their individual stats becomes your own overall performance. There's an awkwardness in this, particularly if you find yourself watching a close game between the Rams and the Giants and the only thing you care about is whether Tyler Higbee catches a pass, forcing you to spend the final fifteen minutes maniacally staring at the tight end and feeling annoyed by any play where Higbee is expected to block. It's like eating a seven-course meal and only paying attention to how much paprika was added to the potatoes. But fantasy potatoes are still small, compared to legitimate sports gambling. Rooting for a random guy on your fantasy team is still less disorienting than hoping to win a bet against the point spread, a sensation so painful and exhilarating it can only be classified as ecstatic evil.

I don't partake in much gambling. I have the wrong personality, the wrong constitution. The more logic I use, the more I lose.* I do, however, *think* about gambling all the time, and I'm part of a (possibly illegal?) pool where I try to pick five games a week against the spread. To win, you need to get all five games correct,† which doesn't sound hard. But it almost

---

*I happened to be watching the NCAA basketball tournament in Las Vegas in March 2023. While strolling through a casino, I noticed the odds for Arch Manning to win the Heisman Trophy that coming autumn were 80-to-1. At the time, Manning was an incoming freshman at Texas. My logic was good: If Manning somehow managed to beat out the incumbent starter, Quinn Ewers, it would automatically indicate that he was exceptional, and because of his last name the media attention around his performance would be ubiquitous. It seemed possible he could become a Heisman candidate by default. I put $100 on Manning to win the Heisman, even though he'd never played a down of college football. Everything about this bet seemed smart. The only problem was that Manning redshirted.

†Anyone reading this probably doesn't need sports gambling explained, but just in case you're a Jehovah's Witness: Sports gambling is almost never concerned with who wins or loses a given game. The wager is over the point spread. If Baltimore is favored to beat Denver by 3.5 points and a bettor selects Baltimore, the Ravens must win by four points or more; if the gambler bets on Denver, the Broncos must either win the game outright or lose by three points or fewer. The idea is that the spread makes every game a 50-50 proposition. If a casino can persuade half its customers to bet on Baltimore and the other half on Denver, the casino is guaranteed to make money, since the casino keeps all the money lost by the losers while still taking a small fee from the winners (this fee is called the "juice" or the "vigorish"). The widespread understanding of this system has generated the belief that a bookmaker never cares who wins or loses any game, since all the casino wants is a balanced ticket (i.e., an equal amount of money wagered on both teams). This is not *totally* accurate, as there are certain situations where bookmakers take a biased position on a game's outcome, based on the belief that they know something most casual gamblers don't. But the conventional wisdom is still more true than false: Most of the time, the line is intended to make every game the equivalent of a coin toss.

ALLEGORY OF THE CAVE

never happens, to me or to any of the other participants in the pool. What's extra-vexing is how knowing almost anything about the teams involved tends to decrease my likelihood for success. In a passive simulation, knowledge can work against you.

Years ago, my brother-in-law (the first real gambler I'd ever met) told me something I was too young to grasp. "You can't understand football if you're not betting on it," he said. "And it's funny, because every asshole in America thinks he understands the NFL. But they don't know anything if they aren't gambling." I didn't believe my brother-in-law when he told me this. I believe him now. In fact, if asked what class of professionals are most consistently competent at their job, my answer would be whoever is setting the betting lines in various Las Vegas casinos. If I had a brain tumor, I'd want a neurosurgeon to handle the operation, but if I wanted to know the likelihood of my post-surgery survival, I'd trust an oddsmaker from Caesars Palace way more than any doctor. Bookmakers know things that cannot be known. At the inception of every college season, there are always a few nonconference games featuring a major powerhouse (say, Alabama or Penn State or Georgia) against a cupcake program who shouldn't even be on their schedule (Louisiana-Monroe, UMass, Kent State). Neither team has played, so there's no way to tell how surprisingly good or exceptionally terrible either school might be. The line will open at 49.5 points, a huge number that feels arbitrary and random. And inevitably, the favored team will win by 48, 49, or 50 points.

How is this accuracy achieved? It doesn't matter how many stories about gambling I read; no one has ever sufficiently elucidated how these lines are drawn with such precision. It's a trade secret shared by the entire industry, but it somehow never leaks to the public, leading me to believe there might be no secret at all. Billy Walters, a convicted felon and the self-styled Michael Jordan of sports betting, wrote a book titled *Gambler: Secrets from a Life at Risk*. Before it was released in 2023, I interacted with

FOOTBALL

Walters's cowriter (the veteran investigative reporter Armen Keteyian) and asked if this book would finally explain how these spreads were created. Keteyian implied that it would, but it really didn't. It only explained Walters's techniques for *beating* the spread, which isn't the same. Every week of the season, there's endless online advice for gamblers on how to find "value" when Vegas gets a spread wrong. The harder question is why Vegas is so often correct. There are only two explanations that make sense. One is that the bookmakers only *appear* accurate due to a combination of confirmation bias (the tendency to notice information that confirms what we already believe) and the availability heuristic (the tendency to base the probable outcome of a future event on a limited number of memorable examples). In other words, I always notice when the spread is set at 49.5 and the final score is 55–7, while thoughtlessly overlooking five other games from the same week where the spread didn't come close. The other explanation is based on the "wisdom of crowds," where the point spread opens* at a neutral number, all the most serious gamblers immediately place bets on either side of the line, and the amount wagered on those bets calibrates the spread until it's perfect. The professional gamblers simulate the game in their mind and place that simulated outcome against the casino's imperfect number, forcing the casino to react accordingly. This works the majority of the time, though it's most instructive when it works *too* well, as was the case with Super Bowl XIII, a game immortalized in gambling lore by the moniker Black Sunday.

The 1979 Super Bowl is the watershed event in the history of gambling on football, a situation so devastating to sports books that it will never be allowed to happen again. The Dallas Cowboys were playing the

---

*The thought leaders for this praxis, setting the table for casinos and U.S. betting markets, are unregulated offshore online sports books in places like Panama and Latvia.

ALLEGORY OF THE CAVE

Pittsburgh Steelers. Dallas had won the previous year's Super Bowl and had the highest scoring offense in the league, but they'd started the season 3-2 and were considered less complete than Pittsburgh. The Steelers had lost only two games all season (by a total of ten points), obliterated both of their playoff opponents, and had already beaten Dallas in Super Bowl X. The betting line opened with Pittsburgh as a 2.5 point favorite. Virtually all the early money was wagered on the Steelers, a dangerous situation for bookmakers if the Steelers won easily. To compensate, casinos started raising the spread to persuade other people to take the Cowboys, but it wasn't working. A few days before the game, the spread had jumped all the way to 5.5 points, prompting a massive number of bettors to suddenly take the Cowboys. The line slipped back to 4.5 and was exactly 4 a few minutes before kickoff. The lack of that final one-half point would be critical.

The game was tight until the fourth quarter, when a series of bad breaks and officiating miscues gave Pittsburgh a 35–17 lead. It looked as if Vegas had avoided disaster, until the final three minutes. The Cowboys staged a furious comeback, recovering an onside kick and scoring twice before losing. The final score was 35–31, an absolute worst-case scenario for bookmakers. Almost no bettors lost money: All the early gamblers who'd picked the Steelers as a 2.5- or 3.5-point favorite were correct, as were all the late gamblers who needed Dallas to lose by less than 4.5 or 5.5. And because the final line hit precisely on the actual margin, everyone who placed a bet on either team at the last possible moment got their money refunded on a push.

The memory of Black Sunday is reintroduced every February, lodged in any story about the huge amount of money being wagered on every new Super Bowl (a number that now stretches way beyond $1 billion). It's the rare high-profile example of Las Vegas losing, so people love the anecdote. It also animates the nuanced mental gymnastics operating inside the mind of every person who believes watching football can make them money.

The average margin of victory in the NFL regular season varies from season to season, but it's usually between nine and twelve points. That average is a little deceptive, since the lowest a margin can be is one while the maximum margin is limitless. If the spread of any NFL game is set at a number greater than nine, it means the contest is expected to be a blowout. But the mind of a gambler rarely simulates a blowout, and what gambling teaches is that blowouts happen less often than we assume, even when one team dominates the other. Instead, the conclusion of many, many games teeters on the cusp of the "backdoor cover," the quintessence of the gambling experience and the wildest outcome to mentally project. A backdoor cover occurs when a team scores (or allows) an inconsequential touchdown late in the game—a touchdown that has no bearing on who wins but huge ramifications for everyone who bet on the spread. Super Bowl XIII was a backdoor cover: Butch Johnson caught a touchdown with 22 seconds remaining, cutting the final score to 35–31. It was a trivial moment that didn't stop Pittsburgh from winning, but it inverted the wager for anyone who'd picked Dallas as a 4.5-point underdog.

This sort of meaningless/meaningful reversal happens constantly, every week of every season. What makes it so intriguing is how it forces a gambler to calculate the existential likelihood of events dictated by apathy and entropy.

There are times when gambling is nothing more than the application of rules that resemble common sense, structured around the game's mathematical quirks. Let's say Team A is playing Team B. Both teams are roughly equal, but Team A is playing at home and Team B's previous game was on Monday night, meaning they had one less day to rest and recover. Team A is justifiably favored, and the bettor's thought process

ALLEGORY OF THE CAVE

becomes transparent: If the spread is 2.5, he takes Team A, since it seems reasonable that a game between two well-matched teams might come down to the home team kicking a late field goal. If the spread is 3.5, he takes Team B, because if the game is decided by a field goal, he'll win either way. It's a conservative, self-evident choice. This, however, is not the true spirit of "gambling." There's risk, but the bettor is merely doing what the percentages suggest should be done. What's harder is a scenario oozing with backdoor potentiality: Team A is better than Team B in every way, and the prevailing sentiment is that Team A will win easily. You agree with this sentiment and decide to bet on Team A, but the spread is 8.5 points. This forces you to follow the game like a meteorologist following a storm cell, fixated on the possibility of Team B scoring an eleventh-hour throwaway touchdown that makes the affair closer than it truly was. It requires the consideration of issues that don't necessarily play a role in winning or losing a football game: how much the involved players care (or don't care) about amassing personal statistics, how much (or how little) the winning head coach wants to embarrass his opponent, the desire (or unwillingness) to attempt an inessential two-point conversion in a game that's already been decided. Every backdoor possibility becomes a simulated game inside the external game. All the players are unknowingly participating in a secondary event, where the motives and the "score" are unseeable to anyone who isn't gambling. On the final weekend of the 2024 season, the 11-5 Baltimore Ravens hosted the 3-13 Cleveland Browns. The matchup was trivial and the Ravens won in a 25-point blowout. It was never close. Yet more than 17 million people watched that meaningless game until the bitter end. Why? In large part because the Ravens were a 20.5-point favorite, the most ostentatious spread of the year. Nobody thought the Browns would win, but many wrongly believed they would lose by less than three touchdowns. The real game was boring. The fake game was drenched in complexity. Two weeks later, in the AFC Divisional

FOOTBALL

Playoff, the Houston Texans trailed Kansas City by 11 with less than two minutes to go, placing the statistical probability of a Chiefs win at 98.7 percent. The game was basically over. But the game *inside* the game remained an electrifying donnybrook. Houston was either an 8.5- or 9.5-point underdog (depending on where and when the bettor placed the bet). When the Texans moved the ball inside the red zone with 2:18 on the clock, analytics advised the Texans to kick a field goal (cutting the margin to 8), opening the door for an onside kick and a desperation Hail Mary. And that's what they tried, though the attempt was blocked. Earlier in the contest, the Texans' kicker had also missed a long field goal and an extra point, making him partially responsible for why Houston lost the game. His influence on the interior game, however, was cataclysmic. That blocked field goal shifted millions of unseen dollars and probably broke up somebody's marriage. Making matters even goofier was what happened on the game's final possession: The Chiefs' punter took an intentional safety with 15 seconds on the clock, moving the final margin to 23–14. That meant all the gamblers who picked the Chiefs to cover by 9.5 *also* lost, on a needless play that represented zilch in the unsimulated world.

This is what my brother-in-law meant when he said, "You can't understand football if you're not betting on it." A normal fan is like a person who listens to Beethoven's Symphony No. 5 and thinks, "This music is beautiful." A gambler is like a person who listens to Symphony No. 5 and thinks, "I don't trust the motives of the bassoonist."

Nationwide sports gambling was legalized by the Supreme Court in 2018. In the years since that decision, gambling has taken over everything, far faster than anyone (except maybe gamblers) imagined. The hobby has become so prevalent that it can feel as though gambling has always been a central part of following sports, and that being against gambling is childish. There are also those who believe the normalization of sports wagering

ALLEGORY OF THE CAVE

will be more destructive than anyone is willing to admit, largely due to the development of betting apps on smartphones that work off credit. I used to be one of those people, and sometimes I still am. It's only a matter of time before a point-fixing scandal damages the credibility of a major sports league, and we're assuredly five or ten years away from a national crisis over gambling addiction. For most of my life, I was of the position that gambling should be legalized, even though it didn't have any social purpose that wasn't negative; my political view on wagering was a little like pro-choice advocates who still think abortion is murder. But I don't think that way anymore, and not because I started gambling and decided it was great. What I've discovered is something I never anticipated: Gambling *enriches* football, at least conversationally. It's an amazing thing to argue about, even for those of us who never risk any money. When I find myself talking about pro or college football with old friends or minor acquaintances, it's astounding how often gambling lines and prop bets infiltrate the dialogue. It's not just an extra topic, added to the list of all other previous topics; it's an entirely separate discussion, connected yet unrelated to the game itself. And unlike talking about fantasy football, talking about gambling is interesting to both involved parties. Listening to someone talk about their fantasy football team is like listening to someone talk about their garden. Listening to that same person talk about their gambling failures is fascinating as hell. Why? Well, mostly because it involves money. But also because it's a stranger, deeper simulation. Gambling on football means you're watching a different game from everyone else. It's a private, passive simulation that only you can see, involving you and you alone, unless you find someone else who made the exact same bet, in which case the two of you are bonded in a temporary, simulated friendship. In his memoir, *Based on a True Story*, compulsive gambler Norm Macdonald (a brilliant guy who lost everything he owned at least three times) describes this unreal sensation with an accuracy that's perhaps too real to handle: "I remember a psychiatrist once telling me that I gamble in order to escape the reality of life. I told him that's why everyone does everything."

▸

Football video games are fun, creative, and addictive. Fantasy football is sometimes fun, sometimes creative, and sometimes addictive. Gambling on football is addictive, addictive, and also addictive. All of those simulations have their place. Still, we all know what the *big* football simulation is, even if we don't talk about it as often as we once did. It's the symbolic simulation that matters most, the one that hauls the water and makes the hay and impregnates the donkey in the back of the barn: It's the ingrained understanding that football is a simulation of warfare, and that football is a way to experience war without the inconvenience of death and destruction. The relationship between football and war is so enduring that it's become cliché, a platitude devoid of insight. The ontolgy, however, is a bit more subterranean. Football is still a metaphor for war, but not the kind of war that still happens. Football is a metaphor for the way war *used to be*, allowing people to feel nostalgia for an experience they never had and would never want.

It is the most powerful mental transubstantiation in all of sport.

There's a long-standing theory that the origin of football is directly and unabashedly tied to military science, specifically to the end of the American Civil War. Instead of relishing the postwar peace, Reconstruction-era thought leaders worried that the next generation of U.S. males would never experience the adversity of combat, and that the absence of this experience would make those men soft and weak. To compensate, college football was invented as a surrogate.

ALLEGORY OF THE CAVE

"Young men could learn the hard lessons of war and develop tough moral character through a battle on the playing field without the actual bloodshed and death of armed conflict," wrote historian George M. Fredrickson in his 1965 book, *The Inner Civil War: Northern Intellectuals and the Crisis of the Union*. This has become the best evidence of football's military genesis. If nothing else, the timing makes sense. The Civil War ended in 1865 and the first college football game was played in 1869. I've referenced this origin story many times, in print and in conversation, and I trust it to be true. The only hitch is that it's impossible to verify. Everyone accepts the correlation, and the logic is (sort of) reasonable. But you can't find much data that suggests this thinking was common at the time. As far as I can tell, nobody in 1866 unambiguously said, "We need football because we no longer have war." There's nothing in Ulysses S. Grant's 584-page autobiography about the patriotic majesty of Spider 2 Y Banana. But as is so often the case with soft history, the received message is more relevant than whatever actually happened. It *feels* like nineteenth-century football would be a practical proxy for the Battle of Gettysburg, so that is what it became. The projection became concrete in 1896, when Walter Camp wrote a book titled *Football*. The book catalogs every detail of the game at the turn of the century, with one subsection brazenly titled "Comparison Between War and Football." Multiple passages from this chapter compliment Napoleon Bonaparte. Camp saw "a very remarkable and interesting likeness between the theories which underlie great battles and the miniature contests on the gridiron," though this vision is muddled by Camp's unconventional worldview. Camp was a proponent of "Muscular Christianity," a late nineteenth-century movement that prioritized the moral value of physicality, self-sacrifice, and institutional loyalty. One of the things Camp loved about Napoleon was the French general's "three to one" ratio, a principle arguing that what an army of soldiers believes is three times more important than their physical resources.

FOOTBALL

What's uncomfortable about this principle is that it implies the key to winning a war is being morally and ideologically correct, thereby suggesting the final result of any war must be its most inherently ethical outcome. Camp wanted to see football as war because Camp saw war as morally good.

Morals aside, some of this relationship is elementary: The goal of football is to incrementally overtake an opponent's homeland, achieved through a combination of force and strategy. The language is unsubtle ("field generals" throw "bombs" over linemen "in the trenches"). The participants wear body armor and are defined only by the color of their clothes.* The hierarchy is militaristic: The head coach is the Secretary of Defense, the offensive coordinator is the five-star general calling the shots, the quarterback is the one-star general who gets the glory, and the other ten guys are grunts who expect to die. Two-a-day practices in August are the high school equivalent of boot camp at Parris Island. Everyone wears a helmet, everyone does calisthenics, and everyone is expected to chant in unison. The best thing you can be is selfless, tough, and committed. The worst thing you can be is self-interested, disloyal, and weak. You can believe this

---

*Because the players are essentially faceless (and because the expression of individual personality is discouraged by the rules), football uniforms matter much more than other sports regalia, particularly at the college level. When someone without a strong rooting interest watches a football game, they're watching a dehumanized battle between groups of colors, with the experience dictated by which colors are involved. Slovenly dudes who hate fashion will still obsess over the visual language of football uniforms. The Platonic ideal is Ole Miss hosting LSU, assuming Ole Miss wears their powder blue jerseys and LSU wears white tops and yellow pants. Clemson (in all-orange) versus UCLA is a matchup that has never historically occurred, but would be deeply satisfying if it did. Tulane (at home) vs. Coastal Carolina skews nontraditional, but the divergence in hue reflects the teal-tinted majesty of the sea. SMU looks amazing when they go all white, as does Colorado. I dislike heavily monochromatic patterns, but a few still work due to the tonal depth: North Carolina, Texas, Penn State. Alabama employs a dismal shade of crimson, but they compensate by putting their players' numbers on the side of their helmets, a timeless accent that overcomes a lot. There are a handful of programs I support primarily because of their aesthetics: Tennessee, Wyoming, Sam Houston. That might sound nonsensical, and in a different sport, it would be. But when the game is college football, I'm not necessarily rooting for the players, whose names I might not recognize and whose faces I cannot see. I'm rooting for the institution itself, making the people wearing the uniforms less meaningful than their visual representation. This is not a flaw. This is a feature.

ALLEGORY OF THE CAVE

is all a social construct, but such a belief is worthless, even if true; most things are social constructs, and things constructed by society are still real enough to kill a man. If football isn't like war, then nothing is like war. It is not, however, like a modern war. It's not shock and awe, and it's not *Call of Duty*. It's closer to the board game Stratego. Modern football can only simulate an ancient war, and that's the attraction. It is not a reconstruction of military maneuvers. It's a reconstruction of military history.

A few months before I was born, Don DeLillo released his second novel, *End Zone*. It's a satiric story about a fictional college football team, similar in tone to Robert Altman's 1970 film *M*A*S*H* (which, somewhat mysteriously, contains a fourteen-minute sequence about a football game that's largely unrelated to the rest of the movie). One of the key characters in *End Zone* is a professor named Major Staley who teaches a class on contemporary warfare, and there are lots of analogies about football and nuclear war. When people criticize this novel, they tend to suggest that such comparisons are trite and a little on the nose, since using football as a metaphor for war is not exactly innovative. What those critics fail to appreciate is that DeLillo realized a very different point, years before anyone else: Warfare had evolved faster than the sport it inspired. There is no nuclear option in football. It can only be done the old way.

"War is the ultimate realization of modern technology," Major Staley explains to a star running back obsessed with atomic annihilation. "For centuries, men have tested themselves in war. War was the final test, the great experience, the privilege, the honor, the self-sacrifice. . . . War was the great challenge and the great evaluator. It told you how much you were worth. But it's different today. Few men want to go off and fight. We prove ourselves, our manhood, in other ways, in making money, in skydiving, in hunting mountain lions with bow and arrow, in acquiring power."

What DeLillo is suggesting (perhaps sardonically) is that football has become one of those "other ways" to prove oneself, and that playing strong safety for Penn State is not altogether different from stalking a cougar in the foothills of Mount Nittany. It aligns with both the notion of football as a postwar replacement and with Walter Camp's vision for Muscular Christianity. But I would take this idea further still. Football is not just a replacement for war. It's a way to connect with how the warlike world used to be, based on values that were once everything and are now nothing. What modern football simulates is the bygone version of warfare imagined by Sun Tzu. That feels good to people, and especially to men.

Stand-up comedian Shane Gillis has a bit where he talks about visiting the former slave quarters of George Washington, and it opens like this: "I'm a bit of a history buff," he says. "Which, by the way, is a sign of early onset Republican. It's a very serious warning sign. If you're a white dude in your twenties and thirties and you can't stop reading about World War II, it's coming." This is clever for multiple reasons, though mainly because it's so obviously true. A less obvious reason is that it describes both the appeal of Gillis and the appeal of football, a sport Gillis briefly played at West Point. Gillis is ideologically liberal, but he looks and sounds like a blue-collar conservative. As a result, he's able to play both sides against the middle by being himself. To intransigent progressives, Gillis is the most palatable version of an anti-woke cis-white alpha male; to a MAGA reactionary, he's a leftist who doesn't take himself seriously and understands why Trump won. He might buy an electric car, but he still knows what a catalytic converter does.

Football balances a similar equation. It is, technically and objectively, the most forward-thinking sport we have. Football constantly adopts new technologies and innovative strategies. The most coveted coaches tend to be the youngest coaches. All thirty-two NFL teams share their TV revenue equally, the most visibly successful example of American socialism. Players wear pink shoes to support breast cancer awareness, and when Michael

ALLEGORY OF THE CAVE

Sam (an openly gay defensive end from Missouri) was taken in the seventh round of the 2014 draft, it was celebrated as a trailblazing moment. Stadium groundskeepers paint END RACISM in the back of end zones. The Rooney Rule requires any team hiring a coach to interview a minimum of two minority candidates, and the longest-tenured head coach is currently Mike Tomlin. Donald Trump once told his followers to stop watching pro football because its players lack patriotism. These are all facts. Yet at the same time, everyone knows that football is *fundamentally* conservative and male-coded, to a depth so deep that mentioning it feels unnecessary. Octogenarian political strategist James Carville has talked about this a lot, sometimes citing anti-pigskin sentiment as part of an existential problem for liberal electability.

"It's what I call coastal condescension," Carville said at the 2024 Aspen Ideas Festival. *"Don't eat hamburgers. Don't watch football. Don't drink beer. . . .* I'm sorry, but Democratic messaging is too feminine. It just is."

Though it didn't make his list of male proclivities, Carville (who attended Louisiana State in the 1960s) could have easily added, "An obsession with warfare that no longer exists." Old men love old wars. They love talking about them and they love reading about them. But here again, the key to this fixation is that those wars are over. If a war is hot and ongoing, it remains off-limits to everybody. The 2003 controversy surrounding Kellen Winslow II is proof.

Winslow is the son of Kellen Winslow Sr., who—at the time of his retirement in 1987—was among the greatest tight ends in history, arguably the very best. Winslow II was another talented tight end, though his pro career would end as a disappointment, further erased by a fourteen-year prison sentence for the rape of an unconscious teenager and the sexual battery of a fifty-four-year-old hitchhiker. Kellen Winslow II is a violent criminal. But in 2003, he was still just a junior at the University of Miami.

FOOTBALL

During a regular season game against Tennessee, a crushing Winslow block injured a Volunteer defensive player. When asked about this injury in a postgame interview, a shirtless Winslow expressed no remorse: "He'd do the same thing to me. This is *war*. They will kill you. They're out there to kill you . . . if I didn't hurt him, he'd hurt me. . . . I'm a fucking *soldier*!"

Now, when Winslow said all this, the United States was only two years removed from the 9/11 terrorist attacks and actively engaged in two ongoing military operations (the war in Afghanistan and the war in Iraq). It was a precarious period for American discourse, with an expectation that support for the troops was universal and nonnegotiable. Winslow was hammered for comparing himself to a military combatant. It was viewed as disrespectful, self-aggrandizing, childish, and untrue. Winslow was forced to apologize, concluding his statement of contrition with, "As for my reference to being a soldier in a war, I meant no disrespect to the men and women who have served, or are currently serving, in the armed forces. I cannot begin to imagine the magnitude of war or its consequences."

Even after his apology, the consensus around Winslow was that he was mentally disturbed, and I suppose the criminal acts he later committed bear this out. But to me, what's crazier is that Winslow had to apologize for saying something about himself that other people say about guys like him all the time. Football players are constantly compared to soldiers. The anecdotal language of football is the nonfigurative language of military history: Edge rushers are "warriors" who "blitz." Guys who cover punts are "gunners." The rivalry between Oregon and Oregon State is referred to as the Civil War. Kansas vs. Missouri is called the Border War, as is Colorado State vs. Wyoming. The annual clash between Texas and Oklahoma is the Red River Shootout. In the 1970s, the rivalry between Woody Hayes's Ohio State and Bo Schembechler's Michigan was known as the Ten Year War, and the definitive book about that rivalry is titled *War as They Knew*

ALLEGORY OF THE CAVE

It. What's ironic about that title is that the Ten Year War, despite starting in 1969, was never thought of like the Vietnam War, even though that war was happening at the same time. Vietnam was a guerrilla war, where revolutionary peasants in black pajamas made unorthodox strikes before disappearing into the night. That was nothing like the Ten Year War between the Buckeyes and the Wolverines. The Ten Year War was like those Napoleonic wars Walter Camp loved, where the tactics were perceptible, the rules of engagement were shared, and Archie Griffin ran to daylight at the point of attack.

I was watching the Army-Navy game a few years back when my young son came downstairs to see what I was doing. He wasn't super-interested in the game, but I told him who was playing and who was winning and that it was evidently quite foggy in upstate New York. He went back upstairs and Army won 15–0. But later that night, when I was putting him to bed beneath his Marvel-themed sheets, he asked why the Army and the Navy would ever be on opposite sides, so I explained the whole deal. My lecture evolved into a longer conversation about war, and nuclear war, and eventually the theory of mutually assured destruction. I worried, because of the name, that he might find the theory of mutually assured destruction troubling or even terrifying. He did not. "That seems like a good system," he said, and I enthusiastically agreed. So then I started explaining how various wars are remembered in different ways, and while everyone concedes that war is terrible, some wars are considered historically good.

"Which ones?" he wondered.

"Well, that depends on who's asking the question," I said, killing the entire conversation. It was time for sleep, at least for him. But the next day, I realized what my answer should have been: Good wars are the wars from the past, where even the people who survived are now dead. Ancient wars

FOOTBALL

are curious and inspiring and dreamlike, and that makes them good. The bad wars are the wars we can remember firsthand, or any wars that are still happening. The very worst wars are the wars that have not happened yet. And this, I could have explained, is why I always watch the Army-Navy game, even if it's not dynamic or competitive: It's a simulation of war, but only the good kind.

6.

This Is Still Your Father's Oldsmobile

AS A MIDDLE-AGED MAN IN CONSTANT INTERACTION WITH OTHER middle-aged people, much of my daily conversation fixates on strangers younger than myself. That's always whom middle-aged people are talking about whenever they discuss the state of the world: people in their twenties they will never actually meet.

This is not a complaint or a problem. It's just life, and it was life long before I was born. Things classified as hot are things that are popular with people in their twenties. A "famous celebrity" is someone who's famous to someone who's twenty-one. Whenever a low-grade futurist monologues about the future of America, what they're describing is how Americans in their late twenties are assumed to be living already. This has been true since the nineteenth century, though you don't fully recognize it until you're at least forty, which means every middle-aged adult is forever forming opinions about the credibility of a demographic who can't grasp how they're already destined to lose the power they don't realize they possess.

FOOTBALL

The enlightened opinion one is supposed to hold about the young is that their provocative ideas are inevitably correct, and that history unfailingly proves that the views of outspoken twentysomethings eventually become the views of everyone else. This take is particularly common among hipster olds who believe aligning themselves with young people keeps them young; they see a college protest or they read a novel from a precocious author or they hear a teenager voicing radical politics, and they say, "The kids know the truth." What's hilarious about this claim is that it only works in the aggregate. Ask any fifty-year-old if he or she (on a personal level) was more intelligent and more ethically sophisticated at the age of twenty-five: They'll always, always, always say no. Somehow, it's possible to imagine that young people are smarter as an amorphous group, even when the individual experience of every midlife adult suggests the opposite. Still, this contradictory outlook is seen as superior to its opposite, which is that all young people are confused and uninformed and lazy and fragile and self-absorbed and narcissistic. Anyone who makes such claims will be told that this is how irrelevant old people always view the encroaching future, and that they're merely repeating the same grievances their own parents made about them (and that their parents' grievances were identical to the complaints once made by their grandparents and great-grandparents). The fact that every fading generation pessimistically concludes the world is getting worse is supposed to prove that these negative categorizations are untrue, though it overlooks the possibility that every generation who criticizes their descendants actually has a point, and that the world *is* continually getting worse.

The crux of this conundrum is not about people or generations, nor is it about the way people and generations change. It's more of a conceptual question—a question that never disappears and applies to almost everything in existence: "Do the old ways still work, or are the new ways better?"

The arc of civilization bends toward the latter. Football coaches do not.

THIS IS STILL YOUR FATHER'S OLDSMOBILE

With the possible exception of used-car salesmen, there's no vocational stereotype quite as fixed as that of a football coach. There are endless examples of real-life coaches who contradict this stereotype, but almost none in fiction, where a coach's personality is always the same. Negative depictions of football coaches (*Dazed and Confused, Varsity Blues, The Slaughter Rule*) present characters with the same core sensibilities as those depicted positively (Eric Taylor in *Friday Night Lights*, Ted Lasso in *Ted Lasso*). Even when a portrayal strives for ambivalence (as with Al Pacino in *Any Given Sunday*), the caricature stays locked. Craig T. Nelson played a problematic antagonist in the movie *All the Right Moves* and an affable protagonist in the TV sitcom *Coach* without changing his baseline persona at all. There are certain traits all football coaches are expected to possess: They're demanding, unapproachable, and obsessed with detail. They are patriarchal realists with juvenile interests. They're emotional, but only demonstrative when the emotion is anger or pride. They refuse to engage with hypothetical questions. They work long hours and are immune to inclement weather. In the morning, they drink whole milk with their kids. In the evening, they drink beer from aluminum cans, alone on the couch. They constantly get fired and are never surprised when it happens. Most critically, they are unsentimentally mired in the past—mistrustful of modernity and indifferent toward the future. Like Tony Soprano, they are history buffs who hate nostalgia; instead of seeing the past as something to remember, they see it as the way things should continue to be done.

What makes this caricature significant is the begrudging acceptance that all of these qualities are necessary, but only in combination and only if possessed by a man whose job is coaching football. It is hard to understand how and why that happened. When a youngish coach like Mike

FOOTBALL

McDaniel or Brandon Staley doesn't fit the archetype, the genuine details of his personality receive less attention than the blanket categorization that he "doesn't come across like a traditional football coach," an optimistic description on the day he gets hired and a pejorative explanation on the day he gets fired. The image matters more than the résumé, even when the résumé is genuine. When Kamala Harris was running for president in 2024 and selected Minnesota governor Tim Walz as her running mate, it was partially because Walz was once employed as an assistant high school football coach for Mankato West High School. During preelection rallies, Harris referred to Walz as "coach" more regularly than she called him "governor," and it became impossible to find any long profile about Walz that didn't note this specific aspect of his biography. In theory, the partnership was supposed to help Harris tap into male voting blocs. In practice, it destroyed her credibility among the specific demographic she wanted to persuade. Walz wasn't pretending; he really was a former football coach. He patterned himself after Nebraska's Tom Osborne, implemented a 4-4 defensive attack, and won a state title. But Walz only seemed like a football coach to voters with no preexisting relationship to football. His image embodied the liberal conception of nontoxic masculinity, a reverse Margaret Thatcher.

What has happened, it seems, is that the meaning of "football coach" has adopted an unusually conflicted taxonomy. As a generic term for a faceless figure, the connotation is bad: The football coach is a retrograde bully, a nonintellectual devoid of empathy. In a more functional scenario, the connotation is good: A football coach gets things done and leads by example. But in a specific sense, when the coach is a real person and not an abstract idea, the negative traits of the generic image *become* the positive traits of the functional image. A football coach is old-fashioned on purpose, because he understands that objective truths don't change. A football coach is not intellectual, but only because he's smart enough to realize you can't learn to plow by reading a book. A football coach is a hard man who believes pain is weakness leaving the body, and what is now considered bullying is what he classifies as motivating. What's crazy is that football coaches (and particularly assistant coaches) who embody problematic traits tend to have longer careers than coaches who do not, even if they experience less success. A traditional coach is seen as an asset even when he loses. A nontraditional coach must win to survive.

In the civilian world, a football coach is granted the status of Colonel Nathan R. Jessep, Jack Nicholson's character from *A Few Good Men*. Jessep throws around terse aphorisms like "You want me on that wall" and "You need me on that wall" and "You can't handle the truth." He's the bad guy in the movie, a chunk of human garbage, but everyone secretly fears he might have a point. Jessep's contention is that certain hard things can only be achieved through the old ways, even if those ways conflict with what society prefers. In *A Few Good Men*, such thinking results in a murder, a suicide, and a prison sentence. But the story's subtextual lesson is perhaps more troubling: The reason Jessep's truth can't be handled is because it's an immoral truth, and the prospect of something both necessary and immoral requires too much cognitive dissonance to casually accept. Such problems can, however, be considered through the many Jessep-like men who coach football, where the stakes are lower but the song remains the same.

▶

What's a bit incongruous about this conjecture is that most real football coaches do not embody their fictional cliché, most of the time. There's now a whole subset to the coaching caricature encompassing younger coaches who specialize in innovation, a loose amalgamation of Sean McVay, Kevin O'Connell, and Kyle Shanahan (though the original models were guys from the seventies like Don Coryell and Bill Walsh). These boy-geniuses tend to be offensive-minded disrupters who treat the sport as a schematic equation, less obsessed with fortitude and more concerned with invention. There's also no consistent relationship between football coaches and political intolerance, despite a paleoconservative desire for this to be the case. While it's true that traditionalists didn't buy Walz as a football diehard, those who connected that failing to his mentorship of the gay-straight alliance at his Minnesota high school were projecting an ahistorical prejudice. Vince Lombardi, the defining figure of the coaching genre, welcomed queer players to his roster when he briefly coached Washington in the late 1960s and made it clear that any teammate who questioned their manhood would be cut from the team.* The nature of the job, and particularly the process of recruiting players at the collegiate level, requires coaches to be open to all types of disparate people. When coaching at the University of Oklahoma in the 1970s and 1980s, Barry Switzer was nationally perceived as a southern redneck but regionally beloved for his ability to relate to minority athletes, many of whom classified him as among the most open-minded white people they'd ever met. Switzer claimed one of his recruiting techniques was to walk through the alley behind a potential recruit's residence before going inside the house. He wanted to see what brand of empty beer bottles were in the trash. This way, if the recruit's father offered him a beer, he could offhandedly request whatever he'd seen in the garbage bin. Some might see this as a deception, and I suppose it technically was. But it's also an example of a person willing to meet strangers on their own terms, in the context of their own lives, without judgment.

In light of all this, one might wonder why the archaic caricature of the football coach continues to exist at all. If most football coaches don't "act

---

*Lombardi's younger brother Harold was gay, undoubtedly shaping Vince's views on this issue.

like football coaches" most of the time, why does it even matter? It matters because *all* football coaches "act like football coaches" *some* of the time, particularly at press conferences, during radio interviews, and in any instance when they're asked about the bad behavior of a different coach. When it comes to supporting their professional peers, football coaches are like cops. The accusation itself is irrelevant. If a football coach is accused of beating his players with a tube sock full of quarters, even his most hated enemies will say, "I wasn't there and can't comment, but I've always respected his commitment to accountability." Such language is always a sign that a football coach is entering "football coach" mode: He will stress *accountability*, he will express concern over *distractions*, and he'll show an utter unwillingness to comment on anything that's happened in the past or anything that might happen in the future. Football coaches "talk like football coaches" for the sole benefit of other football coaches, in the same way fashionable women insist they dress only for other women. There's also a history of coaches who start their careers as outside-the-box iconoclasts and gradually morph into the most predictable incarnation of the classic persona—Chip Kelly, Mike Leach, Jon Gruden, Jerry Glanville, John Madden. At the start of his coaching career, Steve Spurrier ignored tradition, mocked rivals who took themselves seriously, attacked incessantly, benched quarterbacks capriciously, and nicknamed himself Head Ball Coach because he was amused by the way other coaches overused the word "football." He was the rare example of a coach who was entertaining, heretical, and still highly successful. Yet throughout his final seasons as the headman for South Carolina, Spurrier became a staid traditionalist. He focused on defense and downhill running, primordial concepts that still panned out. By the time he retired, broadcasters called him Head Ball Coach without a hint of sarcasm.

 This, as much as anything else, is the underlying condition that bothers progressive ideologues about the mentality of football coaches, and about football in general: The old ways aren't inherently better than the new ways, but they continue to work, regardless of how often society tells us they should not. In 2022, the HBO documentary series *Hard Knocks* spent training camp with the Detroit Lions, led by head coach Dan Campbell. Campbell was in his second year, still looking more like a player than a coach. His intensity throughout *Hard Knocks* was comically insane. Campbell talked about biting kneecaps and playing games in a landfill loaded with trash. He discussed dragging opponents into deep water in order to drown them, and he made a curious reference to not caring if a player had three toes but only one buttock. He exercised alongside his players, doing hundreds of push-ups and sweating like a feral boar. Campbell was constantly swearing, constantly yelling, constantly insisting he was not a lunatic despite a lot of evidence to the contrary. He'd talk about "grit" while on the cusp of tears. It was like watching someone from the 1950s, or maybe from the 1850s.

"This guy is a buffoon," I thought to myself after every new episode. Campbell's personality was the most embarrassing demonstration I'd ever seen in the history of *Hard Knocks*, a show where embarrassing personalities are the norm. I could not comprehend how Campbell got the job and was unsurprised when the Lions started 1-6. But then, somehow, they finished the season 9-8. A year later, they were 12-5, and the year after that, 15-2. Campbell is now considered among the best coaches in the league, loved and respected by his roster and rarely criticized for his reckless play calling. What I saw as buffoonish was actual leadership. So how did I get Dan Campbell so wrong? I suspect it was my inability to accept that his methods—which still strike me as outdated—have more relevance to the material world than I want to admit.

I watch a lot of Notre Dame games, and I watch a lot of LSU games. I've probably watched Brian Kelly coach sixty times this century, if you include the six years he was at Central Michigan and Cincinnati. I've rooted for his team to win in the vast majority of those games, which is curious, considering how unlikable I find Brian Kelly to be. To be fair, he's mellowed a bit over the years, evolving from a frothing red-faced berserker into a more run-of-the-mill jerk. But Kelly still does something that's no longer fashionable: He attempts to terrify his players into execution. He will scream, directly into a linebacker's face, two inches from the kid's face mask. Now, there are many coaches who do things like this on occasion. During any normal football practice on any normal Wednesday, yelling is the principal mode of communication. But Kelly does it all the time, on the sideline in the middle of a game, in front of the cameras, and (seemingly) for the explicit purpose of humiliating whoever fucked up. It seems as if his entire theory of management is built on the belief that there's no motivation more effective than fear, a philosophy that fails in most white-collar circumstances. It does not, however, fail in football. Kelly's teams are always good, always competitive. He took Notre Dame to the 2013 National Championship Game with a roster that was unranked in the first preseason poll. In his final year at Cincinnati, he went undefeated. Kelly can do more with less; in fact, it often appears that scenarios where he's outmanned play to his advantage.

One of Laura Ingalls Wilder's much-loved Little House novels is the 1933 book *Farmer Boy*. In one *Farmer Boy* chapter, the titular character (a nine-year-old named Almanzo) falls through the ice of a frozen pond. He survives, but he's scolded (and physically threatened) by his father for almost dying. When some friends of mine in Brooklyn read *Farmer Boy* to their own young son, they had to explain why a father would get angry at a little boy for an accident that almost killed him. What they told him is that day-to-day life in the 1860s was legitimately dangerous, where one mistake could end a person's life. Almanzo's father needed to scare Almanzo into staying alive. This, certainly, is not the way present-day parenting is handled. But football exists as a surrogate reminder that physical

FOOTBALL

actualities remain uncompromising. If a nine-year-old falls through the ice, he will drown. That fact is brutal and unbending, so Almanzo's father screams him into fearing frozen lakes. For this to work, the father needs to be scarier than the water. That father is Brian Kelly. If a slow, undersized linebacker does not have outside leverage on a four-star tight end, the linebacker will get pulverized and lose his job. That fact is brutal and unbending, so Kelly screams him into proper position. For this to work, the coach needs to be scarier than the mistake.

▸

There's an interpretative risk with any endorsement of "the old ways," and the risk is this: People assume it's coded language for ideas that are too conservative to say directly. Very often, that interpretation is correct. But not always. The gutsiest coaching decision I've ever witnessed happened at halftime of the 2018 NCAA national title game. Georgia was leading Alabama 13–0, and Alabama's coach, Nick Saban, elected to bench starting quarterback Jalen Hurts and replace him with true freshman Tua Tagovailoa. Alabama ended up winning 26–23 in overtime. Knowing what we know now, the decision doesn't seem outlandish. But at the time, in the moment, it felt unthinkable. Alabama trailed by only two scores, and Hurts had lost only two games in two years. Tagovailoa was essentially unknown (I'd followed Alabama all season and did not know who he was). The ESPN announcers struggled with the pronunciation of his last name, opting instead to refer to him as Tua, as if he were already famous. I'd never seen anything close to this kind of decision. I'd never seen a talented, uninjured quarterback benched for a freshman I'd never heard of, in the middle of a winnable championship game. I reflexively anticipated what the media response would be if Tagovailoa sucked and the Bulldogs won by 44. But that kind of thinking is why I would be a bad football coach. I can't stop myself from thinking in a mediacentric way, where the perception of other people matters more than my own internal rationale. Saban was (and is) the opposite. To win, he knew Bama needed to pass more, and he knew Tagovailoa was a better passer than Hurts. He didn't care how this would look or what people (like me) would say. He didn't pretend the position of quarterback was more sacrosanct than any other position on the field. He did what needed to be done, regardless of how that would be viewed by anyone else. It was a thinking so primeval it was radical.

Two days after that 2018 championship, Saban met with his coaching staff and berated them for spending too much time celebrating the victory. He told them they needed to refocus on recruiting. The game they'd allegedly spent too much time celebrating had concluded less than thirty-six hours before this meeting. That draconian work ethic is why Saban is classified as the greatest football coach in NCAA history, a pronouncement often married to a similar assertion about Bill Belichick, commonly considered the greatest pro coach in history.* Those two categorizations, much like the tendency to label Tom Brady the greatest player of all time, always feel slightly wrong to me, simply due to the advantages of modern life and the compound interest of historical knowledge. I also don't know if Belichick or Saban believe all the people who constantly tell them they're the two greatest coaches of all time. I do, however, know this: They would never *say* they believed it, even if they do. Instead, they would discount the question entirely, or they'd make a point of complimenting each other, or they'd robotically list a bunch of famous and obscure coaches from the past. They'd almost certainly reference "Bear" Bryant and Don Shula.

---

*While I was writing this essay, Belichick came out of retirement to take the head coaching job at the University of North Carolina, an unexpected decision that's hard to grasp. He also started dating Jordon Hudson, a woman forty-nine years younger than him. This was an equally unexpected decision that's less difficult to understand.

FOOTBALL

They both might insist the best coach they ever knew was their respective fathers, even though Belichick's dad was only an assistant at the Naval Academy and Saban's dad managed a gas station. This is another element of the "football coach" caricature: No matter how massive a man's ego, he can never say self-aggrandizing things about himself. All credit must go to the players and all failure must be placed on one's own shoulders. It does not matter if no one believes this is sincere.

For the past twenty years, Saban and Belichick have been my two favorite personalities in all of football, far beyond my affinity for any active player or any current team. This is not how it's supposed to be. As fans, we are supposed to root for the players, and I would have never claimed to like a coach more than his quarterback when I was young. But this acquiescent mentality was always inside me, long before it became conscious. In June of 1987, I was at a basketball camp on the campus of North Dakota State, held during the same week as the NBA Finals. Almost everyone in camp watched Game Four of that championship series in the field-house arena on a big-screen TV. About 90 percent of the kids sat on one end of the bleachers, rooting for the Los Angeles Lakers. I was with the remaining 10 percent on the opposite end, rooting for the Boston Celtics. The camp was 99 percent Caucasian, so there was no racial divide dictating who sat where; it was just that most teenagers of the eighties (regardless of ethnicity) preferred the up-tempo Lakers to the workmanlike Celtics. But the thing I remember noticing was how every single coach working at the camp was likewise sitting in the Celtic section. There were no exceptions. "This is so surprising," I thought to myself. "It's funny how all these grown-up coaches think like me." It would be decades before I'd realize I had it backward.

Saban was Belichick's defensive coordinator when Belichick ran the Cleveland Browns in the 1990s. There's a cute picture of them on the internet, awkwardly hugging after beating the Cowboys in 1994. Saban and Belichick are close friends with shared principles (both prioritize defense, depth, and preparation) and a counterintuitive need for attention (both enjoy being on TV far more than their reputations indicate). They venerate competence and excel at glaring. I love lots of things about each of them, but the thing I love most is the way they're very funny despite portraying themselves as utterly humorless. They derive so much unexpressed happiness from self-imposed misery; it's as if they read the myth of Sisyphus and decided Sisyphus had the best life possible. This is especially evident during press conferences, where both men project permanent annoyance for no obvious reason. Belichick, renowned for terse, two-word responses that elucidate nothing, was once asked a technical question about long snappers (specifically if it was really necessary to hold a roster spot for a player whose only job was snapping on kicks). The question was posed sheepishly and without journalistic intent. Belichick proceeded to extemporaneously explain the complete history of kicking for ten minutes. It was meandering and educational and stuffed with specificity, delivered without wit. Yet it was still hilarious, and the subtext was unmistakable: "Thanks for asking me that. Every other question you guys ask is stupid as hell." Saban took this philosophy even further, demanding that reporters stop asking certain questions and once telling the entire Alabama press corps to direct their queries toward a bottle of Coca-Cola, since the bottle would give them the same quality of response. He implied, habitually and unconvincingly, that the only mass media he consumed was the Weather Channel. It is my assumption that if Belichick or Saban were to read this book, they would find it facile, inaccurate, and a waste of time. I'd disagree with that analysis, but I can't lie: Such a reaction would make me respect them more.

A therapist might say an athlete who desires approval from a coach is trying to compensate for a lack of approval from their parents. I'm sure this is true for some, especially if they had a controlling mother or an absentee dad. But that wasn't the case for me. What I saw in coaches as a kid, and what I still see in people like Belichick and Saban, is an ability to understand the difference between how people want the world to be and how the world actually is. This psychological response likely is, on some subliminal level, a reflection of patriarchal respect. It places a male authority figure in control of what is (and is not) true. But this is not a form of adoration, because it's not something I'm happy about. I would prefer to be my own narrator of reality, and that's an increasingly difficult thing to do—except, seemingly, for people who coach football. They are the last radical pragmatists, detached from any notion of an unfixed universe. Bill Parcells, the only NFL coach to lead four different franchises to the playoffs, was known for the zero-sum phrase "You are what your record says you are." This sentiment is both wrong (for approximately nine thousand reasons) and impossible to contradict (for exactly one reason). You can't win an argument against a person who only cares about the one thing they can always prove, for the same reason you can't beat a brick wall at tennis.

I'm writing this essay on a computer. I'm not using a manual typewriter. Does this mean I'm adopting "the new ways"? I suppose it does. I'm also placing this essay inside a book, to be sold as a physical object. I'm not turning it into a podcast or a TED Talk or a collection of TikTok reels. Does that mean I'm preoccupied with "the old ways"? Again, the answer is yes. The new ways and the old ways always coexist. The difference is that embracing change is perceived as a functional inevitability, while sticking with old-fashioned custom is perceived as a choice. This is why "the old ways" are stubbornly glorified and "the new ways" are greeted with distrust: One represents how we view the things we consider valuable while the other represents things that are temporary and cheap. When someone expresses excitement over a new contrivance, it tends to be a trivial tool ("I like how this phone app makes it easier to access my kid's report card"). When someone expresses longing for something that no longer exists, it denotes existential confusion ("I don't understand the way schools teach math nowadays"). The old ways are reserved for things that matter, and that's why football coaches prefer them: Their implementation, in and of itself, makes the game important. If it wasn't important, the new ways would be just as good. Yet this tautological mindset resides within a minefield. When a new idea implodes, the coach who pioneered the idea is ridiculed. It's an embarrassing comeuppance and a lesson to be learned. But when an old idea implodes, the coach implodes with it. There's no coming back.

There's no mystery about what constitutes an old-school mentality: It means the acceptance (or the denial) of what new-school advocates would classify as abuse. What makes that tricky is how the definition of "abuse" never stops changing. Is it abusive to make a high school team practice at 7:00 a.m. during the preseason? Most parents would say it isn't, and that it might actually be good for the kids. What about 6:00 a.m.? That starts to push it. How about 5:00 a.m.? That's twisted and wrong. When he was coaching the Florida Gators to two national titles, Urban Meyer scheduled mandatory two-and-a-half-hour weight-lifting sessions that started at midnight on Fridays and Saturdays, keeping his roster out of the Gainesville nightclubs and fomenting team chemistry. It was not seen as abusive. The workouts became so intense that players sometimes got into fights, punching teammates in the face if they failed to show proper commitment. It was a real-world application of the "code red" scenario from *A Few Good Men*, with Meyer as Jessep. Two decades later, the Gators' midnight lift program seems both crazy and charming (Tim Tebow remembers those sessions as "some of my favorite nights of my life"). It explains how Florida became the best team in the country and why *The Sporting News* named Meyer "Coach of the Decade" in 2009. He understood the old ways. In 2021, when Meyer was fired midseason from a pro job with the Jacksonville Jaguars, his reliance on similar methods was viewed as sophomoric and obsolete. Meyer allegedly kicked one of his own guys in the leg while the player was stretching out. The old ways made him look like an idiot, and Meyer would never coach again. A cynic might say he was only fired because the Jags were 2-11, and that Meyer would have been allowed to kick whomever he desired if they'd been 11-2. There's probably some truth in that. But that's part of what makes the old ways complex: We pretend we're judging behavior, but we're usually judging performance. The question is not necessarily, "Is this wrong?" The question is more like, "Is this worth it?"

There's a wild book about the 1962 Kentucky Wildcat football team titled *The Thin Thirty*, haphazardly written by a disbarred lawyer named Shannon P. Ragland. It's a book about many things (a game that was supposedly fixed, a gay sex scandal involving Rock Hudson) but mainly a chronicle of how the Kentucky roster was physically mistreated by Coach Charlie Bradshaw, a former marine. Bradshaw would make the team do something called the grass drill, where players had to run in place and throw themselves to the ground whenever a whistle was blown. It's a classic old-school drill, one I vividly remember from junior high. What was different about Bradshaw's version of the grass drill was that it did not involve grass; he made the team do it indoors, without pads, on hardwood floors. Bradshaw ran his kids until they vomited on a daily basis, causing some players to lose more than forty pounds and prompting fifty-eight of the original eighty-eight team members to quit the team (hence the title of the book). Bradshaw's 1962 conduct was so barbaric that a psychological study in 2007 concluded the majority of his surviving players were still suffering from post-traumatic stress disorders. This, quite obviously, is not what anyone celebrates when they yearn for "the old ways." There is no wistful longing for the ways of Charlie Bradshaw, particularly since he wasn't even that successful (in his 14-year career, he won 66 games while losing 68). A more muddled example is the case of Ohio State's Woody Hayes, a beloved maniac most remembered for assaulting an opposing player in the 1978 Gator Bowl.

To this day, Hayes is the first example employed in any discussion regarding what a football coach cannot do. You absolutely cannot "pull a Woody Hayes," and any coach who does is certain to be fired. Yet Hayes was nonetheless inducted into the College Football Hall of Fame in 1983, and many of his transgressions* have morphed into a legacy of perverse nostalgia. Everyone knows Hayes punched a kid out of frustration, on national TV. Everyone knows he did the one thing a coach can never do. But because *everyone* knows this, and because Hayes was terminated for that mistake, and because that termination became the first paragraph of his obituary, there's a desire to retcon Woody Hayes as a symbolic concept: He was the very best of the very worst. His inability to change destroyed his career, making Hayes the darkest timeline of the classic coaching caricature.

But was it worth it?

Hayes won five national championships by refusing to accept the modern age. He did everything the old way, until society decided the oldest ways were too cruel to continue. His unacceptable methods had to be eradicated. Which, to those who live for this kind of life, only proves they'd still probably work. Forty-six years after the Gator Bowl that cost Hayes his

---

*He assaulted multiple journalists, claimed the 1968 My Lai massacre in Vietnam was justified, and would not allow his team to watch the Paul Newman film *Slap Shot* because of its references to lesbians and its glorification of mooning.

career, another Ohio State football coach, Ryan Day, was preparing to play OSU's despised rival Michigan. At the time, the Buckeyes were ranked No. 2 in the nation, and Day's career winning percentage at Ohio State (88 percent) was higher than Hayes's (76 percent). But beating Michigan matters more to Ohioans than every other game on the schedule, and when Day talked to reporters about the Michigan game, he used the prehistoric language of Hayes: "This game is a war, and any time there's a war, there are consequences and casualties, and then there's the plunder and the rewards that come with it. That's what it is. I just think that's what it comes down to. As I said in my introductory press conference, the number one job is to win this game."

Day talked tough, but to no avail. Michigan won 13–10. It was the fourth year in a row the Wolverines defeated the Bucks, validating what many Ohio State fans had always quietly suspected: Day does not truly believe beating Michigan is his "number one" job. Michigan builds its roster with the sole goal of beating Ohio State. Day builds his roster to beat everyone else and win the national playoff. And you know, that's precisely what happened. Ohio State won the 2024 national title after losing to a Michigan team that finished 5-4 in the Big Ten. By any modern standard, Ryan Day did what mattered most. He won it all and kept his job.

But was it worth it?

7.

Drinking Hot Coffee Through a Straw

COMIC BOOK COLLECTORS LIKE TO SAY THE GOLDEN AGE OF comics is not a decade or an era, but whatever year it happened to be when a person first starts buying comic books. This axiom can be applied to many collectible things, including football cards, thereby making 1980 my *annus mirabilis*. Many of my automatic thoughts about the composition of pro football are still tied to how it was presented through little cardboard rectangles that smelled of chewable dust. Because of how network television operated in 1980, I could usually see only two and a half games a week—the Vikings at noon on Sunday, whatever was slated as the late afternoon game (usually Dallas or Denver), and the first half of *Monday Night Football* (I had to go to bed immediately after Howard Cosell's halftime highlights). It was a limited worldview. Still, football cards allowed me to have a full portrait of the entire league, with an emphasis on statistical output and how various players looked while standing around without a helmet. It was the only time in my life when I could have picked the majority of the league out of a police lineup. Which is why, if my eight-year-old self had been granted access to a magical portal that allowed me to see what the NFL was going to look like when I was fifty, my first reaction would have been provocative. It would not have focused on how the passing game had advanced or how the players had gotten bigger, or even that there were now four new teams that did not previously exist. I know what my first thought would have been: "How is it possible that the best running back is a fast white guy?"

Within the rubber bands of my cardboard universe, there were only five white running backs on earth, and none of them were fast. One was Rob Carpenter, Earl Campbell's blocking back in Houston (the ubiquity of Carpenter's card annoyed me, because there was no 1980 Campbell card available; he was in a contract dispute with Topps). Another was the Raiders' Mark van Eeghen, a ham-and-egger who was already washed. A third was Rocky Bleier, a balding Steeler best known for being wounded by a grenade in Vietnam. Larry Csonka (a superstar in the early 1970s) had deteriorated into a short-yardage specialist, waiting to retire. The only legitimately great white runner was John Riggins, who skipped the entire 1980 season over a contract dispute. In the 1982 NFL playoffs, a revamped Riggo rushed for 610 yards over the course of four games and was named Super Bowl MVP, but Riggins was an I-back who played like a fullback. He was all downhill power, an exception proving the rule.

Throughout the entire Super Bowl era, no white player ever led the NFL in rushing—until 2023. In 2023, Christian McCaffrey ran for 1,459 yards and caught 67 passes for 564 more. He was Offensive Player of the Year, the cover model for *Madden NFL 25*, and the highest-scoring fantasy option, rewarded by the 49ers with the largest contract ever given to a running back. His status was universally recognized, though undoubtedly temporary; the shelf life of NFL running backs is short, and the likelihood that McCaffrey is still the best running back in the league by the time this book gets released approaches zero. A pair of Achilles injuries undercut most of his 2024 season, and Saquon Barkley had a 2,000-yard campaign for the Eagles while McCaffrey sat idle. But still: McCaffrey was *once* the best runner in the league, albeit briefly, and everybody could plainly see that. He's also white, which everyone sees while pretending not to notice. His whiteness is something that's supposed to be unremarkable, something not worth thinking about. The most important aspect of McCaffrey's whiteness is that it's not supposed to have any meaning at all—and that's true, most of the time. But in the same way that classifying oneself as apolitical is its own version of politics, prioritizing the unimportance of an observable truth has the opposite effect. The idea, it seems, is that if everyone *pretends* not to notice something, the entire process of noticing uncomfortable things will eventually disappear. This has never happened and never will. But this is the way football deals with race, which is also the way society deals with race, which is yet another example of how football explains reality by adopting and perfecting its most difficult contradictions.

▶

Part of what makes social prejudice so demoralizing is the assumption that it's inherently built in to human nature, and that the power of an illogical bias is the way it's immune to all evidence contradicting its illogical premise. This is also why the volatility increases whenever a bias is overcome.

For decades, women's basketball repeated an argument about its own cultural perception, over and over and over again: "Our product is awesome, but almost no one wants to watch it, and the explanation is institutional sexism." It was an impossible claim to dispute, tacitly accepted by both advocates and naysayers. But then Caitlin Clark started playing for Iowa, and—suddenly—women's college basketball became more popular than men's college basketball. The 2024 Iowa–South Carolina championship was watched by almost 19 million people, while the men's title drew an audience of fewer than 15 million in prime time. It should have been the greatest moment in women's hoops history. But the intensity of Clark's stardom exacerbated the original conflict. The claim had always been that the women's game was amazing, but sexism kept it from finding an audience. Now its audience was huge, temporarily larger than the audience for the men. This placed feminists in a tenuous position. How could this explosion of interest be explained? There was no way anyone was going to claim institutional sexism was over, because no marginalized group would ever do that; in the history of humankind, there's never been an example of an oppressed group conceding that society had improved and their oppression was over. This meant the only other explanation for the long-standing disinterest in women's basketball was that the pre-Caitlin product *wasn't* irrefutably awesome, and that women's basketball was finally being watched because it had finally become watchable. And that, for understandable reasons, was insulting to every other female basketball player on the planet. Clark's early career was permeated by petty criticisms from older WNBA stars and premeditated on-court collisions with resentful rivals, eventually forcing pundits to find new ways to explain why the most electrifying women's shooter anyone had ever seen was secretly overrated. A few blamed her heteronormativity, but most focused on race, eventually making Clark's whiteness the sole explanation driving her popularity. Which, in basketball, is how this process always works, regardless of gender. Every ideological argument about pro basketball eventually becomes an argument about race, simply because the sport's demographics provide such a perfect photo negative of how the rest of society normally looks. Black people are 14 percent of the U.S. population and 70 percent of the NBA, and the handful of white stars competing at the highest level are rarely native-born Americans. It's a straightforward racial inversion of the country as a whole, making it easy to evaluate the underpinnings of any conflict: Take any position normally expressed by a minority activist and provisionally reverse it.

With football, however, such straightforward reversals don't work. The racial components are not as symmetrical. There are more Black players in the NFL than white players, but the proportion is not overwhelming: The percentage usually falls between 53 and 58 percent, though if you include other nonwhite groups the number approaches 70, skewed by the remarkably high number of Samoans (who manage to make up 3 percent of the NFL despite having fewer than 225,000 total citizens). There's also convoluted segregation within various position groups. Offensive linemen, and especially centers, tend to be white. Defensive linemen are predominantly Black. The NFL went eighteen years without a viable white cornerback, yet punters and kickers are almost never Black. There are many established theories as to why these variances exist, though these theories are rarely expressed, since any attempt at explanation can be reframed as insidious. The most disorienting imbalance involves quarterbacking, a position that gets 70 percent of the public's attention and is 70 percent white. The genesis for this discrepancy was unambiguously racist. It then became "accidentally racist" for a transitory period before entering a long stretch of ethereal racism that was more implicit than explicit. Today, a quarterback's race is still sometimes discussed, though never in a context suggesting a Black quarterback can't play or can't win. Instead, the player's race is discussed *stylistically*, sometimes accompanied by the implication that a Black quarterback is even preferable, for the same reasons originally used as anti-Black weapons in the era of unabashed discrimination.

What all this means is that the racial dynamics in football are more irrational than the racial dynamics in basketball. That perplexity, somewhat ironically, makes football a better conduit for thinking about society, even though race has served as basketball's defining narrative since Texas Western beat Kentucky in 1966. Race is so intertwined with basketball that it's impossible to have an academic hoops conversation without referencing race directly, an obligation that deflates the tension. There's nothing befuddling about Caitlin Clark's whiteness. It's assumed, because she plays basketball, that her racial identity carries a meaning everyone understands. But what does it mean that there are almost no Black punters? Is that proof of prejudice, or is it a denigration of punting? Does the fact that there are almost no white cornerbacks insinuate that cornerback is the most physically demanding position in the defensive secondary, since white guys often thrive at strong safety and free safety? If so, why is the average salary of a safety higher than the average salary for a corner? Why is there perpetual skepticism about Lamar Jackson's capability as a quarterback, expressed by many of the same people who've twice voted him league MVP? Would the same thing happen to a white version of Lamar Jackson, playing in the exact same style? Maybe, but that's tricky to say, particularly since a "white Lamar Jackson" doesn't seem like a person who could possibly exist. But then again, it once seemed like Christian McCaffrey couldn't exist, and now he does and nobody acts surprised.

Football's relationship to race is confusing, inconsistent, and willfully misread. Which is how it must be, in order for it to feel like life.

▸

The amount that race is discussed by media has increased dramatically over the past twenty years, with the biggest jump in 2016, the year Donald Trump was elected president and 49er quarterback Colin Kaepernick started kneeling during the national anthem. An article by Zach Goldberg in *Tablet* magazine calculated that—between the years 2011 and 2019—

usage of the terms "racist/racists/racism" increased by more than 700 percent in *The New York Times* and almost 1,000 percent in *The Washington Post*. Though there's no isolated data on this, the uptick felt even greater in football-related journalism, particularly due to the coverage surrounding Kaepernick. Yet there's something about this increase that's deceptive: Almost all the references to race focus on aspects ancillary to football itself. There are countless debates about the way race impacts salaries, medical care, coaching vacancies, team nicknames, TV ratings, vaccine compliance, franchise ownership, fan perception, and the semantics of how players are criticized or complimented. But what is no longer discussed (or even fleetingly referenced) is why the majority of elite football players are Black. We simply accept that this is how it is, and that all those ancillary conflicts arise from a natural condition that isn't supposed to be mentioned or even perceived. In 2023, former Pittsburgh Steeler running back Rashard Mendenhall went on social media to propose replacing the Pro Bowl with an all-star game between an all-Black team and an all-white team. Mendenhall was crushed for this post, with critics expressing disbelief that he'd even speculate about a world where such a game would be possible. Still, within hours of the Mendenhall post, other press outlets started projecting what the two respective rosters might look like, delighted that they were now "forced" to consider a verboten issue (as long as they made it clear they were also fundamentally and morally opposed to the entire premise).

Mendenhall's mistake was expressing himself too clearly. It's always possible to inject race into sports talk, but—unless you're making the safest possible argument—some misdirection is both necessary and expected. For example, when television broadcasters want to note the uniqueness of McCaffrey's whiteness without mentioning that he's white, they instead mention his parents. His father was a Pro Bowl receiver with the Denver

Broncos. His uncle was an All-American basketball player in the SEC. His mother was a college soccer standout at Stanford, and his mother's father was a world-class sprinter who medaled at the 1960 Olympics. Taken in aggregate, it's not remotely surprising that McCaffrey is an extremely fast mammal with elite hand-eye coordination, though the same biographical information can be used to position him as yet another exception that proves the rule: His natural speed is not "natural," since his body is the final outcome of a sui generis genetic superstructure. It's the perfect noncommittal factoid, supportive of every race-based sports opinion without mentioning race at all.

Such levels of evasiveness have not always been required.

In 1988, Doug Williams of the Washington Redskins became the first Black quarterback to start a Super Bowl. Throughout the two weeks preceding the game, the color of his skin was just about the only thing anyone asked him about (though the big question everyone remembers, "How long have you been a Black quarterback?," was a question never actually asked* at all). There was no avoidance of the issue, almost to a point of overkill. On the song "She Watch Channel Zero?!," Public Enemy rapped about Williams's Super Bowl appearance so casually that Flavor Flav didn't even feel obligated to mention him by name. His Blackness was the only relevant detail.

The late eighties were a high-water mark for racial debates that were both mildly uncomfortable and completely mainstream. In 1989, NBC aired a prime-time documentary titled *Black Athletes: Fact & Fiction*.

---

*There's an apocryphal belief, even today, that the most insulting question asked of Williams during Super Bowl media day was, "How long have you been a Black quarterback?" What appears to have happened is that Williams misheard the following semisarcastic question from Butch John of the Jackson *Clarion-Ledger*: "So, Doug, it's obvious you've been a black quarterback for quite some time, when did that start to matter?" The language of John's query was likely based on something Williams himself had said earlier in his career, when he noted that he'd been defined simply as a quarterback in high school and at Grambling but was constantly recast as a *Black* quarterback upon being drafted by the Tampa Bay Buccaneers in 1978.

DRINKING HOT COFFEE THROUGH A STRAW

Hosted by Tom Brokaw, the program examined the role of race in sports, starting from the position that Black superiority was anthropological and self-evident.

"Tonight we will introduce you to scientists who believe, by and large, that Black athletes do have a genetic edge," Brokaw intones in the introduction, while skeptics of that notion (like the Stanford track coach Brooks Johnson) are positioned as naive contrarians. Much is made about the density of fast-twitch muscle fibers in Black people versus the preponderance of slow-twitch fibers in white people. The report touches on the recent firing of the oddsmaker Jimmy "the Greek" Snyder from *The NFL Today*, terminated by CBS for asserting that Civil War–era slaves had been "bred" to have bigger, stronger thighs. What feels retroactively strange is how Snyder's comments are not criticized or unpacked but merely framed as an uncouth description of something most people assumed to be accurate. When *The New York Times* reviewed *Black Athletes: Fact & Fiction*, the TV critic's complaint was that the program behaved like a person "walking-on-eggs" and that it "treads so carefully that you can't always be sure whether it is inviting controversy or evading it." The perceived weakness of *Fact & Fiction* was (at the time) its unwillingness to fully concede Black athletes were naturally better, and that Brokaw's evenhanded reluctance stopped him from addressing the harder question of why this is true.

To the modern viewer, watching *Black Athletes: Fact & Fiction* on YouTube generates one of two reactions, based on the response that viewer assumes a person of their political ideology is supposed to hold. Some would see the documentary as a creepy artifact from a less enlightened time, when racism could be masked as science and white subjectivity was classified as objective news. It's equally possible to see it as a candid, thoughtful conversation about something everyone recognizes but can no longer discuss. Either way, it's lumped into the category of "something that could only have been made in the past." It is not, however, from the *distant* past. The language used throughout the telecast is identical to the lexicon that would be used today (particularly the refutations expressed by sociologist Harry Edwards). The content itself is still relevant. The reason it feels anachronistic is its obsession with the *cause* of racial disparity, as opposed to the *outcome* of racial disparity. In 1989, a documentary like *Fact & Fiction* could ask the question, "Why does 13 percent of the population make up over 60 percent of the NFL?" That was the crux. If made today, such a doc would more likely ask, "If the vast majority of NFL players are nonwhite, why are only 28 percent of the head coaches minorities? Why are there no Black owners? Why are Black athletes funneled toward positions that have the highest injury rates?" And while all of those questions are valid, they're contingent on the antiquated question of why these disproportions originally emerged, a disparity we've just decided to stop publicly wondering about.

▸

It's a weird question, but I'm going to ask it anyway: How many NFL quarterbacks *should* be Black?

There are many diplomatic responses to this question, all of which get easier if you confidently express nothing at all. A safe answer would be, "More." An even safer answer would be, "All who deserve the job." The absolute safest reply would be, "The question is racist," though I have no idea why that would be the case, outside the fact that it involves race and makes me nervous. But this inquiry is the heart of the complexity—a specific question that's discussed only in the abstract. Prejudice against Black quarterbacking has delineated football's relationship to racial diversity for almost a century. It's the most traceable example of the problems of the past and the progress of the present, a prism for every negative stereotype, every recanted philosophy, and every inch of political progress. As recently as 1967, entire NFL seasons could unfold without a Black man attempting a single pass. In 2023, both starting QBs in the Super Bowl were Black. The world has changed. Yet the discomfort around this issue has nonetheless increased, and it's impossible to imagine what would need to happen for the discomfort to end.

Everyone knows that Jackie Robinson broke baseball's color barrier in 1947, a factoid so familiar that it would be worth only $200 on *Jeopardy!* The ubiquity of this knowledge is ironic, as Major League Baseball is now only 6 percent Black (roughly one-third of what it was in the mid-1980s). Integration in football is less familiar and harder to pinpoint. Technically, the first Black pro football players were Fritz Pollard and Bobby Marshall in 1920, but neither is granted the historical status of Robinson. The running back Kenny Washington was the first Black player to sign an official NFL contract, joining the Rams in 1946; that same year, Bill Willis and Marion Motley signed contracts in the All-American Football Conference, where Motley quickly established himself as a Hall of Fame fullback. These are all meaningful milestones. What's unique about football, however, is that the position of quarterback is viewed so separately from every other job that it has its own gravity, often greater than the sum of the remaining roster. If, for example, the Washington Redskins had played the 1988 Super Bowl with (white) Mark Rypien at QB and a Black starter at every other position, it's plausible race would not have been mentioned once in any pregame press conference. What's even more telling is how the reluctance to play a Black man at quarterback managed to endure long after integration had been accepted in every other context. The first Black player in Big Ten history was a beloved halfback/kicker named George Jewett, starring for Michigan in 1890. The first Black man to start at quarterback for the Wolverines was Dennis Franklin, who didn't show up on campus until 1972.

There's a temptation (and an enforced pressure) to explain why this happened in the simplest way possible: *America was and is racist.* The more complete answer is harder, although not really any less racist. The first level of prejudice was a belief that Black people weren't smart enough to call the plays and run the offense. This rationale was boosted by segregationists like George Preston Marshall, the founder and owner of the Redskins franchise. Marshall believed every white player was as racist as he was and would attempt to injure Black quarterbacks on purpose, likely presenting him with mixed emotions. The first Black person to start at quarterback in the modern NFL was George Taliaferro in 1950, but he'd spend the majority of his pro career at halfback. A Pynchonian character named Willie Thrower got a fleeting chance with the Chicago Bears in 1953 before trying his luck in Canada. In the late sixties, Marlin "the Magician" Briscoe started five games under center for the Broncos, though he played cornerback as a rookie and eventually became a wide receiver. The first Black quarterback to have a "normal" career was James Harris, who started for three different teams throughout the seventies and led the NFC in passing in 1974. Unlike Taliaferro and Briscoe, Harris refused to switch positions, a rare refutation of a coaching preoccupation that played a huge role in keeping this prejudice alive.

It's common for high school quarterbacks to change positions when they get to college, and for college quarterbacks to change positions if they make the NFL. There are myriad examples of this, many involving white players. Paul Hornung won the Heisman as a Notre Dame quarterback but moved to halfback for the Packers. Nolan Cromwell was an All-American quarterback for Kansas before spending his career as an All-Pro safety with the Rams. Julian Edelman, a QB at Kent State, was a Super Bowl MVP as a Patriots receiver. Travis Kelce played quarterback for his suburban Ohio high school. Quite often, the best athlete in a small school is automatically slotted into the role of quarterback; the kid survives off pure physicality until the level of competition improves, when he's then reassigned to a different position. It's not a grand conspiracy. But this happened to Black athletes so frequently it altered the entire history of the sport. Eldridge Dickey threw for more than 6,500 yards at Tennessee State and led the TSU Tigers to the 1966 National Black College Football Championship. He was ambidextrous (even as a downfield passer), rumored to have an IQ of 130, and drafted in the first round by the Oakland Raiders. But in the second round of that same draft the Raiders also selected Kenny "the Snake" Stabler from Alabama. A boozehound womanizer, Stabler became the most storied quarterback in Raider history. Eldridge was moved to wide receiver and never found success. Drew Pearson was a quarterback at Tulsa before converting to receiver, eventually making the Hall of Fame. Freddie Solomon broke records as the quarterback for the University of Tampa but jumped to WR upon graduation. As a Florida high school senior, Deion Sanders played under center as an undefendable wishbone assassin. The number of Black dudes who fit in this category could be listed ad nauseam: Jimmy Raye. Gene Washington. Brian Mitchell. Josh Cribbs. There have been numerous books written about Black quarterbacking, but it would be just as possible to write a book about all the Black quarterbacks who never got the chance. This positional apartheid was strengthened by the success undersized Black quarterbacks experienced at colleges that ran the option, calcifying the belief that Black athletes were terrific runners and flawed passers. Homer Jordan of Clemson, Jamelle Holieway of Oklahoma, Tony Rice of Notre Dame, and Tommie Frazier of Nebraska all won national titles, but none were drafted by the NFL.

This critical stretch of time—roughly starting with Dickey's failure in 1968 and ending with Randall Cunningham's MVP season with the Eagles in 1990—can be seen as pro football's Brad Paisley era, when some of the racism against Black quarterbacks could duly be classified as "accidental" (though I'm sure some will find such a claim offensive and overly generous). The ingrained belief about how Black quarterbacks played did not align with the ingrained belief about what skills an elite quarterback needed to possess, despite both of those ingrained assumptions being inaccurate. For all of the seventies and eighties (and even through most of the nineties), the prototypical professional quarterback was tall, durable, and predisposed to staying in the pocket. The key qualities were "mechanics" and "poise." At 6-foot-4 and 220 pounds, Doug Williams fit the classic mode, so the Bucs took him 17th overall in 1978. The fact that Williams rushed for −37 yards as a senior at Grambling weirdly helped his cause; at the time, building an offense around a running quarterback was considered foolish. Fran Tarkenton scrambled the Vikings to three Super Bowls and retired with every major passing record, but he was seen as an anomaly (who not coincidentally lost all three of those title games).

College quarterbacks who racked up big yards on the ground were suspected of being misplaced running backs who passed out of desperation, and that was the perceived résumé for many Black QBs. Coercing someone like Antwaan Randle El to switch positions was pitched as a career opportunity, and sometimes no coercion was necessary. Anquan Boldin was among the most lauded high school quarterbacks in Florida history, a fast-and-physical option runner for Pahokee High who passed for nearly 3,000 yards as a senior. Yet when Boldin enrolled at Florida State in 1999, he immediately asked the coaching staff to move him to safety. Head coach Bobby Bowden convinced him that transitioning to receiver was the better move. Boldin played fourteen years in the NFL, retiring with more than 1,000 receptions. He'll probably make the Hall of Fame. But is it possible he'd have gotten there just as readily as a quarterback? Is it possible he played his entire career at the wrong position?

Cunningham's 1990 MVP coincided with Houston's Warren Moon leading the league in passing, a pair of events unofficially terminating any notion that Black players were intrinsically inferior quarterbacks. The culture and language around this issue started to change, although not

DRINKING HOT COFFEE THROUGH A STRAW

quickly and not always for noble motives. Throughout the nineties, a handful of high-profile Black quarterbacks played exceptionally well, making it seem like Black quarterbacks had a higher rate of success than their white contemporaries. But this was partially because the only Black quarterbacks able to stick around were the ones who excelled; if they were average, they disappeared (the percentage of Black starting QBs is always higher than the percentage of Black backup QBs). The calculus didn't fully shift until the twenty-first century, when a new generation of offensive coordinators stopped believing pocket mobility was a negative trait. Utilizing the quarterback as a primary runner, once considered a death wish, was cautiously reconsidered around 2010. By 2020, it was reframed as essential. For five decades, Black quarterbacks fought the stereotype that they were raw athletes who wanted to run as much as they wanted to pass. Now that stereotype is positive, perhaps even overvalued. On opening day of 2025, there were sixteen Black starting quarterbacks, the most in NFL history. Which brings us back to my original awkward question: How many NFL quarterbacks *should* be Black?

This is not a question about representation. It might seem like it is, but it's not, and things would actually be easier if it was. When you hear a person insisting that "representation matters," they're discussing something that doesn't apply to this particular dispute. Black quarterbacks are mathematically overrepresented, relative to the population at large. No one is worried that young Black kids don't have enough quarterbacking role models. The problem is how this query forces any analyst to auto-accept many of the same principles that make *Black Athletes: Fact & Fiction* untenable to modern thinking. If roughly 6 out of 10 players in the NFL are Black, it stands to reason that roughly 6 out of 10 quarterbacks should be Black, meaning the whole conflict would be objectively solved if 19 teams started a Black quarterback, 19 teams carried a Black backup, and no one thought about those 38 Black quarterbacks any differently than the remaining 26 white quarterbacks. But this solution requires total acceptance of the original ratio. It only works if 60 percent of the NFL being Black is, in fact, the correct percentage. And why would that be? How can this be explained without making sweeping, troubling statements about racial essentialism? Such acceptance also means that this same thinking should be applied across the entirety of every roster, meaning 13 starting NFL running backs should be white and the majority of punters should be Black. These are quotas no one expects or wants. There's also a practical imbalance: If we accept that 60 percent of the league being Black is normal and unremarkable, we're obviously accepting that one minority makes up the majority of good football players. If we likewise accept that certain football positions are more important than others, it stands to reason that the most critical positions should attract the best athletes. That would mean the number of Black quarterbacks should probably be *higher* than 60 percent, despite Black people representing only 14 percent of the overall populace. But here again: This "logic" is based on the premise that Black people are inherently better at football, and that's a troubling concept. It opens a door to the possibility of other races being inherently superior (or inferior) at other jobs and activities, which is pretty much the bedrock of racist ideology. The only way this imbalance can be discussed is to blame social engineering, built off the inference that American society limits Black mobility in intellectual fields while pushing them toward sports and entertainment. It would further indicate that any political progress overturning this engineering should therefore make society more equitable, increasing the number of Black people in professions where they were once denied access (like finance) while decreasing Black prevalence in professions where they're already overrepresented (like quarterbacking). It would mean, logically but unreasonably, that the number of Black NFL quarterbacks should actually be going *down*, assuming the world is getting better. But the number of Black quarterbacks continues to go up, indicating that the problem must be getting worse and that it's wrong to want more Black NFL quarterbacks. But, of course, no one believes this, nor does anyone think that if the number of Black starting quarterbacks suddenly went from sixteen to six, it would mean society has improved.

So how many NFL quarterbacks should be Black?

There is no acceptable answer to this question. I'm probably racist for wondering about it, and my inability to understand why such wondering is bad probably makes it worse. When one is considering demographic representation, math is never helpful. The population of Samoa is only around 220,000, yet there are 30 Samoans currently playing pro football. An astounding 5.1 percent of players selected in the 2024 draft were Polynesian. The likelihood of a Samoan teenager making the NFL is around 56 times greater than a teenager from the U.S. mainland, a disparity seen as both a positive reflection on Samoan athletes and a negative reflection on the limited opportunities for young Samoan males. It's a cool thing we're not supposed to be happy about.

▶

There is, I suppose, another potential answer to the question over how many NFL quarterbacks should be Black, though this response is the opposite of safe or sensible: "I don't care, as long as one of them is Colin Kaepernick." As I write this paragraph, Kaepernick has been out of the league for a decade and is almost forty years old, but many people still want to see him on an NFL roster, particularly the morning after any especially terrible game from a subpar white quarterback. Such a scenario would actually be terrible for Kaepernick. He was already regressing when he left the 49ers in 2017. Moreover, the memory of his skill as a player has improved in the years since he last played, bordering on Hall of Fame–level respect. And

FOOTBALL

you know, someday Kaepernick *will* make the Hall of Fame, probably just before he dies, and he *will* deserve it, although not because he was an elite football player. He will deserve it for some of the same reasons Curt Flood should be in the Baseball Hall of Fame; he will deserve it because he changed the way people think about the meaning of football, even if he didn't change many minds about the things he cared about more.

It's bizarre, and historically embarrassing, to consider how understated Kaepernick's protest against police violence actually was. He didn't stand up for the national anthem during a preseason game. That was the inception. After that, he started kneeling during the national anthem and did so for the remainder of the 2016 season. If reporters had not asked him why he was doing this, it's possible no one would have noticed. Kaepernick would explain his reasoning when asked directly, but he rarely gave interviews and often let his girlfriend speak on his behalf. There's a misplaced belief that Kaepernick's actions were related to the killing of George Floyd by a Minneapolis police officer, but this is totally false; Kap's kneeling occurred more than three years earlier. He was completely out of the league at the time of Floyd's death, having already received a financial settlement from the NFL, the result of alleged collusion by team owners to keep him unemployed. How much Kaepernick received from this settlement remains unknown, though the most popular estimate was usually under $10 million total, split between Kap and his teammate Eric Reid (who co-filed the grievance). He was, and will remain, the central figure in a controversy that's still referenced incessantly—a cultural superstar whose unobtrusive protest erased an unorthodox football career that was pretty fascinating before becoming inessential.

I first became aware of Kaepernick when he was at Nevada. He was a guy you saw on ESPN2 at weird times on weird days. To increase national exposure, the Western Athletic Conference liked to schedule a few games on Friday nights. I was living on the East Coast, so he'd still be playing when I got home from the bar. At the time, Nevada was the only team in the country running the pistol offense* almost exclusively, a scheme perfectly suited for a quarterback like Kaepernick. He had a crude throwing motion (it always looked as if he were chucking a baseball) but he wasn't inaccurate. He was fast and hard to get on the ground. As a senior in 2010, he beat the No. 3–ranked Boise State Broncos on the night after Thanksgiving, a heartbreaking 34–31 overtime thriller that killed Boise's one true shot at a national title. I did not assume Kaepernick would succeed as a pro, but I'm also not a scout. He was drafted by the 49ers in the second round, the sixth of twelve quarterbacks taken. On draft day, details about his personal life became known: He was biologically biracial, the adopted son of two white parents. He was a 4.0 student throughout high school and college. He owned a gargantuan pet tortoise that will likely outlive him. None of these factoids seemed radical at the time, although they all do now, if you try hard enough to make them seem provocative.

Under the tutelage of brilliant psychopath Jim Harbaugh, Kaepernick broke into the San Francisco lineup midway through his second season, when starter Alex Smith suffered a concussion. What became controversial (relatively speaking) was Harbaugh's decision to keep Kap as the starter following Smith's recovery. Conventional wisdom has always avowed no player should ever lose his job due to injury, presumably to stop a starter from hiding an injury out of occupational anxiety. Smith was also having a nice season, leading the league in completion percentage at the time of his concussion. Alex Smith's strength was competent consistency.

---

*The pistol is a combination of the shotgun and the I formation. The quarterback lines up three and a half yards behind the center, with a running back directly behind him, about eight yards deep. When I first saw this formation, it struck me as the worst of both worlds: The QB wasn't deep enough to see the full secondary and still needed to take a three-step drop after catching the snap, while the RB didn't have a blocking fullback and was aligned too far from the line of scrimmage. I hated it. But I was wrong. The pistol offers more versatility than almost any other formation, particularly if your quarterback is mobile.

But Kaepernick offered high risk with high reward, qualities more in line with Harbaugh's pigskin libido. There was uncertainty over Harbaugh's choice, and it always seemed possible that Smith could win his job back, until the 49ers reached the playoffs and faced Green Bay: With the score tied at 24 in the third quarter, Kaepernick obliterated the Packers with one play. Operating out of the pistol, the Niners ran a read option, a simple (almost high school–ish) play that was extremely in vogue in 2012. Kaepernick kept the ball, sprinted right, hit the corner, and made the Packer defense look like giant sloths in the La Brea Tar Pits. That 56-yard run is the pinnacle of Kap's on-field career, the ultimate manifestation of his speed and judgment. Three weeks later, San Francisco lost to Baltimore in the Super Bowl, but the game was close. If the Niners had won, Kap would have been MVP.

Kaepernick opened the following season with a 412-yard passing game. Golden Gate optimism was supersonic. He was good (and sometimes great) for two years, widely viewed as a Top 15 quarterback with potential still unlocked. He signed a $126 million contract before the 2014 season. It seemed justified. But the team went 8-8 and Harbaugh left to coach the University of Michigan. The world stopped talking about Kaepernick as a meaningful football player (or anything else) for the next three years, until he started kneeling during "The Star-Spangled Banner" and nobody could talk about anything else.

Kaepernick the player and Kaepernick the activist are not disconnected concepts. They must be considered together. And that's what makes this so hard, particularly as it applies to race.

Prior to Kaepernick, the football player most associated with race-focused politics was Jim Brown, the gridiron corollary to Muhammad Ali and Bill Russell. Brown was a progressive icon for decades. That prominence became compromised in his later years, when many of his "less progressive" activities from the past received more and more attention, such as the time he threw his girlfriend off a second-story balcony in 1968. What is undeniable, however, is that Brown's status as an activist was more acceptable—particularly by those who disagreed with him—because of his unimpeachable excellence as a running back. It's still possible to argue that Brown is the greatest runner who ever lived, magnified by his decision to retire at the peak of his powers, a decision he later classified as political. This, in a rational universe, should not matter. A man's opinion on gang violence should not be taken more seriously if he leads the league in rushing. But of course it *does* matter, for irrational reasons that are easy to understand. Team sports, and football in particular, are systematically grounded in elements we don't normally accept in regular life. Sports are hierarchical, playfully fascist, and fundamentally artificial. We accept these things in football for one reason: Sports are a meritocracy, at least when compared with society as a whole. It's not a perfect meritocracy (as illustrated by the history of Black quarterbacks), and every imperfection can be used as a means for disqualifying the larger notion. We all know the only time anyone is supposed to reference the term "meritocracy" is when they're insisting it doesn't exist and never has. But exceptions don't negate the larger actuality. Unlike life, football is a series of games, and games are won or lost in nonnegotiable terms. There is no equality in football, ever, on any level. That makes it possible (and maybe natural) to view similar people quite differently, based on how well they break tackles. So when someone like Colin Kaepernick stages a protest, he is not seen as a human interested in human rights. He is seen as a football player interested in human rights, which is not the same thing.

This is how Kaepernick publicly described his protest, after that first preseason game where he didn't stand for the anthem: "I am not going to stand up to show pride in a flag for a country that oppresses black people and people of color. To me, this is bigger than football and it would be selfish on my part to look the other way. There are bodies in the street and

FOOTBALL

people getting paid leave and getting away with murder." Parts of the message are unambiguous while others are more difficult to parse. His main issue focuses on police violence and its racial implications, a category of argument in which every statement implicitly begins with the words "of course" or "however." For example:

1. **OF COURSE** everyone believes that police shouldn't kill civilians or target minority groups.

2. **HOWEVER**, this very real problem is also statistically less overwhelming than most activists and news consumers tend to believe.*

3. **OF COURSE**, statistics shouldn't matter in this case, because even one unjust murder is a tragedy.

4. **HOWEVER**, in a country with 340 million people and 393 million firearms, a certain number of police shootings are inevitable, and some of those are going to involve human error.

What this means is that Kap's take is debatable. But in this particular scenario, that shouldn't matter. There is no reason an NFL player shouldn't be able to stage an unintrusive protest for whatever reason he wants. The big complaint about Kaepernick's action was that it was disrespectful, and that it "politicized" an event consumers want to see as apolitical.

---

*The Washington Post has tracked every fatal shooting by on-duty police officers since 2015. This tracking collects *all* fatal shootings—cases where a cop kills an innocent kid, cases where the victim is not innocent at all, cases where cops shoot people who are actively shooting other cops, cases where cops inadvertently shoot bystanders, etc. According to the *Post*, the annual number of police-generated homicides stays within a surprisingly tight range: more than nine hundred but fewer than twelve hundred. This is roughly the same number of Americans who die on bicycles in any given year, and around a quarter the number of Americans who die from choking on food. That said, the rate of Black people killed by police is more than twice the rate of white people killed by police, even though white people constitute the largest overall chunk of deaths. It's also possible to question the validity of the *Post*'s numbers and to argue that police cannot be trusted to report their own activities.

DRINKING HOT COFFEE THROUGH A STRAW

But his actions were coordinated with the pregame performance of "The Star-Spangled Banner," an inherently political (and completely unnecessary) tradition. A large segment of the populace disagreed with Kap's protest, but that supports his rationale. If Kaepernick had been kneeling to promote something nobody is against—say, "world peace" or "an end to hunger"—a critic could reasonably claim what he was doing *was* a distraction, because it would be drawing attention to an individual for no vital reason. That was not the case with Kaepernick. This was a textbook example of a well-executed protest: A person did something that interfered with nothing and harmed no one, with the sole intent of persuading the media to ask, "Why are you doing this?" Had no one tried to stop him, it would have been a moral, short-lived, nonviolent demonstration. But (of course) people *did* try to stop him, and they succeeded. That changed what the protest meant, how important it would become, and why Kap would never again make an NFL roster. It was, as Kaepernick told reporters, "bigger than football."

Yet there was still a football aspect to all this.

It became impossible to discuss, but it was there.

The public response to any protest—or really to *any* political moment, small or large—always breaks into three camps. The first comprises activists who unequivocally support the protester's message and view them as a hero. The second are those who automatically hate the protest and see it as an ungrateful attack on a society they value. These two camps dominate the discourse. But they live on the margins, and their opinions are taken seriously only by those who already agree or are looking for a fight. The people who matter are the people in Camp Three, where the reactions are less predictable, though not necessarily because the constituents are more open-minded or better at critical thinking. More often, responses emerging from Camp Three are based on something personal or arbitrary. Such a person might support a violent protest when they see it on the news, but not if the riot is happening too close to their own neighborhood. They might disagree with a protest in theory, but they'll sympathize with an especially earnest protester who reminds them of a younger version of themselves. They might have no fixed opinion at all, but they'll create an irretractable one if they go to a dinner party and that's the topic of conversation. Mainstream traction for any movement inevitably comes down to how convincing it appears to the uninvested residents of Camp Three. The defining perception of a political idea is dictated by the people who don't particularly care about the idea itself. For someone like Kaepernick, that posed an impossible obstacle.

Kaepernick was protesting on behalf of oppressed minorities, coming from the perspective of a Black man. But as a pro athlete, he was not considered and described in that context. Instead, Kaepernick was seen as a Black *football player*, which is different. His credibility and social standing are established not by his personal character but by his quantifiable ability as a quarterback. This is true for all pro athletes, but especially for football players. It's taken for granted that football requires a subjugation of individualism and a fealty to authority. It is, rightly or wrongly, understood as a conservative idiom with traditional values. When a football player breaks from that—when a player rejects this dogmatic illusion, for any reason—his thoughts are evaluated through the lens of his on-field ability. Jim Brown's political leverage came from his status as the best player of his era, a classification Kaepernick was nowhere close to in 2016. Would his protest have been taken differently had it occurred in the summer of 2013, during the preseason following his Super Bowl appearance? Yes (if nothing else, he would have had the support of everyone who wanted the 49ers to win games, irrespective of their views on police violence). Would it be taken differently if instead of Kaepernick, the protester was Patrick Mahomes, another biracial QB expressing his views identically to how they'd been expressed by Kap? Absolutely. But those hypotheticals change nothing. Kaepernick's protest began when his professional future was on the decline, making his politics vulnerable to football-related attacks: He was doing this to stay relevant, he was doing this because he had nothing else to offer, he was doing this because he'd lost his desire, he was doing this to get traded. Over time, the criticism adopted prejudiced coding: He was ungrateful, he was underinformed, and he was overpaid. He was no longer a football player who mattered.

Kaepernick's protest began as a commentary on race. It ended as a disputed requiem over his own Blackness. In between, it involved a lot of different things, many of which were convoluted, some of which weren't about race at all, and most of which were disconnected from the original issue. It was not simple, in any way. But it was simple in the beginning and it was simple in the end, and those are the only parts most people remember.

When I say football reflects the day-to-day American projection of race, this is what I mean.

The settlement paid to Kaepernick serves as evidence that he was blackballed by the league's owners, a monetary concession that explains why he couldn't get a job despite being better than many (or even most) of the backup QBs who never protested anything. This is true, though also misleading. What happened to Kap's career was not some unforeseen twist. Immediately after that first protest in the 2016 preseason, Kaepernick told reporter Steve Wyche of the NFL Network, "If they take football away, my endorsements from me, I know that I stood up for what is right." This is the kind of statement made by a person who already knows what the outcome is going to be, almost as if that outcome were interwoven with the aspiration. Kaepernick's physical talent was, in those first years after his forced retirement, good enough to make an NFL roster. But no team wants a situation where the backup quarterback gets more attention than the starter, and no coach wants to spend a week answering divisive questions about a player who might not play a single down. A similar situation occurred with the NFL's second best-known kneeler, Tim Tebow. Tebow was not as good as Kaepernick, but he went 8-6 as a starter and won a playoff game. He was superb in goal line scenarios and could have served many teams as a multipurpose utility knife. But Tebow was not worth the trouble. His high-profile Christianity polarized the same people in 2011 who would be polarized by Kap five years later. Tebow was a distraction. Why would any franchise want their fortieth best player to be more famous than every other guy on the roster? The only justification for keeping a Kaepernick or a Tebow is that they're too unstoppable to cut, and that wasn't the case for either. One of the maddening things about meritocracies is that merit only dominates at the top of the pyramid; once you move off the apex, it's the demerits that matter more. Kaepernick's protest would have been acceptable if he'd still been among the fifteen best quarterbacks on the planet, but he wasn't, so it wasn't. And that, somewhat perversely, is why he warrants consideration for the Pro Football Hall of Fame. If Kaepernick had staged his protest as a superstar, it would not have carried a fraction of the risk. As it was, Kap sacrificed a potentially long career as a backup or marginal starter, in service of an unpopular political message that became a common opinion within four years. The impact of this exceeds almost anything he could have accomplished as a player.

"But that's ridiculous," you say. "The Hall of Fame is not supposed to reward people for being *impactful*. It's supposed to reward people for being awesome football players."

Sure. But if that's the case, why does the HOF occasionally induct owners and referees and scouts? It's because those inductees altered the trajectory of the league. And no matter how one feels about Kaeper-

DRINKING HOT COFFEE THROUGH A STRAW

nick's persona, it cannot be disputed that he did the same. The NFL, at least on a surface level, has increasingly aligned itself with Kaepernick's ideology, the ironic outcome of his banishment. What that ideology advances is the conviction that *any* issue involving a pro football player is—at least partially—a racial issue that cannot be interpreted as subtext. It must be interpreted as text. Skepticism about the playoff viability of Lamar Jackson's playing style* is not the unspoken residue of antiquated beliefs about Black quarterbacks; it is a function of his Blackness *right now*, forwarded by those who privately believe certain antiquated beliefs are not antiquated. The firestorm around Tebow initially seemed like a firestorm over ostentatious religiosity; fifteen years later, it seems equally shaped by the fact that Tebow was a white quarterback, and that his mechanical limitations might have been treated differently if he was not. The main reason we've entered the era of "player empowerment" is that it's hard to sanction any player whose point of view encompasses racial consciousness, and that's now every issue that football touches. It happens by default. And Kaepernick is the guy who made that happen, and that will not (and should not) be forgotten, regardless of how it makes you feel.

---

*I've now referenced this vague criticism twice without explaining what it is, but I think most fans know what I'm referring to: Jackson won the Heisman at Louisville and the NFL's MVP trophy twice. I consider him the best running quarterback to ever play, though some might place him No. 2 behind Michael Vick. He's also an accurate passer who rarely throws picks. Jackson's quickness and agility allow Baltimore to run plays you'd normally expect from a Pop Warner team; they spread the field with four WRs, place Jackson in the shotgun, and just let him take the snap and immediately bust up the breadbasket. There's almost no way to defend this, and no one argues that Jackson isn't elite. Yet there's also a persistent theory that his greatness is overly reliant on athleticism, and that a disciplined, well-coached defense can goad him into playing a more conventional style that makes his physical gifts extraneous. I don't agree with that assessment, but Jackson happens to be my favorite current player, so maybe I'm blind to this. I must also concede that a critical fourth-quarter interception against the Kansas City Chiefs in the 2023 AFC championship was probably the worst pass I'd ever seen him make, coming at the worst possible moment.

FOOTBALL

▸

I'm thinking about race and football not because I want to but because it has to be part of this. It's too important to circumvent, even when it's unentertaining. Every assertion in this book is embedded with subjective racial implications, the majority of which I'm oblivious to. It's a strange sensation to know that whatever I write is going to be viewed as partially wrong, simply because my identity dictates a perceived incompleteness to my understanding, and that even my attempts to compensate for this will fail, since I'll still be the person making the compensations.

But that said: Let's imagine a premier twenty-first-century college football program that started only white quarterbacks for almost a decade. Let's imagine this university started six different white guys in a row, and all of them were very good—good enough to make the NFL. However, let's also imagine the very *best* quarterback to pass through that program was Black, and he barely played, and in order to get on the field at all, he had to transfer to a different school in a different conference. Two years after that transfer, he emerged as the best passer in FBS history, was awarded the Heisman Trophy, and won an NCAA championship.

Would this appear too coincidental to be normal? Would this scenario ooze with racial overtones? I think that it would, and I would think, "This must have some kind of meaning." Yet the scenario I'm describing actually did happen, except in reverse. From 2012 to 2022, every starting quarterback for Ohio State was Black. All of them were varying degrees of excellent: Braxton Miller, J. T. Barrett, Cardale Jones, Dwayne Haskins, Justin Fields, and C. J. Stroud. Over that span, Ohio State went 128-15 and won two national titles. Still, it's hard to ignore that the best quarterback to pass through the OSU program during this stretch was Joe Burrow, who never started a game and attempted fewer than 40 passes during his three years in Columbus. Burrow transferred to LSU with two years of

DRINKING HOT COFFEE THROUGH A STRAW

eligibility remaining. In 2019, he threw for 5,671 yards and 60 touchdowns, the greatest season any college quarterback has ever produced. And you know what's bizarre? I watched this happen in real time, and it never once made me think, "This must have some kind of meaning." It felt devoid of meaning, and easy to explain away. I did not see this as "reverse racism," nor did it make me think that society had inverted. If this inconsistency had not been pointed out to me by a friend who attended Ohio State, I'm not sure I would have noticed at all. So then I wonder something else: Was my unwillingness to detect this contradiction *also* a form of anti-Black prejudice? Does it suggest I only project racism onto situations when it's safe and uncomplicated? Is it condescending to accept Burrow's transfer to LSU as unremarkable, even though I'd see the inverse as insidious? Why do I only see meaning where I can also see conflict?

These are rhetorical questions, a literary device I often employ whenever I'm afraid to examine my deepest feelings. There are thirty-three question marks contained in this essay, which would make for some brilliant closure if Christian McCaffrey wore No. 33, but he doesn't. I carry some guilt about dragging McCaffrey's name into this at all. He hasn't done anything except play great while being the only color he can be. It degrades his talent and makes him seem sardonically symbolic, and part of me wonders if I should do something equally symbolic to compensate. Maybe I should get in my car, drive to a hobby shop, buy McCaffrey's 2023 football card, and give it to my kid. "Check out this dude," I'd say to my son. "He was the best running back in the NFL." But my son would look at the image and see nothing surprising or controversial, and I would have to live with the sad realization that I always will.

8.
The Cottage Life

THE SIGNATURE TRACK FROM THE BRITISH METAL BAND DEEP Purple is "Smoke on the Water," a masterwork that will outlive its creators. This is largely due to the song's relationship to guitar instruction. Released in 1972, its opening four chords still represent the first real rock riff most novice guitarists are expected to master, meaning "Smoke on the Water" will never disappear, even if no one remembers who wrote it. In another fifty years, it will be the six-string equivalent to "Chopsticks" on piano. And like so much of human civilization, one of its most delightful characteristics is a mistake that cannot be fixed.

The lyrics to "Smoke on the Water" are a direct narrative about how the song itself was recorded in Switzerland, with more expository detail than most songwriters would deem necessary. Its third verse, for example, mentions how the band had borrowed a mobile recording studio from the Rolling Stones: This was a truck with a control room built into it, allowing Deep Purple to record a new album while still on tour. However, Deep Purple vocalist Ian Gillan made a mistake during the recording process,

FOOTBALL

singing a key line from the song as "With the Rolling truck Stones thing just outside." One assumes he meant to say, "With the Rolling Stones truck-thing just outside," or maybe even the more coherent "With the Rolling Stones' truck parked just outside." But that's not what he sang, and the band elected not to fix it, understandably unaware that this would become the most timeless material they would ever create. There are many people who can't name any Deep Purple songs except this one, and there will never be a Deep Purple concert where "Smoke on the Water" is not performed. Which means Ian Gillan has been forced to repeat this nonsensical lyrical mistake around three thousand times throughout his career, and he must continue to do so, until the day he dies. He has to live with this error forever, because the error is part of what "Smoke on the Water" is: the first idea and the last idea.

Canadian football has the same relationship with downs.

▸

There's something I do every summer, and I've done it for so many years that I can no longer convince myself I'm serious. It generally happens in the third week of June, right after the NBA Finals: I'll be sitting in front of the television, wondering if I should read some book I purchased two months ago but still haven't opened. I start flipping through the TV channels (because I'm still the type of person who does that), and I suddenly realize a football game is happening. It surprises me, every time. The uniforms look collegiate, the score is something like 15–4, and I recognize one of the quarterbacks as a dude who had a few decent games for Iowa State or Eastern Washington or Cal-Davis. It always feels like I found something I forgot that I lost—an understated jolt of euphoria melding curiosity with relief. I pull the phone out of my cargo shorts and text three of my friends. *This is it*, I write with my thumbs. *This is the year I start watching Canadian football*. And that's what I do, for maybe forty minutes. I never reach the end of the game. Somebody punts on 3rd and 5, and it dawns on me that the reason these games feel like finding something I'd forgotten I lost is because I lost it on purpose, the previous summer.

I understand why Canadians believed three downs would be better than four. Even Walter Camp, the Vito Corleone of American football, initially thought three downs was the correct number, though he thought this during an era when teams needed only five yards for a first down. In 1912, Camp's version of football added a fourth down, along with doubling the necessary distance for a fresh set of attempts and decreasing the size of the field from 110 yards to 100. The Canadians had already adopted the premise of 10 yards to move the chains, having implemented a battery of new regulations called the Burnside rules* in 1903. But they didn't change the size of the field and they didn't add the extra down, and that has hounded Canada forever. Like that awkwardly transposed lyric in "Smoke on the Water," the Three-Down Problem is an immutable CFL trait, compressing the identity of Canadian football into something that looks familiar but still feels demented and strange. It is the bell Canadians cannot unring.

What's tragic about the Three-Down Problem is how—when described only as a concept—it makes so much sense. I understand why they thought it was the better option. The passing game is more visibly entertaining than the running game, so any rule encouraging teams to pass has immediate appeal. Because Canadians play with twelve men per side, the extra eligible receiver (maneuvering on a longer, wider field) makes throwing easier and more effective, compensating for the missing down. Once non-stop passing became the factory setting, everything else became more

---

*These rules, designed to separate football from rugby, were named after John Thrift Meldrum Burnside, a star athlete for the University of Toronto.

FOOTBALL

wide open. In 1998, a running back named Mike Pringle of the Montreal Alouettes rushed for 2,065 yards, despite averaging just 20 carries per game. It could be argued that playing with only three downs forces football to embrace the best parts of itself, in the same way I can almost convince myself that "Smoke on the Water" might be marginally improved had it been written by Rush. Yet I know all this is false. I know that the most interesting feature of Canadian football is the same feature that makes it too goofy to love, and that's a disenchanting truth. What it does, however, is inadvertently illustrate another truth that might otherwise go unconsidered: Football is fragile. It's a collision sport played by massive men, but its internal structure is brittle. Certain conditions can't be altered, and if they are, the whole thing shatters into something unrecognizable.

Canada did its best, but Canada fucked up. And now the Canadians just have to live with it.

▸

I went to college eighty miles from the Canadian border. I've met my share of Canadians. And though I know this will sound unoriginal and forced, it must be said: I love the people of Canada. They are self-deprecating, well informed, and open to drinking in the afternoon. I've spent time in Montreal and Winnipeg, I consider Vancouver the continent's most beautiful city, and I've seen most episodes of *Letterkenny*. If I'm ever trampled to death by an animal, I hope it's a moose. I prefer the climate of the Great White North, and I appreciate how Canadians can adore their homeland while still making fun of it. Deceased Canadian actor Donald Sutherland used to tell an old joke about three soldiers—one British, one Canadian, and one French—who were captured during wartime and about to be executed.

THE COTTAGE LIFE

"They were each given an opportunity to have a last wish," Sutherland would say. "The Brit asked for a cup of tea, the Canadian asked for fifteen minutes to talk about Canadian identity, and the Frenchman asked to be shot before the Canadian."

This joke reminds me of something I've often wondered about. There's a pattern I've noticed among Canadian nationals living in the United States that has always puzzled me, though perhaps Sutherland's willingness to make that joke is a partial clarification. My evidence is anecdotal and not absolute, but I don't think it's imaginary. What I've noticed is this: Canadian women living in the U.S. tend to be critical of the United States, for all the predictable reasons—the health-care system, the political climate, and the overall disinterest in non-American news. Despite these complaints, Canadian women usually want to remain in the United States and will do whatever it takes to continue living here, even as they bemoan day-to-day conditions they see as inferior to their place of origin. Canadian men, conversely, typically appear to *love* America, sometimes more than they should. They note qualities about the United States that are better than their Canadian equivalents and often convey bemused admiration for American culture. But what's odd is that most of those American-loving Canadian men never seem to stay here. They eventually move back to Canada, still expressing more positivity about the U.S. than those who elect to remain.

My data on this is purely observational, which means it doesn't really qualify as data. It might just seem this way to me because—particularly during college—I knew more Canadian males than Canadian females, making their departures more abundant and easier to notice. Still, it was always interesting to me how so many of those male Canucks were quietly fatalistic about the prospect of living there. They were resigned to returning, never explaining why. Sometimes I'd watch the NFL with these resigned Canadians (they never cared much about college ball), and I'd ask a lot of questions about the CFL, always expecting them to claim that its flawed rules made the game more charming, in the same way that a three-legged dog is impossible not to pet. It never happened. They never defended it. At the time, one inescapable joke about the CFL was that it only had nine franchises, yet two of the nine teams had virtually identical nicknames: the Saskatchewan Roughriders and the Ottawa Rough Riders.

"Don't Canadians realize how weird that is?" I would ask.

"Of course we do," they'd say in response. "Everyone does. That's just how it is."

This nickname duplication existed for sixty-five years, until the club from Ottawa folded in 1996. Six years after that, the franchise was rebooted, and the new owner tried to (again) name the team the Rough Riders, only to be thwarted by Saskatchewan's enforcement of modern-day copyright laws. Ottawa is now known as the Redblacks, a neologism they concocted out of thin air. Is it better to have a nickname that's willfully confusing, or is it better to have a nickname that means nothing at all? Americans usually take the latter option. But I suspect CFL fans would have preferred the former, for the same reason they play with three downs: "That's just how it is."

▶

The Three-Down Problem is a problem of proportionality. Passing is more important than rushing in American football, but only marginally, and that was an evolution that happened over time. Passing is more important than rushing in Canadian football because passing and kicking are the entire game. In the United States, running the ball twice and gaining four yards on each carry places the offense in a position to run the ball again; in the CFL, the same scenario forces a decision, and (depending on field position) probably a punt. Superficially, that doesn't sound troublesome;

to an informal consumer, it might sound preferable. But it has a rippling impact that makes everything else about Canadian football wonkier and unreasonable. Since passing has to be everything, offensive schemes are designed with only passing in mind, prompting teams to stress finesse over power. That emphasis prioritizes smaller players over larger players, making physicality cheaper and less essential. To facilitate the centrality of passing, the CFL allows multiple players to go in motion simultaneously and get a running start toward the line of scrimmage before the snap, sometimes making the moment before a play distracting and more chaotic than the play itself. Even the rules governing alignment are designed for wide-open action: Instead of the offensive and defensive linemen placed nose-to-nose, all defenders must start one full yard away from the line of scrimmage, a real defensive handicap in short-yardage scenarios. Making it easier for teams to convert short-yardage situations is necessary, as it decreases the insane number of punts that come as a consequence of using only three downs. In 1988, Bob Cameron of the Winnipeg Blue Bombers averaged more than ten punts per game, on a team that won the league championship. Punting is so crucial to Canadian football that a team can get an extra point just by kicking the ball into the end zone (this is known as a rouge), though their opponent can nullify this action by fielding the ball and punting it back in the opposite direction. In the final moments of a 2017 game between Winnipeg and Montreal, the ball was kicked back and forth four times on a single play. On the last night of the 2024 CFL season, Edmonton defeated Toronto 31–30 on a "walk-off rouge," meaning they scored on the game's final play by punting the ball to no one.

If an NFL fan was informed of these concepts—but somehow didn't know they came from Canada—they'd assume they must be exploratory rule changes intended to *modernize* football. They'd think the elimination of fourth down was a way to juice passing statistics, that adding a yard of

FOOTBALL

separation at the line of scrimmage was a safety precaution, that all the pre-snap motion was a way to make the sport look like a video game, and that the rouge was an attempt to inject excitement into punting. All those measures seem like disposable ideas an upstart football league would implement in an attempt to attract younger viewers, since young people are always assumed to be impatient and susceptible to gimmickry. The irony is that Canadian football only looks futuristic because it's so old. The CFL's version of the Super Bowl, the Grey Cup, was first played in 1909, and there'd already been 54* Grey Cups before the first Super Bowl. Canadian football has existed longer than American football and adheres more closely to its original model. Canada is the country most responsible for football's existence. Yet this chronology generates a paradox: Every year, around 8.5 million Canadians watch the Super Bowl, while only 4 million Canadians watch the Grey Cup. It's a ratio that exists despite a CFL quota requiring every team to have at least twenty-one Canadian players (and no fewer than eight Canadian starters) on every roster. So why is this the case? Why did the upstart American version of football come to dominate its more classic Canadian equivalent, *even in Canada?*

Science historian Jared Diamond won the Pulitzer Prize in 1998 for his book *Guns, Germs, and Steel: The Fates of Human Societies*, a 480-page explanation for why Eurasian countries managed to seize so much of the globe. Diamond points to many factors—the advantage of certain geographies, the directional axis upon which a continent is situated, different forms of agriculture and technology, and the asymmetrical spread of disease and illness. It's an immersive work of scholarship, though the book is now criticized as often as it's praised.† Still, *Guns, Germs, and Steel* is a

---

*A few Grey Cups were canceled in the early twentieth century because of World War I, the 1919 flu pandemic, and disputes over the rules.

†Attempts to disparage Diamond's work are usually framed as criticisms of his academic rigor, though the underlying reasons are almost always political. What's surprising, however, is how

great example of a writer trying to isolate the historical nature of cause and effect. Early in the book, Diamond suggests a certain inescapability to how the modern world came into being. When considering Francisco Pizarro's conquering of the Incas in the sixteenth century, Diamond starts with a thought experiment: What stopped the Incas from conquering Spain? What gave Spain such an overwhelming colonial advantage, and why does world history so often move in only one direction? The problem with this conjecture, according to half of Diamond's critics, is that his query implies colonialism is an inevitability, stemming from a belief that any society would overtake a rival society if given the opportunity. They argue there's no reason to believe a group like the Incas would have even considered conquering Spain, and that wondering why they didn't strips Pizarro of accountability.

I realize this ideological conflict over colonialism is not *exactly* like the conflict between U.S. and Canadian football. It's not as if Bud Grant attacked the CFL with a cavalry and the Canadian players lost their minds when they saw horses for the first time. American football did not "conquer" Canadian football. But there are a few parallel questions, related to the flow of culture across borders. Did the NFL-CFL relationship become unbalanced because American football did something right? Or did it become unbalanced because American football is intertwined with the superstructure of America as a nation, and that makes it right, even when it isn't? Power can make the unnatural feel predestined. Am I refusing to see what's obvious? Do I overrate the Three-Down Problem by underrating the hegemony of U.S. sovereignty? Did American football overtake Canadian football solely because it happened to be played in the more

---

the attacks come from both sides of the political spectrum, with equal ferocity. Those on the hard left think Guns, Germs, and Steel is racist, condescending, and historically capricious. Those on the hard right see Guns, Germs, and Steel as the worst example of white guilt—an attempt to erase the agency and accomplishments of Europeans and proof of how American education has become self-hating and delusional.

dominant country? If Canada had added a fourth down and U.S. football had stayed with the traditional three, would I be writing an essay explaining why three downs are better than four, blindly convinced that the way things worked out is the only way that makes sense?

Actually, no.

▶

In his book *The Fourth Dimension*, mathematician Rudy Rucker explains how the only way anyone living in our three-dimensional world can attempt to understand how a fourth dimension would function is by visualizing how a familiar three-dimensional object would appear to someone trapped in a two-dimensional world.* In the same way, the only method for understanding the consequences of the Three-Down Problem is to consider something equally imperfect: a hypothetical variation of football with *five* downs.

Imagine this: It's 1912, and Walter Camp rethinks his view on how many downs should be used in American football. Because the distance for a first down has doubled from 5 yards to 10, Camp concludes a fifth down is necessary, lest the advantage swing too far to the defense. Five downs, 10 yards—the math feels balanced. U.S. football becomes a five-down sport while Canadian football remains a three-down sport, and for the next forty years both versions evolve and progress in the same fashion we currently understand. By the time we reach the middle of the twen-

---

*What Rucker means is that, because we live in a three-dimensional spatial reality, the concept of a fourth dimension (whatever that might be) would only be visible to us in a manner that we're already accustomed to experiencing. In order to visualize how a fourth dimension would appear in our three-dimensional universe, we must imagine what it would be like to live in a 2D world that suddenly encountered a 3D object. His example was a sphere moving through a flat plane (which, to someone living in a two-dimensional plane, would look like a dot that expands into a circle before shrinking back to a dot).

THE COTTAGE LIFE

tieth century, American football would be increasingly uninteresting, particularly when compared to its Canadian equivalent. The best American players would be bulldozers, with every play taking place inside the hash marks. Passing would become a novelty, and all the quarterbacks would look and play like Tim Tebow. America's status as a media and economic superpower would not be enough to overcome the straitjacket of a fifth down. By 1980, the United States would need to either convert to the Canadian rules or become a fringe concern.

Four is the magic number. It had to be four.

Part of the reason American football so aptly reflects American society is that both entities share an inability to find a center path. There's a tendency in U.S. society, and in U.S. football, to remain as conservative as possible for as long as possible, only to suddenly redirect that inertia by massively overcorrecting the previous condition. Football's relationship to passing is a good illustration. Considering how the game is now played, it's crazy to think how much the mid-century men who controlled football hated passing. In 1963, the Texas Longhorns' head coach, Darrell Royal, wrote a book that claimed, "I've always felt that three things can happen to you whenever you throw the football, and two of them are bad." This quote was later attributed to Ohio State coach Woody Hayes, and Royal admitted he might have originally heard the axiom from Hayes. But it really doesn't matter who said it first: The sentiment encapsulates how the majority of college coaches felt throughout the sixties and seventies. It's impossible to find a national championship team from this period that heavily relied on throwing the football. There was more downfield passing at the pro level, but just barely; for six straight seasons in the 1970s, the NFL leader in receptions was always a running back. Buffalo's O. J. Simpson ran for more than 2,000 yards in 1973 while his quarterback passed for less than 1,000. Meanwhile, in Canada, passing was already all pervading. Pete Liske, a quarterback from Penn State who couldn't stick in either the NFL or the AFL, threw for 4,479 yards with the Calgary Stampeders in 1967 (by comparison, the Packers won the Super Bowl that season with Bart Starr throwing for only 1,823 yards).

What statistics from this period suggest is that, if given a viable excuse, American football coaches might never have started passing at all. They resisted for as long as they could. If coaches like Royal and Hayes had been granted the luxury of five downs, the game would never have evolved beyond the 1930s. It would have been more brutal and less creative, with all strategy geared toward controlling the ball and eating the clock. An extra down would have made run-oriented schemes like the single wing and the triple option unstoppable, effectively eliminating any need for the development of passers or pass catchers or pass rushers. Virtually every play in a five-down universe would resemble a short-yardage plunge, and no amount of TV coverage or collegiate spirit would make that appealing to casual consumers. Football would have never usurped baseball as America's favorite sport, and the difference between the U.S. version and the Canadian rendering would have grown increasingly vast. By 1980, fans in both countries would have deemed the CFL more watchable than the NFL, and if the CFL had expanded into a handful of U.S. cities—as it briefly and unsuccessfully attempted in the mid-nineties—the transition would have worked. I would not be a guy who texts his friends every summer to claim I'm about to start watching Canadian football. I would be a guy who texts them every September, insincerely claiming I was going to start watching the SEC.

What I'm arguing is both obvious and ignored: Sometimes, the reason something happens isn't sociological or subtextual. Sometimes the reason is concrete: Three downs is better than five downs, but neither is as good as four. There's always an intellectual temptation to anatomize any situation by considering everything except the situation itself, forever preoccupied with the possibility that one event is either upstream or downstream from something ostensibly unrelated. It's certainly possible to come up with nonfootball reasons for why Canadian football's stature is so much smaller than its younger relative: The difference in population. The difference in demographics. The reach of American television* and the popularity of U.S. newspapers in Canada, a relationship that does not go both ways. Money. Weather. Asymmetrical xenophobia. In his book about the history of the CFL, author Steve O'Brien addresses this directly in a chapter titled "Battling the American Influence":

> In some ways, threats (real or imagined) of American dominance have produced the same fears, reactions and handwringing as witnessed with other forms of Canadian pop culture and the Canadian sense of identity. . . . The NFL relentlessly hypes itself as the ultimate sports league in the world. They have convinced the public and media that they have the best game, the best athletes, the most elaborate TV production, the most workable business model, salary structure and lucrative pay cheques. Therefore, people are convinced that it is the best league.

One of O'Brien's points is that American prejudices infiltrate the CFL in backhanded ways, highlighting disparities by perpetuating them. In the same way American coaches once believed Black athletes were not suited to play the position of quarterback, it was believed (particularly by U.S. coaches working in the CFL) that Canadians were likewise unsuited to play QB. Despite the rule requiring twenty-one Canadians on every

---

*This is a common argument, but it has a flaw: In 1954, NBC lost the television rights for college football to ABC, a loss that equated to only one game per week. Meanwhile, NFL franchises were able to set up their own TV deals, and most teams signed with a now-defunct television network called DuMont. To compensate for the loss of college football, NBC crafted a partnership with the CFL. The irony was that NBC had 120 affiliates across the country, while DuMont had only 18. What this means is that throughout the 1950s it was much easier for Americans to watch Canadian football than it was to watch American football. But they still didn't want to.

roster, the CFL hasn't featured a Canadian-born superstar quarterback since Ottawa's Russ Jackson, who retired in 1969. It was broadly assumed that the only way to win in Canada was to find a quarterback from the States, which (somewhat ironically) caused many Black quarterbacks frozen out of the NFL to migrate to Canada and take Canadian jobs. Such views were reinforced by the way any American QB who excelled in Canada—Joe Kapp, Joe Theismann, Dieter Brock, Warren Moon, Doug Flutie—inevitably returned to the U.S. and signed with an NFL club. The reason most of those quarterbacks ended up in Canada in the first place was that they were undersized, cementing the belief that the CFL was (at best) a minor league whose wide-open play made it possible for a small quarterback to put up big numbers. The math driving that theory doesn't always make sense: Warren Moon led the CFL in passing yards (twice) as an Edmonton Eskimo and the NFL in passing yards (twice) as a Houston Oiler. Still, Moon's Eskimo statistics mean less, and not because of prejudice or patriotism. They mean less because they were achieved in a form of football that's like poutine without gravy.

The problem is the three downs. It isn't anything else.

▸

My all-time favorite CFL player is Vince Ferragamo. This is due to many factors, though the only one that matters is my age. Ferragamo unexpectedly took the Los Angeles Rams to the Super Bowl in 1979 and would have been named MVP if the game had ended in the third quarter. A premed student when he played college ball for Nebraska, Ferragamo was the most handsome quarterback of the post-punk era, incessantly likened to Warren Beatty, a movie star who'd coincidentally played a Rams signal-caller in the recently released *Heaven Can Wait*. Ferragamo threw for 30 touchdowns in 1980 and looked like the future face of the league, only to change leagues entirely; he signed with the Montreal Alouettes in 1981 for $600,000 (roughly twelve times the amount he was making in L.A.). Because his departure occurred during a summer when Major League Baseball players were on strike, Ferragamo's exodus received inordinate media attention, amplified by his subsequent failure. He threw 25 interceptions against 7 touchdowns and was humiliatingly replaced by Gerry Dattilio, a guy from (gasp!) Quebec. Ferragamo was a classic drop-back passer who lacked the rollout mobility needed for a three-down league. Some claimed the extra defensive back confused him, though Vince never claimed that. What's often forgotten is that when Ferragamo sheepishly returned to the NFL, everyone assumed he was cooked, but he was still better than decent; on the day after Christmas in 1982, he threw for 509 yards against the Bears.

I bring this up not to criticize or compliment Ferragamo, nor as an excuse to needlessly include a fellow I considered cool when I was nine. I bring it up to undermine any accusation that Canadian football is less valuable because the game is too easy, or that my criticism of the CFL derives from some disinterested notion that it isn't "real" football. There are more elite athletes in the NFL than there are in the CFL, but that barely matters; there are more elite athletes in pro football than in college, and almost anyone who seriously watches both versions prefers the latter. Despite his arm talent, Ferragamo struggled in Canada because he couldn't adjust to a configuration of a sport that's more dissimilar than it appears on TV. The downs were too different. Canucks stuck with the number 3 and we picked the number 4, and that altered everything about both versions. It's not a subjective divergence. It's not a relativist dispute. And this should make you feel good, even if you live in suburban Regina.

It's proof that premodernism is still possible.

For much of the eighties and all of the nineties, anything strange or compelling was classified as postmodern, often as a misdirected modifier that meant "We don't quite understand why this strange thing is compelling." As a journalist throughout this period, I was fanatically obsessed with postmodern ideas, as were many other journalists similarly bamboozled. We wanted everything to be postmodern, until everything actually was, at which point we insisted that it wasn't our fault. By now, referring to the world as postmodern is like referring to R. Kelly as divisive. It's the accepted underlying premise of every debate, regardless of the issue. If, for example, a city has experienced an uptick in criminal activity, there'll be an avalanche of possible arguments explaining the root cause of the spike: a failure in policing, a shift in population, increased poverty, decreased housing, an influx of opioids, the decriminalization of marijuana, inequality, lax prosecution, the overzealous enforcement of trivialities, and the coalescence of random statistical anomalies. Any one of those factors can be used as a tool to explain why the uptick happened. Yet the preponderance of competing possibilities forces a postmodern reading of why *anything* now happens: It could be all of these things or none of them, or some combination that depends on how the circumstance is perceived (and by who is perceiving it). If one explanation feels true, that makes it true (at least for you, which is enough). It's also possible that crime isn't going up at all, or that it only seems like a problem because of how it's presented through social media, or that crime *is* increasing but the increase is somehow good, or that certain crimes should be reconsidered if the criminal is self-aware of the crime's meaning. It's common to claim there's a singular answer that explains why any problem exists, but somehow unsophisticated to believe such an answer can exist at all.

Again: I'm not blasting anyone for thinking this way. I think this way all the time. *I made myself think this way.* Which is why, a few thousand words ago, I nearly shifted the entire focus of this essay away from the Three-Down Problem and toward the postmodern prospect of American supremacy, where Canadian football has been wrongly subjugated for a multitude of non-football reasons. There is an unwritten version of this story where I do exactly that. But that unwritten argument is a prisoner of the postmodern dungeon. It is a criminal in leg irons who's unwilling to confess that—sometimes—the truth is not debatable and decisions have meanings.

Football can be played with three downs. Three-down football is still football, in the same way the opening to "Smoke on the Water" can (almost) be played with only three chords and most audiences would still recognize what song you're trying to perform. These are things that can be done. They're possible possibilities. But it won't feel the same and it won't be the same, and if you still require a rationalization more elucidating than "That's just how it is," try watching the CFL next June. Prove me wrong. I'm not nervous.

9.
The Question

CHRONIC TRAUMATIC ENCEPHALOPATHY, ABBREVIATED AS CTE, is a real thing that's happening to real people who play football. It's not a theory or a talking point. It's a degenerative brain disease resulting from head trauma, specifically concussions. CTE can also (possibly, probably, almost certainly) be caused by so-called micro concussions, where the brain absorbs an impact but there are no immediate or noticeable symptoms. The result of CTE is brain fog, memory loss, erratic behavior, depression, dementia, and suicidal thoughts. It's impossible to prove someone has CTE until they die and their brain is sliced up, a process allowing researchers to test for the presence of specific proteins associated with the disease. Not surprisingly, these tests are usually conducted on deceased people who showed palpable signs of CTE while still alive, so the vast majority of CTE investigations prove positive. As of this writing, 376 deceased NFL players have had their brain autopsied and 345 of those brains showed evidence of CTE. The best-known cases involve the Hall of Fame Steeler center Mike Webster (who was severely mentally impaired before dying from a heart attack at age fifty), heavy-hitting Eagle safety

Andre Waters (who died by suicide at forty-four), and Junior Seau (the NFL's Man of the Year in 1994, who killed himself in 2012). An especially moving example was the suicide of former Bear defensive back Dave Duerson, who purposefully shot himself in the chest so that his brain remained intact and could be tested for a disease he was certain he had.

In other words, the question is never, "Is chronic traumatic encephalopathy real?" Because that answer is yes.

The question is also not, "How can this be prevented?" Because it can't be prevented in a football context, particularly if CTE is a manifestation of micro concussions. Every play at the line of scrimmage is a synchronized collection of micro concussions. That's what the sport is.

The question is also not, "Should the NFL accept financial responsibility for all victims of CTE?" Because the short answer is yes and the long answer is (a) it's hard to prove that a person deserves compensation for a disease that can only be verified after his death and (b) trying to isolate the financial value of a human mind is both impossible and beside the point.

These are the wrong questions.

This right question is this: Should strangers be allowed to do very dangerous, very popular things?

▸

Including the words "very popular" in the previous sentence will seem confusing to some and distasteful to others. It is a bit craven, a bit grotesque. Why should the *popularity* of football have anything to do with its morality? A nonsensical act doesn't become reasonable simply because people enjoy nonsense. In the case of football, however, mass popularity is the element that matters most. There are lots of dangerous, unpopular activities that virtually no one worries about. There are people who think we should ban

THE QUESTION

tourists from climbing Mount Everest, but the argument almost always comes from an environmental perspective, inevitably citing the forty tons of frozen garbage that now despoil South Col, the penultimate settlement of base camps just below the summit. That 2 percent of all Everest climbers die in their attempt is rarely employed as a reason for stopping other people from trying. The list of nonessential activities deadlier than football is lengthy: BASE jumping, wingsuit flying, scuba diving. Trying to ride a 2,300-pound Brahman bull is unambiguously more dangerous than trying to block a 230-pound strong safety. Supermoto cycle racing is predictably risky, but so is riding a normal motorcycle on a regular road (there are more than 300,000 motorcycle fatalities every year). Recreational skateboarding is alleged to cause 7,600 annual concussions, though it can be assumed the real figure is higher (most skateboarding mishaps are never reported). The risks inherent to football do not make football unique. What makes football unique is the colossal audience that views it as entertainment, making millions of seemingly uninvolved people complicit in whatever damage it incurs. On the surface, it might seem like this alleviates the sport's accountability, since football cannot control the level of its own success. But the levers of control are irrelevant. Regardless of the reason, football *is* the most popular institution in the United States, and that alters the meaning of its consequence.

The sweep of its magnitude spills into the lives of even the most casual of consumers, turning every football death (at any level) into a coast-to-coast moral crisis. This doesn't happen with more insular sports. Dale Earnhardt, the Elvis Presley of NASCAR, was killed at the Daytona International Speedway in 2001, preceded in death by his colleague and close friend, Neil Bonnett, in 1994. They died on the same track, on the same turn. It was as if Eli and Peyton Manning both died in the Super Bowl, seven seasons apart. The racing community mourned the deaths of Earnhardt and Bonnett, but neither incident was seen as a requiem on the sport itself. Earnhardt competed in a race just six days after Bonnett's funeral, and Dale's own son drove at the Rockingham Speedway a week after his dad's fatal crash. NASCAR can compartmentalize tragedy in a way football cannot.

Whenever I chat about sports with the parents of adolescent boys, the possibility of their own son playing tackle football is often part of the conversation, and the spectrum of responses is consistent. A few parents say yes or no immediately, almost as if the question were self-evident. Other fathers will say "probably not" and tacitly blame their spouse. However, the most common response is for the parent to concede they'd allow their kid to play football if football was truly important to their kid, even though that wouldn't be their preference. "There are so many other extracurricular options," they say. "Why does it have to be football?" This is a compelling question for America as a whole. There are many, many things that could serve as bell cow for the U.S. monoculture. Why has society coalesced around a sport that wrecks people's brains? Why does it have to be football?

The mainstream appeal of boxing began in the early twentieth century and continued until the 1980s, fading to the fringes as football took full control of the zeitgeist. To some, this suggests there will always be at least one public fascination directly connected to physical risk—and if that's true, there's not much more to argue about. If this is indeed the case, even the elimination of football would have little social impact, since the public appetite for violent entertainment would immediately be replenished by something else (mixed martial arts, competitive Power Slap, bum fights). But this is a misreading of the conflict. I don't think the relationship between football and violence is a fraction as straightforward as the relationship between violence and boxing. A correlation exists, but it's more theoretical. Football is never watched as a blood sport; fans want a spectacle where the *possibility* of injury is omnipresent, but without any-

THE QUESTION

one getting seriously hurt. What they love about football is the strategy and the skill, and those qualities only have meaning when pursued under dangerous circumstances. The violence is necessary, but not desired. It's a little like those bozos trying to climb Everest: They don't *want* to die, or even come close to dying, yet they realize the achievement would mean less if that possibility wasn't on the table. Football's predicament is that the game itself is what people love, but the game becomes uninteresting if the level of physicality falls below a certain undefinable threshold. This is why every rule change introduced to improve player safety is immediately unpopular. It's not that fans want to see guys get hurt. It's that every incremental move away from high-risk physicality makes the sport less like itself.

There is, I cannot deny, a bit of circular logic here. What I'm arguing is that football is not popular *because* it's violent, but that violence is a critical component to the other qualities that make its popularity possible. The distinction is subtle, but that's not the problem. The problem is that its violence-adjacent popularity has grown so gigantic that every detail related to football has taken on an outsized importance, most notably the moral ramifications of 150 million Americans choosing to spend their weekends watching healthy people pulverize their brains. Which is why I must ask the same question for a second time: Should strangers be allowed to do very dangerous, very popular things?

▸

Perhaps you wonder why I keep using the word "strangers" in my query, instead of a more communal noun like "people." I do this to emphasize the difference between thinking about a problem coldly and thinking about a problem emotionally. I realize some will read that sentiment and insist the latter is preferable to the former, and that removing the emotional component is antihuman. Those readers are correct. That's why I'm doing it.

In 1988, George H. W. Bush ran for president against Massachusetts governor Michael Dukakis, a candidate maligned as soft on crime. Bush and Dukakis had two debates, and the second debate opened with moderator Bernard Shaw throwing Dukakis a hard hypothetical: Shaw asked if Dukakis, a lifelong critic of capital punishment, would support employing the death penalty if someone raped and murdered his wife. "No I don't, Bernard," responded Dukakis, and his subsequent explanation did not play well with anyone. By saying no, Dukakis seemed like a guy who cared about public policy more than his own spouse. Had he said yes, it would have made him a hypocrite and obliterated his platform. It was an unfair question, no different than if Shaw had asked Bush if he'd still support capital punishment if his son was wrongly convicted of murder. But there was one way out of this. There was one answer Dukakis could have provided that would have worked: "Bernard, I would want to kill that criminal with my own hands. I would want him beaten with motorcycle chains and a lead pipe, without a trial. I'd want to pour boiling oil on his genitals. I would want his death to be excruciating. *And that is exactly why I would be the least qualified person to make this decision*, if such an event happened to my actual family."

There's a desire to view moral conflict through the eyes of whoever is most negatively impacted, based on the premise that their perception is the most relevant. But the truth is closer to the opposite. The more a person personalizes a conflict, the less they can be trusted to think analytically. My daughter loves to climb tall trees, a normal activity that makes me nervous. If something terrible resulted from this preoccupation, critics would be justifiably skeptical of my next book, *Against Lumber*. Only a person who experiences tragedy can understand how the experience feels, but the intensity of that understanding is what disqualifies them from seeing a situation in

THE QUESTION

reasonable, practical terms. That's why I use the word "strangers" instead of "people." I'm trying to depersonalize the problem.

I know it's callous to consciously dehumanize something that's happening to actual humans. It's hard to look at the life of legendary tight end John Mackey (a dementia victim for years before dying in 2011) and argue the Mackey family is less qualified to comment on CTE than a guy whose principal understanding of his condition comes from an episode of HBO's *Real Sports*. It seems arrogant and willfully unempathetic. Yet this is how it must be considered. The existential crisis with football and CTE is not that it happened to John Mackey (or to Tyler Sash, or Ken Stabler, or Aaron Hernandez, or whomever you want to pick). The existential crisis is the possibility that it's happening to all football players, all the time (on every play), and that half the U.S. population is complicit in this by watching (and caring about) a mode of entertainment that requires this to continue. Individual narratives can't dictate the conclusion. They need to be strangers.

This doesn't mean personal feelings don't matter. It only means personal feelings are a separate conversation. Every parent has the right to conclude that their own kid will never step on a football field, and the spouse of any NFL player has the right to tell her husband to retire. Whatever argument they use is valid, within the strictures of their own lives. But those arguments have little relationship to anyone else, in the same way the hypothetical rape and murder of a governor's wife can't change the meaning of crime and punishment for anyone who isn't her husband.

▶

The most easily understood argument for allowing strangers to pursue dangerous things is the concept of free will. It feels basic: If someone understands the risk of what they're doing, they have the right to do it, assuming what they're doing doesn't pose a risk for anyone else. Football is well suited for this argument, since it's conducted in a space meticulously separate from the balance of society. You can't play football by accident. It is always a choice. Yet this supposedly straightforward logic might be the trickiest aspect of the entire debate.

It's hard to imagine a modern pro football player who has no idea that concussions are serious, if for no reasons other than the NFL's enforcement of its concussion protocols and the existence of Tua Tagovailoa. In terms of injury concerns, it's the risk they are most consistently and pedantically informed about. This is also true at the college level and (increasingly) at the high school level. But what these players *actually* know, in specific terms, ranges anywhere between a first-year med student and a second-year cadaver. In the summer of 2024, former Pittsburgh Steeler receiver Antonio Brown was on a podcast with former Steeler running back Le'Veon Bell. They ended up having a conversation about CTE that was both illuminating and tragic, a combination that somehow became hilarious. Brown, who'd previously implied on social media that he has CTE and that it helps him receive sexual favors from women, seemed to believe it was not that bad and not that rare. "I don't want to say it's brain damage because you can't live if it's brain damage," said Brown. "I feel like it's a characteristic of traumas that we all go through."

I would never classify Antonio Brown as a proxy for all football players. He's been charged with numerous crimes, accused of sexual assault by multiple women, once threw an ottoman out of a fourteen-story window, and was banned for life from a Holiday Inn Express in Albany, New York. He's not the average guy, in any way. But Brown's response is indicative of something that's true in all walks of life—successfully establishing that something is dangerous doesn't mean people will accurately comprehend what that danger entails. Football players know that concussions can lead to a disease called CTE, but that's not the same as proving

THE QUESTION

every individual "understands the risk of what they are doing," particularly since even those in the medical community sometimes disagree on what the relationship between concussions, CTE, and dementia truly is. So if no one *completely* understands this—if the objective consequence is either much worse or much less awful than science has the capacity to explain, forcing players to interpret the hazard through their own worldview—it becomes difficult to argue that personal agency matters at all. Free will is a detriment to the man who doesn't realize he's confused. And even if that man is *not* confused—even if that man has a complete and realistic understanding of what football could do to his brain and his life—it likely wouldn't matter, anyway. The incentives to play football have become so titanic that it's irrational to expect a normal twenty-year-old male not to do it, assuming they have the skills and opportunity. Yes, it's still (technically) their choice. Yes, they still (technically) have agency. But the equation is unbalanced. The overwhelming majority of pro football players could never build a better life than the one afforded by the NFL, in terms of wealth and prestige. Even if the risk of CTE was five times greater than it appears, the short-term payoff would seem greater than the long-term risk, particularly since one in seven Americans living past the age of seventy will be diagnosed with dementia no matter how they live or what they do. At the college level, football provides a free education, an incredible campus experience, more money than any normal job, and an outside chance at a pro career. At the high school level, football provides identity, status, action, and the possibility of attending a college that might be otherwise out of reach. There's no knowledge or data that would dissuade most young football players from wanting to play football. We know this because—in a nonspecific sense—such knowledge and data have *always* been available. In 1978, a New England Patriot receiver named Darryl Stingley was paralyzed for life by Jack "the Assassin" Tatum in an exhibition game. It was, for decades, the most glaring example of football's risk.

FOOTBALL

But one of Stingley's three sons still ended up playing pro football in the Arena League, and Stingley's grandson recently became an All-Pro cornerback with the Los Angeles Chargers. In sports, there's no such thing as generational trauma.

Researchers keep trying to prove that football is too hazardous to play, a difficult task that's also unnecessary. It's a little like the relationship between science and smoking cigarettes. A direct link between smoking and lung cancer was not officially established by the U.S. surgeon general until 1964. Prior to that definitive proof, cigarettes were issued to military personnel to deal with anxiety. There were ashtrays in schools and libraries and hospital waiting rooms. I can remember my high school chemistry teacher (born in 1952) telling us how her own mother told her to start smoking as a way to stay thin. Society did not officially comprehend the danger of cigarettes until the mid-sixties. But at the same time, there were certain things people *always* knew about smoking: They knew it involved the inhalation of smoke, they knew inhaling smoke made novice smokers cough, and they knew people who smoked for decades usually spent their final years coughing incessantly. It wasn't necessary to *prove* smoking was bad in order to detect that it wasn't healthy (and even when the proof was confirmed, millions of people kept doing it). Football's risk falls into the same category: There has never been a time when football wasn't understood to be dangerous. No neurosurgeon's opinion was necessary. The sport was nearly outlawed in 1905 when 18 college players died in a single season. *The Violent World of Sam Huff,* a harrowing 30-minute TV documentary about an undersized New York Giants linebacker, was nationally broadcast on CBS in 1960. In 1978, *Sports Illustrated* ran a cover story headlined BRUTALITY: THE CRISIS IN FOOTBALL. In 1993, another *SI* cover rhetorically pondered if 185-pound defensive back Chuck Cecil was "too vicious" for the NFL (Cecil had acquired the nickname "Scud" due to his

THE QUESTION

habit of turning himself into a misguided human missile). Luke Kuechly of the Carolina Panthers, regularly classified as the smartest defensive player of his generation, suffered a glancing concussion against the Saints on a Thursday night in 2016. Kuechly started spontaneously weeping on the field, an involuntary reaction he couldn't stop or understand.

Le'Veon Bell and Antonio Brown might not be able to explain why football is dangerous, but they clearly know that it is. We all do. You can't know what football is without recognizing that it's an unnatural act, predicated on collisions and endangerment. It's all part of the same package. Watching football carries the nonzero possibility that the watcher will one day witness a death on live TV.

This is a hard thing to accept. That, however, is not the same as deeming it unacceptable.

▶

Trying to establish consistent moral parameters for how much (or how little) society should protect people from themselves is frustrating and unworkable, unless you're the kind of consequentialist who loves repeating the words "Yes, but then what about *this*?" Every specific example can be rejected by a counterexample that's equally valid. I never wore a seat belt until I took driver's education in tenth grade, when we were all forced to do so. Growing up, I didn't know anyone who wore seat belts on a regular basis; there was one guy in my hometown who hated seat belts so much he supposedly cut them out of his truck with a hacksaw. This now seems absurd. I accept seat belt laws unconditionally, for all of the most obvious reasons (prevention of harm, protection of the uninformed, the cost to the public). Forcing people to wear seat belts stops people from dying. But then why do we let people swim? Thousands of people die from drowning every year, yet we'd never ban swimming. Closing public pools or outlawing the ocean seems way crazier than not wearing a seat belt. And why is that? Probably because people love swimming, and the physical gratification of swimming compensates for the risk that accompanies it. Yet couldn't the same thing be said about cocaine? It's illegal to take antibiotics without a prescription. It's not illegal to own a cobra in the state of Texas if you pay a $20 fee and live outside the city limits of Houston. Skydiving is allowed in every state. Fireworks are not. There is no end to this strain of whataboutism. You can do it all night.

The likelihood of football being banned outright is akin to the likelihood of the Second Amendment being eliminated. It will never happen, and any humanist who argues that it should fuels the fire within all those who'd rather die than compromise. The legality of football is not something to worry about. But even so: Asking oneself if the social and individual value of football outweighs the toll it takes on its participants is a worthwhile exercise. It forces a person to confront what values they *actually* value, as opposed to the values they feel obligated to accept and promote.

Here are the arguments in favor of football's existence, despite any negative consequences they entail:

1. It's fun and rewarding for the participants, due in part to the physical demands intrinsic to the experience.

2. It provides career opportunities for low-income athletes with otherwise limited options.

3. It's entertaining and enriching for nonparticipants.

4. It has aesthetic and intellectual value that's specific to itself.

5. It teaches things that are difficult to learn otherwise, particularly in the modern world.

THE QUESTION

6. It has economic ramifications that stretch beyond sports.

7. It's woven into the fabric of American culture and American identity.

8. People should be allowed to do what they want, even if what they want is sometimes bad for them.

Here are the opposing arguments:

1. Football is an unnecessary endeavor that injures people, sometimes seriously.

2. The people most at risk may not understand the severity of that risk.

3. Even if those at risk fully understand the game's potential danger, they might be compelled to participate through social and economic forces that do not have their best interest in mind.

4. It's possible the risks are actually greater than we realize or suspect.

5. Because the nature of football is integrally violent, its participants are required to commit violent acts against their opponents, making them potentially responsible for another person's injury or death.

6. Because football exists as a form of entertainment, anyone who watches football is promoting and supporting its mechanics, making all fans complicit in any damage deriving from those mechanics.

7. Because football (as an organized game) is so intertwined with dominance and brutality, the disorganized culture surrounding football adopts those same qualities, pushing them into aspects of life that have nothing to do with sports.

8. People should not be allowed to do dangerous things simply because they want to do them.

FOOTBALL

Because these are arguments (as opposed to universally agreed-upon facts), most of them are disputable, particularly those in the first category. Is football objectively *fun?* Maybe, but maybe not.

"Anybody who tells me that they go out there to have fun playing football is a liar," claimed Lyle Alzado, an ultra-hostile defensive lineman who played fifteen years in the AFC before dying from a brain tumor in 1992, a condition he attributed to steroids. Alzado once ripped the helmet off an opposing player and threw it at the guy's face. "This game isn't fun. This game is a war."

While it's undeniable that football has improved the lives of countless kids born into poverty, an academic might assert the money those players earned for themselves pales in comparison to the revenue they've generated for others who've risked nothing, making pro and college football exploitative (and since Black players play an outsized role in the overall football population, it would also mean that football is structurally racist). Ethical absolutists will claim qualities like entertainment value and fiscal impact have no place in a debate about morality, and people who hate populist American culture view football's place in that culture as extra distasteful. Arguments in the second category are more durable, but only slightly. Any point hinging on "complicity" is automatically suspect, as there's no limit to how far that accusation can be extended (a homeless man stealing a Snickers bar in Seattle can be cited as "complicit" in the Israeli war against Gaza, if one strains hard enough). The only immutable statements are the final declarations in each class: Either people should be allowed to do dangerous things, or people should not. When all other concepts are stripped away, that's the question that remains.

My answer is a conditional "yes," though I admit my condition is somewhat unusual: People should be allowed to do dangerous things, but only if we're making that decision from a purely secular perspective.

THE QUESTION

About 80 percent of Americans believe in God. That percentage is higher among football players (it's been estimated that 40 percent of NFL players identify as full-on evangelical, a number far above the national average). The sports world is about as secular as Iran. But to examine this question pragmatically, we must accept or fantasize that God (or any supernatural equivalent to God) does not exist. Because if God exists, it means God created humankind, and if God created humankind, the laws for human behavior aren't flexible; they're just unknown or unverifiable. Logic and reason become extraneous. If it turned out that the one true religion is (say) Jainism, which teaches that any living creature (including protozoa) cannot be deliberately damaged in any way, football becomes untenable. The Islamic faith forbids self-harm, so any devout Islamic nickelback who believes micro concussions lead to brain damage would be committing a grave sin anytime he was flagged for targeting. Quakers oppose the use of force as a way to resolve conflict, and every conflict in football is decided by force. The rules of many religions, if interpreted literally, make a litany of sports morally unacceptable. And since any belief in an unspecific higher power allows for the possibility that one of these religions is, in fact, metaphysically correct and unimpeachable, the only option is to delete that entire side of the equation. When considering the acceptability of allowing strangers to do dangerous things, the assumption has to be that "human life" is nothing more than the end result of a capricious series of random evolutions, and that there's no greater force providing guidance or demanding compliance. The only rules are the rules we create for ourselves.

Under these parameters, an answer becomes clear.

In any secular mindset, two competing paradigms emerge, and both support football. The first is that existence is unintentional, nothing matters (or has the potential to matter), morals and ethics are constructs, and life can offer nothing more than a hallucinatory meaning. It's a Crowley-esque worldview that permits any activity that society isn't compelled to stop through legal means. This includes self-destruction, consensual sexual deviance, and paralyzing Darryl Stingley. The second paradigm, preferred by most atheists, is that life has *more* meaning in the absence of God, because the meaning is not just a list of instructions. The rules are not inborn. The rules must be built. And though it might seem shallow, football can play a role in that construction.

If there's no universal path to self-actualization, a path must be creatively forged by every individual, and anything that exists can be transformed into a vessel of meaning. It could be art or commerce. It could be raising kids or rescuing puppies. But it could also be playing football, or even watching football. All that's required is an ability to access something within the experience that transcends the ever-creeping suspicion that reality is a pointless accident. And you know what? The violence within football is part of that, for everybody involved. I hate admitting it, but it is. It escalates the stakes, and it allows for a different kind of meaning to be imposed upon its nature. *Football is fucking dangerous.* Its physicality is uncompromising, and no one knows if the reward trumps the risk. It's crazy that we do it at all. It's crazy that it controls the culture. It's crazy that it defines huge swaths of the country, including some swaths that barely care. It's crazy that so many men play a brutal game, end up with incurable dementia, and still insist they'd do it all over again in the exact same way, despite the awareness that they'll eventually be unable to remember the very thing they fell in love with. *It's crazy.* Football is crazy. But it is an insanity we must accept and permit ourselves to enjoy, unless we believe people are obligated to remove every unessential hazard from day-to-day existence. And I just don't believe that obligation is valid. I don't believe human life can be fulfilling if the only goal is ensuring that it lasts as long as possible.

THE QUESTION

I've had two concussions in my life. I mean, I *think* they were concussions. I don't actually know. I never saw a doctor or entered the blue tent. One happened when I was sixteen, walking through the shelterbelt behind my house. A shelterbelt is a long line of trees planted in a row, usually three or four rows deep, designed to block the wind and limit erosion (my family always referred to this particular shelterbelt as "the grove," though that term might be technically incorrect). I was aimlessly walking through this shelterbelt, daydreaming about whatever a sixteen-year-old daydreams about, when I inadvertently stepped on a rabbit. The rabbit freaked out and jumped forward. I freaked out and jumped vertically. By chance, this event occurred as I was walking beneath a box elder tree that featured a thick horizontal branch about eight feet off the ground, and I jumped straight into it, hitting the overhanging branch with the top of my head like Wile E. Coyote. I knocked myself unconscious for somewhere between three seconds and three minutes (probably closer to the former, but who knows?). I still can't believe any of that happened. I can't believe I accidentally stepped on a rabbit and I can't believe I got coldcocked by a tree. It felt like a sledgehammer that fell from a helicopter, though the hilarity of the circumstance compensated for the pain.

The other concussion was football related.

It was 1985. I was in seventh grade. The afternoon was cold and overcast and foreboding, a description that could be applied to almost every football practice I remember, except for the ones that were hot and humid and dehydrating. We were doing a three-man open-field tackling drill that didn't have a proper name: The offensive player would catch a ball thrown high in the air, simulating a punt return. The two defensive players would sprint at him from 25 yards away, simulating punt coverage. The offensive player was supposed to catch the ball and return it up the middle. The two defenders were supposed to converge on the ballcarrier and kill him. The technical nuance was absolute zero.

Our coach was in a sadistic mood that afternoon, which is a little like saying Bob Marley was high that time he wrote a song about social unrest in Jamaica. We were all informed, in terrifyingly colorful language, that the consequence of allowing any kick returner to score would far exceed whatever we imagined might be an equitable response to failing at a drill we did almost every day. It was my turn to serve as one of the gunners. I weighed around 100 pounds, maybe less. The return man weighed around 150 pounds, maybe more. I sprinted as hard as I could and tried to drive the crown of my helmet through the middle of his body, my spine parallel to the ground at impact. This was how hitting was taught at the time (you'd go to Gitmo for teaching it like that now). The return man, a lineman nicknamed "Noot" who was fast for his size, dropped his oversized head to the same level as mine. We collided like bighorn sheep in a commercial for Dodge pickup trucks. The physics played out in a predictable fashion. I'd like to say we both went down, though that can't be verified. I saw stars, a sensation I'd previously assumed was a colloquialism and not a verbatim description of what happens when your retinas are disturbed. It was like sitting in the cockpit of the Millennium Falcon when it jumped into hyperspace, except in slow motion. My mouth guard tasted like I'd just had dental work. But I remained conscious and my fingers didn't fence. Noot helped me to my feet and I woozily walked to the back of the line and waited to do it again, because that was the expectation. I don't remember anything else from that day, though that isn't connected to the concussion. I don't remember most of seventh grade. It's more because this sort of thing used to happen all the time. The only reason I specifically remember this incident is because it specifically happened to me.

Do not misread what I'm saying here. I'm not trying to mitigate the

THE QUESTION

severity of head trauma, nor am I pretending to compare something that happened to me in seventh grade with anything that happens to NFL football players. I mention it only because I still think about it, and I sometimes wonder if my opinion about this stuff would be different if my own experience had been worse. What if I'd been momentarily incapacitated? What if I developed lifelong issues with my neck? What if I'd shown up at school the next day and couldn't remember how to multiply fractions? Would my views on all of this be different? Probably. Would I still insist we must "depersonalize" the issue if I couldn't do that myself? Probably not, and I might even insist that *only* people who've dealt with a traumatic head injury are in a position to weigh the pros and cons of allowing this to happen to others, despite my current inclination to argue the opposite. Everything I believe is based only on what I think I know, the only system available and the worst system possible.

I was watching *Monday Night Football* on the evening Damar Hamlin almost died, an event that felt apocalyptic but has already devolved into a trivia question. Hamlin, a safety for the Buffalo Bills, made a routine tackle on Cincinnati Bengal receiver Tee Higgins. Hamlin then stood up, fell down, and went into cardiac arrest. He had no pulse and was administered CPR. "I died on national TV," he would later remark, and that was absolutely what everyone thought at the time. There had always been a (rarely spoken) awareness that—at some point—people who watch a lot of NFL football would see a player die on the field. It appeared that Hamlin was the final manifestation of that inevitability. As the ambulance left the stadium, optimism was low. The game was suspended and eventually canceled. I flipped over to CNN and Fox and MSNBC to see if the story had crossed into non-sports media, and it had, with all the broadcasters using the somber voice typically reserved for assassinations. There was sadness for Hamlin and confusion over what had transpired. But there was also sadness and confusion for a different reason—a reason so bleak and verboten that it could only be discussed in private conversation: If Hamlin died, would football die with him? There had always been an understanding that this outcome was possible, but no one really knew what the response would be. That part had never *really* been deliberated. We all knew a player could die and we all knew we'd have to see it, but that was about as far as the speculation extended. Perhaps it would become something impossible to unsee. This event was also happening in January 2023, a period when the term "reckoning" was an inescapable part of the discourse; it wasn't unthinkable to imagine Hamlin's death forcing football to reckon with itself. The play had looked so standard and unremarkable. If this level of contact was enough to kill a man, what part of football *couldn't* kill a man?

But then, as we all now know, everything changed in seventy-two hours. It turned out Hamlin's heart attack was caused by a rare condition called "commotio cordis," the result of a meticulous blow to the middle of the chest at a precise moment in the ventricular repolarization phase of the cardiac cycle. The rarity of this condition is so extreme that it will possibly never happen again to another NFL player for the rest of time. Hamlin not only survived but returned to the Bills. He became a starter in 2024 and developed a nonprofit charity, jump-started by the $10 million donated to him from people who watched him (almost) die on TV. In the end, we did not see a person killed by football, allowing us to continue watching strangers do very dangerous, very popular things. I'm able to write this particular essay in this particular book, and my argument is acceptable, until something happens in the future that will make it obscene, at which point however correct I was in the past will no longer matter at all.

10.

Nuclear Football

BECAUSE FOOTBALL IS SO POPULAR, A LOT OF ENERGY IS invested in trying to unpack the roots of that popularity, working from the premise that understanding what society loves is a way to understand what society values. Something that often comes up in these explorations is a reference to the three sports most popular in America a hundred years ago—baseball, boxing, and horse racing. This specific bit of knowledge has become one of those factoids everyone seems to know, typically cited as proof that nothing lasts forever. Baseball is still considered one of the country's three major sports, but it's a distant third, a victim of gradual erosion. A 2024 World Series matchup involving the country's two biggest media markets (as well as the sport's two biggest superstars) was watched by roughly the same number of people who tuned in to a run-of-the-mill *Monday Night Football* game coincidentally airing at the same time. Boxing is now a niche concern, decimated by self-inflicted wounds and disparaged as corrupt, dependent on gimmicky pay-per-view events that only generate revenue and disappointment. Trying to trace the decline of baseball and boxing is convoluted, usually requiring analysis of how the sports have changed and evolved. It's also a bit contentious, since it still feels possible that either sport could, theoretically, return to prominence.

A more instructive deterioration is what happened to horse racing.

The modern mind can't envision horse racing as a major spectator sport. It's an isolated pastime that grows more insular with every successive generation. Mainstream interest will spike if a Thoroughbred challenges (or attains) the Triple Crown. But when this happens, as it did in 2015 and 2018, public fascination with the respective horses—American Pharoah and Justify—was nowhere close to the attention superlative horses were afforded in the seventies, to the same degree that the finest horses of the seventies (Secretariat in '73, Seattle Slew in '77, Affirmed and Alydar in '78) were not as celebrated as Man o' War in 1920. In 1938, Seabiscuit was as famous as Babe Ruth. There's no way a contemporary horse could become that iconic, unless it started a horse flu pandemic or learned how to talk. In the early 1920s, there were almost four hundred active racetracks in the United States. Today, there's fewer than seventy. Horse racing is now exclusively tied to in-person and off-track betting. It has no other purpose, and it's hard to argue it's still among the country's ten most-loved sports, despite evolving the least. There's a difference between watching the 1875 Kentucky Derby and watching the Kentucky Derby today, but the difference is minor, even in terms of athletic performance. It's fundamentally the same sport. But something else about the world changed completely, and that's what caused the shift: A normal American no longer has any relationship to horses.

If you were alive in 1900, you didn't necessarily own a horse. But you undoubtedly knew people who did, and you encountered horses constantly. Your father had a horse, or your grandfather owned a horse farm, or you worked a blue-collar job where horses did the labor. The country was still 60 percent rural, but even if you were born in Chicago, the nickname of your hometown was the City of Horses and you needed to avoid piles of horse dung whenever you crossed the street. In 1900, the U.S. Agricultural Census estimated there were around 21 million horses in the country, at a time when the human population was 76 million. There are now fewer than 7 million horses in a country with 340 million people. By 1935, automobiles had replaced equines almost entirely. But most Americans still had a relationship to the *culture* of horses. The average citizen could visually recognize the difference between a Quarter horse, a Morgan horse, and a Thoroughbred. They'd know that a horse's muzzle is softer than cashmere, and they'd know that horse sweat is white and frothy. They'd know to never mount a horse from its right side, or to walk around the back of a horse without touching its rump. Even if they hadn't ridden a horse in years, they'd remember how it felt to sit upon a thousand-pound mammal that's both overpowering and subservient, and they'd recognize what it takes to control that mammal. They'd have a realistic sense of what horses cost, and they'd respect a horse more than other animals. In 1920, and perhaps as late as 1940, the majority of Americans were Horse People by default, and that default knowledge fueled the appetite for racing. The action at Saratoga or Pimlico or Santa Anita was the competitive version of an experience they fully understood, and the hooved competitors were creatures from their own memory. This collective familiarity will never happen again. When a twenty-first-century person watches a horse race, they're watching something antiquated and peculiar—a remnant of the preindustrial past, centered on an alien ungulate they recognize but cannot appreciate. Modern horse racing can be only a peripheral pastime, explicitly intended for millionaires who love to spend money and degenerates who love to lose it.

FOOTBALL

▶

Within the penitentiary of our current moment, football appears invincible. It doesn't seem plausible, or even possible, that it could become irrelevant or niche. If everything about society remained as it is, it appears more likely that football will consume its competition and become the *only* sport anyone in the United States cares about at all. But that won't happen. Society *will* change, and societal transformations impact what's popular more than what's obscure.

I don't know how long I'm going to live. But if I make it to a hundred, I believe I'll die in a world where football has surrendered its monocultural grip. It will no longer serve as a practical means for understanding American life, and no one will mind if my funeral forces them to miss the Iron Bowl.

This will happen for two reasons.

The first reason is elaborate, multifaceted, and speculative. It's more a conjecture than a prediction, and it probably won't unspool precisely the way I propose. But I'm confident something along these lines will transpire, with a net effect identical to the one I suggest.

The second reason is closer to what happened to horse racing. I'm more confident about this one, because the process has already started.

▶

So this is how the future will go . . .

For the next five to fifteen years, football becomes even more dominant than it is right now. This, incongruously, results from the mismanagement of college football. Every twenty-first-century policy decision involving NCAA football has been wonderful for the players and terrible for the game: the destruction of traditional conferences, the 2018 introduction of the transfer portal, and the 2021 legal decision allowing college players to financially benefit from their name, image, and likeness (a sensible modification that was immediately misused). These changes push college football in a more professional direction, a depressing shift that works to a sport's short-term benefit. Casual fans prefer pro sports to their collegiate equivalent; pro sports are a zero-sum game that don't depend on regional history or symbolic value. The expansion of the college playoff increases the number of relevant regular-season games, expanding the fan base to schools without tradition. Any remaining connection between "going to college" and "going to college to play football" becomes immaterial, making the governing relationship between the NCAA and college football unnecessary. There's no reason for college football to remain tied to an organization that only hinders its economic potential. The forty strongest programs break away from the NCAA and start their own autonomous league.

Once college football becomes a freestanding entity, universities can pay their athletes a direct salary and employ players who are not enrolled in the school (the quarterback at Oregon or Auburn or Minnesota "represents" that institution, but isn't necessarily a registered member of the student body). The transformation feels apocalyptic to diehards, but national interest surges, and taking a stand against these changes is viewed as naive and repressive. The changes are classified as progress. But this progress injects a cancer, some of which is obvious and some of which is unseen. What happens to college football is what happened to men's college basketball after the "one-and-done" rule was implemented in 2006: It devolves into a quasi-professional version of the sport that ceases to differentiate itself from the professional version. All recruiting is national and every team plays the same way, overhauling its roster at the end of every season. The contrast in style between a triple-option team and a Veer-and-Shoot team disappears, as does any semblance of geographic representation or historical weight. College football becomes a less interesting version of pro football, nothing more than a feeder system for the NFL. That's the part that's visible. The invisible part is the corrosion of football participation at the high school level. In places where football is not culturally emphasized (the Pacific Northwest, the non-Jersey Northeast), a bias against allowing children to play football becomes the normal opinion to express. Every new study about CTE asserts that every collision increases the possibility of suicide and dementia, and—even if a mother disagrees with those findings or diagnostically accepts the risk—there's mounting social pressure *from other parents* to dissuade that mom from allowing her son to play a game that necessitates (and sometimes glorifies) high-speed hitting. In some regions of the country, the shift doesn't happen. There are still certain communities where football is the only thing that matters, and attempts to eradicate that sentiment are ridiculed. But places like Dublin, Georgia, and Jourdanton, Texas, become the contrarian outliers, disconnected from the bulk of America. By 2040, the football landscape has adopted a radical asymmetry: The NFL remains huge, despite diminished interest in the college version and the disappearance of football as a high school activity.

For a while, this barely matters. For another ten to twenty years, the NFL prospers while youth participation dwindles. The number of available players decreases, but the size and skill level of those who remain continues to advance, just as it has for the previous eight decades. Innovations in technology and training push physicality forward. The mental part of the sport becomes more and more sophisticated. To the consumer, the pro game looks better, or at least unchanged, and there's temporary moral comfort in this bifurcated system. Football is now an *exclusively* professional pursuit, watched and supported by millions of fans who have no personal relationship to the game itself. The sport has progressed to its social and economic end point.

NUCLEAR FOOTBALL

This is where the plane hits the mountain.

Economic escalation has made pro sports fragile. That fragility became obvious during the COVID pandemic, when the NFL, the NBA, and Major League Baseball all realized they *had* to keep playing games, even if the stadiums were empty and the outcomes were compromised. It's common to classify an entity like the NFL as "too big to fail," but it's actually too big to *stop*. The economic superstructure is so extensive that the cultivation of revenue can never relent or plateau. And for a long time, that goal was achievable. The NFL's total revenue hit $1 billion for the first time in 1989. By 2001, it had grown to $4.3 billion. Ten years after that, it had doubled to $9 billion. In 2019, the mark was $15 billion. It was $18.6 billion in 2023, projected to hit $25 billion in 2027. The rate of increase has slowed, but only because the numbers became too large to sustain exponential growth. By 2050, the statistics have gone ballistic: In order to stay on its trajectory, the NFL needs to make *at least* $100 billion every season. By 2065, the number will be $200 billion, and the face value for a ticket will exceed $3,000.

The impetus for this escalation is television. Live sporting events are the only way to consistently force mass audiences to sit through commercials. The ascendency of on-demand streaming services and the decline of traditional networks made advertising on television a hopeless proposition for any event that isn't both popular and live, and pro football is hyperpopular and always live. Whatever price* the NFL sets for the broadcast rights to pro football is expected to be accepted, over and over and over again. League revenue continues to rise, as long as companies need a media platform to advertise whatever it is they hope to sell.

But what happens when they don't?

---

*As I write this footnote, NBC is paying the league $1.7 billion a year to show one game a week. By the time this book is published and you read this footnote for the first time, some other network or platform will undoubtedly be paying more than that for a similar opportunity.

FOOTBALL

Somewhere in the middle of the current century, there will be a panoramic realization about TV advertising. The realization will be this: It doesn't work, at least when compared with what it costs. It's always been understood that advertising is a lagging indicator, reflecting the past more than the future. This, however, will be a more extreme comprehension of its limitations. There's never been irrefutable evidence that TV advertising is effective at anything except introducing a new product to those who have never seen that product before. How much (or how little) audiences see a commercial does not consistently correlate with how much they want the product. It *seems* like advertising works, and there's a circular argument insisting it must ("Why would Procter & Gamble spend $109 million a month on TV commercials if it wasn't a good idea?"). No one has come up with a better plan. But at some point between 2040 and 2060, the money required for the production and distribution of televised advertising becomes too expensive to justify the continuance of a never-proven strategy. Corporations conclude that paying huge sums of money for thirty seconds of (mostly ignored) exposure is a bad investment, forcing TV networks and streaming services to conclude that paying far larger sums for the rights to NFL football is no longer sensible. These sweeping conclusions happen overnight, as is so often the case with media sea changes. When its existing TV deals expire and the new deals are negotiated, the NFL finds itself without leverage; for the first time, the new offers are smaller than the expired contracts. The perceived value of the league plummets. And this, somewhat predictably, is when the mass of an empire portends its own annihilation: For more than a hundred years, the National Football League only got bigger and richer. It was designed only for imperial expansion, which is the only thing it did. But now it has to somehow get smaller, and that's something it cannot do. It is too brittle to contract. It can only shatter.

Way back in 2022, the yearly operating costs for an average NFL franchise were already exceeding $400 million.* By 2062, that figure is three times larger. Ticket prices are raised, but the number of seats and luxury boxes in any stadium is finite. Merchandising is a tiny fraction of the overall portfolio, and corporate sponsorship has inherent boundaries (there are only thirty-two buildings available for garish renaming). The only viable option is to cut player salaries, eliminate all contractual guarantees, increase the yearly schedule to twenty-two games, and eliminate multiple franchises and hundreds of jobs. The players strike, but this isn't like the strikes of 1982 and 1987. This time, the players want a larger share of a smaller pie, and that can't happen. The best counteroffer from ownership is still a major pay cut, and the owners are not motivated to get players back on the field. They will lose money by hosting games. It's like a strike and a lockout at the same time, and the work stoppage becomes interminable.

In fact, it becomes more than interminable.

It never ends.

▶

Now, I know what you're thinking (or at least I think I do).

You're thinking, "Even if all this happens exactly as you say, it would not end football. Destroying the delivery mechanism for a popular product does not destroy the desire for that product. People love football too much. They need it to give their weekends meaning. They need it for gambling. If there was no better option, the NFL could sell the games themselves, straight to people's phones and VR goggles, without any need for a third-party platform. If every game became an à la carte pay-per-view event,

---

*This is based on the 2022 operating costs of the Green Bay Packers, the league's only publicly owned team that still qualifies as a nonprofit corporation (and must therefore publish its expenditures).

FOOTBALL

people would pay whatever it cost, every week. If a consumer had to pay $1,000 or $5,000 or $10,000 for a subscription to the whole season, and if that was the only way to get access, hundreds of thousands of people would do so without hesitation. There are limitless ways to make money from an enterprise that's more popular than everything it competes against. How much would people pay to watch a game through a tiny camera mounted on the quarterback's helmet? How much would Saudi Arabia or Dubai pay to host a Super Bowl? *People will always need to watch football.* It's not like other things. It's not normal entertainment."

This, I must concede, is true—if the scenario I described were happening today. But it's not happening today. It's something that will happen in the future, to different people, and those future people will not be like you. They will live in a version of society where football stops and no one cares. And that inevitability is why I wrote this book.

▸

I don't like using the term "late capitalism," mainly because I don't believe it's an accurate description of where the world is. I don't think we're in the "late" stage of capitalism. I think we're much closer to the middle. But some principles of capitalism are already warping, in a pretty obvious way. The most rudimentary laws of inflation—that prices double about every twenty years, and that the buying power of one dollar decreases by 50 percent over the same span—have become increasingly unreliable. A lot of capitalistic enterprises are going to crash in the next three or four decades, with professional sports leagues among the most noticeable. Sports leagues are micro models for how unsustainable systems play out on a larger scale. Right now, the pro league most vulnerable to this is the National Basketball Association. The NBA will likely fall into crisis before the NFL. Football has kept salaries lower and avoids guaranteed contracts, obstructions that are bad for individual players but good for the stability of the league. Enforced frugality will buy the NFL an extra decade. But football has a second problem, churning and swelling beneath the crust. It is an infrastructural problem, though that language makes it sound more complex than it is. What is already happening, and what will continue to happen, is that the evolution of American culture is in direct opposition to the culture of American football. The sport, in almost every way, is a contradiction of what enlightened people are supposed to want. It conflicts with how modern people are socialized to think, subverting the symbolic meaning of what football represents. This dissonance amplifies football's current popularity, because it's the only high-profile oasis for certain verboten ideologies. But as the chasm between society and football continues to widen, the human connection to the game will erode. It won't be readily noticeable for many years, because football's TV ratings will still be higher than all the alternatives and the media will still cover the games like monoliths of interest (the media, like advertising, is another lagging indicator). It will be assumed that a lengthy NFL work stoppage would be treated like a national emergency and that the public will panic if football disappears. But then such an event will actually happen, and when it happens, the reaction will be startling, unexpected indifference.

Horse racing receded from prominence when average people lost their relationship to horses, an observable transition that happened gradually. Football will recede from prominence as average people lose their relationship to the sport's interior culture, a gradual transition that will remain cloaked until the point of economic crisis. When that point is hit, a new realization will be swift and dumbfounding. It will become obvious that football's century of supremacy, originally built off the game's ability to reflect and simulate society, had sustained itself through illusory means.

FOOTBALL

Since the era of Jim Thorpe, football has served many different functions, one being a source of entertainment. In the future, that's all it will be. It will *only* be entertainment, perpetuating its popularity through tautological habit. People will watch the NFL on Sundays because that's the thing people watch on Sundays. The Super Bowl will serve as an unofficial holiday because we've agreed it's an acceptable excuse for behaving as if a holiday were happening. The top quarterbacks will be tabloid celebrities because we're accustomed to seeing quarterbacks in a celebrity context. But these things will no longer be organic extensions of public desire. They will not be extensions of a national passion. They will be ancillary activities, tied to a sport the majority of the populace neither consciously nor unconsciously engages with on an ontological level.

▸

Football is an ethnocentric game, beloved in only one country. This is not what we want. Football is violent, and its violence is sometimes praised. This is not what we want. Football is an exclusionary activity, exclusively played by men. This is not what we want. Football does not reject "toxic masculinity." This is not what we want. Football celebrates the ability to ignore injury and accept pain. This is not what we want. Football rewards domination of the weak. This is not what we want. Football shuns individualism and identity. This is not what we want. Football is authoritarian and militaristic. This is not what we want. Football is hierarchically controlled, with objective outcomes. This is not what we want. Football is uncomfortable, uncompromising, demoralizing. This is not what we want. Football, from a structural vantage point, is fascist and reactionary. This is not what we want. Nothing about the culture of football is what we want, or what we are told to want, or what we are supposed to want.

NUCLEAR FOOTBALL

It's possible you disagree with these assertions, for any number of reasons. Perhaps you have semantic qualms with my inclusion of certain words. Perhaps you think the accusations are inaccurate (or perhaps misleading). Maybe you disagree with the assertion that "this is not what we want," because you believe society really does want those things. Maybe they're things *you* want, a set of desires I understand. But the specific veracity of these allegations is not the issue. The issue is that this is the perception of football culture, particularly among those with no affiliation to that world. It's how football appears to any disinterested bystander, and it's how football is explained by academics. It's also, somewhat ironically, how football demands to perceive itself. When Jim Harbaugh became the head coach at Michigan in 2015, he described football as "the last bastion of hope for toughness in American men," an opinion that made Harbaugh sound like a nutcase to anyone who assumed football was just a game. Traits seen as negative by non-football people are the same traits a football traditionalist views as positive, and that discord cannot be fixed. There are no rule changes or branding initiatives that could ever reverse the fundamental reading of what football culture is, unless the entire game was reinvented in totality, in which case the people who love football most would lose interest (since it would no longer resemble the thing they love). For football to remain football, it must maintain its connection to not just the past, but to the problematic past. It needs to sustain the conventions that are now seen as transgressions, at least as a posture; it can condemn those traditions, but it can't remove them. Even if the game is made less dangerous and more inclusive, it must present itself as a dangerous, separatist game. Even if the way football coaches behave becomes more benevolent and empathic, the stereotype of the football coach needs to stick. The political meaning of football cannot change, and that will make it too unstable to withstand the evolution of everything else around it.

FOOTBALL

"But hasn't that happened already? Aren't all the things you're saying about the future already happening now?"

Yes. Exactly. The future has already started, and football only seems bigger. But that's because football operates within a state of perpetual momentum. It is a car headed toward a distant cliff with a brick on the accelerator, comfortable with the sensation that everything is still perfect. There's an inescapability to football's present-day dominance, accepted by everyone. But like horse racing in 1935, the root of that dominance is becoming distant from the lived experience of its fan base. A link still exists, but it's intangible, imaginative, almost sci-fi. It's no longer a game many people played in high school, or even a game their fathers played in high school. It's something your family watched on TV, so you do the same, mostly out of habit. It's a live-action video game. It's a fantasy league your coworker persuaded you to join. It's an excuse to make a wager on your phone. It's a series of three-hour reality shows airing every autumn weekend, and its narrative is the culture that football controls. But that culture is increasingly foreign to those who digest it. What football values, how it's systematized, the polarizing allegory of what it means to play and what it means to care—these are antiquated, pre-internet ideologies that will signify nothing in the year 2065. Future people will still *like* football, but their psychological investment will be zilch, and when some economic disaster makes football disappear, they won't mind if it never comes back. It will just be the loss of an entertaining distraction, and distractions are replaceable.

▸

What I'm arguing here, perhaps melodramatically, is that I see football doomed by its own unreasonable success. It's a sport so commercial and expansive that it can no longer function in any other way, trapped by its

NUCLEAR FOOTBALL

own necessity for autocatalytic growth. That success was built off its ability to reflect twentieth-century America, an accidental synchronicity that became profound. But because that synchronicity was unintentional, it can't resynchronize on command. As generations change, football fundamentally stays the same, turning it into a $25 billion simulacrum—a disconnected metaphor for a society that no longer exists, rocketing on autopilot, oblivious to the growing distance between itself and the future. Which is disheartening, but also what I love about it: I love that even in the future, football will live in the past.

Like a prospector who didn't reach California until 1855, my obsession with football started after the peak had already passed. It was a relationship sustained by television, molded and manipulated by books and magazines and newspapers. My belief system came from overheard conversations and misinterpreted myths. I always wanted to be older, to actually remember the things I had to learn secondhand. Many of my favorite players were retired before I turned ten. I had pictures on my bedroom wall of legends I never saw play. I will always view the 1970s as football's zenith, and that's because I was barely there. If I'd been born ten years earlier, I'd likely think the same thing about the sixties. Tomorrow can never matter as much as yesterday. The great football games I've seen can't match the great football games I've missed, and I've missed so many.

I missed a game when I was twelve. It was the Friday after Thanksgiving. I don't recall where I'd been that afternoon, but it was dark when I got home. My father was in front of the TV when I came through the front door. I could hear Brent Musburger's voice, so I walked straight into the living room, still wearing my stocking cap. It was a college game. It was Miami versus Boston College. There were six seconds on the clock with the ball at midfield. Miami was winning 45–41. I asked what was happening.

"Boston College played hard," said my father. "But this one is over."

FOOTBALL

I'd missed the game, but I saw one play. The last play. Doug Flutie, Boston College's 5-foot-9 quarterback, took the snap and avoided a sack. He sprinted right and heaved the ball sixty-five yards to no one in particular, the desperate act of a desperate gnome. It landed in the outstretched paws of his roommate, an All-American receiver named Gerard Phelan (a man whose renown is defined by this one catch). It was amazing, unbelievable, iconic. It was all the clichés we always use whenever we pretend something that just happened will never happen again. I thought my dad would be overjoyed by this miracle, because he hated Miami and loved that Flutie was Catholic and short. Maybe it did make him happy, on some level. But what he said about Doug Flutie immediately after that touchdown did not sound like joy, nor did it sound like he was talking about football.

"Well, there you go," he said without affect, still staring at the screen. "I gave up, but he did not. And that's why he is who he is, and that's why I am who I am."

It was an odd thing to hear. It was disturbing. It was out of character for my dad to say something like this, though not out of character for him to believe it. My father was born in February 1928, and his own father died two months later. He lived through the poverty of the Great Depression and cared about horse racing long after it was practical. He was a chronically depressed workaholic who was usually in a good mood. His darkest thoughts were still amusing. But this thought was different. What did it mean? Was this what he thought about when he watched college football? It didn't seem possible. Why did he tell me that? Was he talking to himself, or was he talking to me?

I had no idea in 1984, but I know now: His past was my future, and the intersection was this.

11.

A Rose by Any Other Name Would Not Impact the Rose Bowl

MITCH HEDBERG DIED IN A HOTEL ROOM IN 2005, THE CONSEquence of acute drug intoxication (which, were he still alive, he'd compare and contrast with obtuse drug intoxication). He was, and will likely remain, the only stand-up comedian I ever loved systematically. What I mean by this is that I didn't just love his material, as there are many comedians whose work makes me laugh almost as much. It means I loved his jokes even when they weren't funny. There's a throwaway line on his first album where he sheepishly admits how excited he'd feel whenever he stumbled into an opportunity to make himself hallucinate. It was like hearing a recording of my own inner monologue, spoken by a man I didn't know and would never meet. I loved the essence of Hedberg: the way he talked, the way he viewed the world, the dissonance between his onstage demeanor and his offstage sadness, and the level of sophistication he applied to unsophisticated material. I loved how he denied his own wisdom. And while I don't have a favorite Hedberg joke, this one is in the AP Top 20:

FOOTBALL

They call corn on the cob, "corn on the cob." But that's just how it comes out of the ground, man. They should call that "corn." They should call every other version "corn *off* the cob." If you cut off my arm, it's not like you'd call my arm "Mitch," but then reattach it and suddenly call me, "Mitch all together."

This joke slides into my mind whenever I get trapped in a conversation about why football is called "football," the single most untenable conundrum within the sport. I've been avoiding it for this entire book, but I've run out of real estate. There are, certainly, other issues more ominous: Words are not violence, and Will Smith will never make a movie where he plays a renegade Nigerian linguist. But unlike every other football-related dispute, this one offers no rebuttal. In every other conflict, there's always a way to reframe the problem as either (a) not real or (b) not as simple as it seems. But the problem with using the word "football" to describe football is distinct. Referring to football as "football" is closer to the incongruity Hedberg noticed about corn on the cob. It makes no sense for multiple reasons, any of which should end the argument before it even begins.

The most glaring contradiction is that lionizing the word "foot" is a lionization of kicking, and kicking happens on only about 17 percent of all football plays, unless you only watch games coached by Kirk Ferentz. Kickoffs and field goals are performed by specialists divorced from the rest of the roster, injecting an odd etymological emphasis upon a few dozen feet. We call the game football, yet striking the ball with one's foot in any non-kicking situation incurs a 10-yard penalty. This almost qualifies as dialectic sarcasm. And even if we pretend all of this is fine, the function of the foot is still overrated: For forty-three years, the longest field goal in NFL history was kicked by Tom Dempsey of the Saints, a guy born with no toes. For a whole host of mechanical and philosophical reasons, it's straight-up irrational to call football "football." Almost any expos-

A ROSE BY ANY OTHER NAME

itory alternative ("runball," "hitball," "turfball") would be more accurate.*
But all this ingrained absurdity still pales in comparison to the final contradiction: Outside of the United States, Canada, South Africa, and certain sectors of Australia, any earthling talking about football is actually talking about soccer, though putting it in those terms is a little like classifying 99.8 percent of the world population as "non-Jews" or "non-Mormons" or "non-Juggalos." This incompatibility is magnified by the historical timeline, since (what I call) soccer was already prevalent before (what I call) football had even been invented. It doesn't help that (what I call) soccer also happens to be the world's most popular sport, whereas global interest in (what I call) football equates to the status of bullfighting anywhere that isn't Spain.

The explanation as to how and why this happened is no conspiracy, nor is the explanation particularly clear. The website for the Pro Football Hall of Fame has an explainer page titled "Why Is the Game Called Football?," but it's only four paragraphs long and explains almost nothing. It was not a case of brazen theft, because nobody living in the nineteenth century was territorial about what various sports should be named. People of the nineteenth century weren't even territorial about what they should name territories ("Hey, this place has cactuses, like Mexico. Let's call it *New* Mexico."). The only truly audacious detail is that we just keep doing this, even though it undermines the worldview of eight billion non-Americans living in the Eastern and Southern Hemispheres. Americans call football "football" because that's what Americans want to call it. We offer no cogent clarification as to why this is, nor do we insist that other

---

*To be fair, this is not the only example of a sport whose name has become nonsensical over time. The term "stock car racing" originated because the cars used in races were required to be normal, unmodified vehicles that could be purchased by anyone off the street, hence the term "stock." But by the end of the 1980s, the cars used in NASCAR events were built and designed exclusively for racing and had almost no relationship to any sedan you'd get from a dealer. The one thing you will never see in a stock car race is a stock car.

nations do the same, nor do we spend much time considering how this might seem to anyone who isn't us.

This is educational.

It's not good and it's not bad. But it is important, which quietly makes it both.

⯈

One does not hear much about American exceptionalism these days. This is not surprising, since the only thing everyone seems to know about American exceptionalism is that it does not exist. The first time I encountered the phrase "American exceptionalism" was in the early 1990s, explained as a form of jingoistic propaganda. I was told it promoted the illusion of the United States being structurally and morally unique. I accepted that critique, mostly because it had never occurred to me that the United States might be viewed as well organized or moral. I didn't think that it was and I didn't think that it wasn't—I'd just never considered the premise at all, until I was informed the premise was false. It's always awkward when this type of contextual education works in reverse. As a child of the seventies, I was taught that Christopher Columbus was an explorer who discovered North America and that it was essential to memorize the names of all three of his ships. Years later, midway through high school, we were informed he was also a murderer and a rapist and not even the first explorer to arrive in the New World. But when my kids learned about Columbus, the *first* things they were taught focused on the raping and the murdering and the myth of his discovery, prompting them to wonder why they needed to learn about some random sea criminal who evidently deserved no credit for anything (and the names of his boats weren't mentioned at all). I had a similar sensation with my introduction to American exceptionalism: I was told to stop believing in something I'd never believed to begin with.

A ROSE BY ANY OTHER NAME

Over time, I've found myself reevaluating the theory of American exceptionalism, though not in the way it's usually described. The problem, in my view, has to do with an extraneous suffix. Instead of using the word "exceptionalism," we should use the word "exception." When the concept is phrased as American *exceptionalism*, it has a positive connotation built in, prompting anyone with a negative view of the United States to insist the entire notion must be false. The premise is rejected within the same moment it's considered, killing the conversation before it begins. Yet if we tweak the phrasing ever so slightly—if we instead use the phrase "the American exception"—it supports the same kind of dialogue in a neutral way, erasing any intrinsic merit without denying any flaws. To categorize something as exceptional is an autocompliment. To categorize something as an exception simply means it needs to be considered as a deviation from the norm, in a manner that might be better and might be worse.

This is how we should think about the American experience.

It should also be the way we think about American football, including the semantic irrationality of its name.

American football is not inherently "exceptional," but it's an exception to every other game and every other pastime. It does not fit on the omnifarious spectrum of sport. Even the ball itself, a noncircular prolate spheroid, is incompatible with almost any other athletic endeavor, even in an emergency. You can play baseball with a tennis ball. You can play basketball with a volleyball. You can play soccer with an unripe coconut. But a prolate spheroid works only for football or rugby, and you can't count rugby, since rugby can be played with anything. Rugby is like type O blood. You can play rugby with a rotting pumpkin or a radial tire or a human skull. The participants might not even notice.

Like so much U.S. culture, American football operates from a position of internal confidence and global disinterest. Now, to a certain kind of person, those modifiers are inaccurate. A certain kind of person reads that

FOOTBALL

sentence and thinks, "What the author actually means is *arrogance* and *incuriosity*." And you know, if that's your take, that's fine. Those alternatives are valid, because the connotations are not my concern. The theoretical problem with football calling itself "football," even though there's already a more popular sport with the same name, is unrelated to the pragmatic explanation, which is that football's relationship to soccer is completely unlike soccer's relationship to football.

I've written about soccer in the past, sometimes pejoratively. I wrote about it so pejoratively that some soccer fans have never forgiven me. I have a few regrets about that, although not enough to retract anything I wrote, including the stuff I got wrong. The biggest thing I got wrong was my insistence that people of the United States would *never* care about soccer, predicated on how soccer had been (incessantly and unsuccessfully) marketed throughout the last three decades of the twentieth century. Over and over, the media told American consumers that soccer was The Sport Of The Future, and that this destiny would be fulfilled whether they wanted it or not. This strategy failed for so many years that I assumed it would fail forever. But then, sometime during the second Bush administration, the indoctrination worked, for a variety of off-kilter reasons. Part of it had to do with soccer's saturation of youth sports and its willingness to include women. Another key was the game itself, which does have a few benefits (it's nice to start watching a sporting event at 5:00 p.m. with absolute certainly it will be over by 7:05). Yet the most critical factor was something I didn't anticipate at all. I could not foresee how the symbolic meaning of loving soccer in the United States would become so diametrically unlike how it's loved anywhere else in the world.

In most other countries, the caricature of a hardcore soccer fan is the portrait of a deranged hooligan. Bill Buford's *Among the Thugs* is the lodestar text, though such images are perpetuated in every news report of a stadium riot in Indonesia or Croatia or Poland, or whenever some African midfielder gets pelted with bananas while playing in Italy. But those incidents are the dark exceptions. Those are the worst outliers. Remove the most savage examples of intoxicated psychosis, and what remains is the (generally positive) perception of soccer as the passion of the working class. Five of the founding twelve English soccer clubs were formed in northern mill towns. In 1996, I didn't follow European soccer at all, but I still knew the bloke-coded populists in the Brit-pop band Oasis rooted for Man City. It was also known that the singer from their rival group Blur preferred Chelsea, but he was an elitist with artistic parents. His fandom meant less. Soccer was a game available to all, but it mattered most to those who were lower class, less educated, and excluded from other extensions of art and culture. Virtually all the legends of South American soccer—Pelé, Maradona, Messi—emerged from poverty. That is soccer's romantic appeal. But (of course) there's one glaring exception to this, and (of course) it's the American Exception.

The American soccer fan is a different caricature: a well-educated progressive whose nontoxic sensitivity allows them to appreciate a more beautiful game. Regardless of where they live, they're envisioned as white suburbanites from blue cities, though they choose to see themselves as citizens of the world. They've read *Among the Thugs*, but they can't relate to it. They prefer Franklin Foer's *How Soccer Explains the World*. A 2023 research paper by Johan Rewilak at the University of South Carolina was unable to prove that watching soccer makes a person liberal, but it accepted the preexisting link between soccer and leftism as a given ("It is well established that there is a strong correlation between those who follow soccer and those who vote Democrat," writes Rewilak). For the U.S. soccer fan, part of the sport's appeal is America's international inferiority at the men's game, providing a rare opportunity to see the United States as an underdog on the world stage. Most critically, the American soccer zealot feels habitually mocked by fans of American football, prompting them to see anti-soccer critics as both xenophobic and dumb (an argument easily illustrated by our unwillingness to call soccer by its proper name). This has become the U.S. soccer community's de facto relationship to football: as that of an oppressed underclass, informed by a global mentality. But for this to make symmetric sense, American football needs to see soccer in similar terms, either by affirming the accusation ("Yes, we are your oppressors") or smugly denying it ("You are not oppressed in any way"). That has never happened, in either direction. The master-slave relationship has never been consummated. Instead, football views soccer the way most Americans view the metric system: as an alleged inevitability that's okay for people in other places, but which fails to reflect our own specific connection to the world.

Nobody attacks the metric system for not making sense. Making sense is its singular purpose, so criticizing the system feels like a criticism of reason itself. Water freezes at a temperature of 0°C and boils at a temperature of 100°C, and those numeric digits were applied *in response* to the properties of water. A person did not make that decision. Water made that decision. A meter was originally designated as 1/10,000,000th of the distance from the North Pole to the equator, a French attempt at imposing scientific rationality upon an unforgiving planet. When using the metric system, earth itself is always in control. But the English imperial system functions in reverse. The imperial system generates weights and distances from imperfect representations of daily life—a foot is roughly the length of a man's foot, a yard is roughly the length of a man's stride, and a hand is four inches long and applied only to horses. The imperial system is hard to learn and frustrating to explain, but it allows for something the metric system does not: It allows individuals to *invent* which calculations are meaningful. There's an understood meaning to being six feet tall. There is no social meaning to being 1.83 meters tall. The ability to throw a baseball 100 miles per hour is an excellent benchmark for delineating arm strength,

A ROSE BY ANY OTHER NAME

just as the ability to dunk on a 10-foot basket is an ideal gauge for jumping prowess. Running one mile in four minutes will always be a touchstone for middle-distance runners, even though the mile is no longer a standard racing distance. Fahrenheit is bad for the various phases of water but better for everything else: The difference between a sweltering 100-degree afternoon, a perfect 70-degree evening, and a chilly 20-degree morning has an explicit dialectical clarity that disappears if those same digits become 38, 21, and –7. The metric system is designed for scientists. The imperial system is designed for people.

▸

Now, before you throw this book into the fireplace, allow me to project the nine reactions most people will have upon reading the previous paragraph:

1. That's true, kind of. I can almost see his point, sort of.

2. This writer is a moron.

3. This writer is an *American* moron, to the level of parody.

4. Isn't this just an unfunny version of that *Saturday Night Live* sketch where Nate Bargatze pretends to be George Washington?

5. If the difference between 38°C and 21°C lacks "explicit dialectical clarity," why not use 40 and 20? That translates to 104 and 68 in Fahrenheit, which is almost the same.

6. Who cares about the four-minute mile? It's not 1954. This argument actually makes me want to use the metric system more.

7. Does ascribing a universal social meaning to being six feet tall indicate heightism, misogyny, or both?

FOOTBALL

8. Why is this guy insulting the properties of water?

9. I really, really don't see how this has anything to do with football.

Let me state, for the record (which is, technically, this book), that I understand all nine of those reactions. I halfway support six of them. It's also true that the examples I cite as inventions made possible by the imperial system are trivial, whereas the advantages of the metric system tend to focus on things like cooking, chemistry, physics, industrial mechanics, international trade, space travel, and large plastic bottles of Mountain Dew. If someone prefers the metric system's coldly clinical logic, there is no counterpunch. It's more logical, in every dimension. But whenever someone declares that the United States should *unilaterally* adopt the metric system because everyone else in the world has already done so, they're considering the issue from a position of creative weakness. They're ceding their day-to-day relationship with reality to the inhumanity of math. And there's simply no good reason to do this, other than an insecure desire to conform with everyone else. There's no downside to "illogically" measuring weights and distances within an insular society, and the upside is psychologically massive: It allows humankind to project a sense of self onto the physical world, as opposed to having the parameters of existence imposed upon us. Moreover, it's not as if the United States *can't* use the metric system whenever it wants; it's always there, and any benefit it provides can be exploited at our own convenience.

It's easy to admit you're wrong if you don't care about being right. That's the key to language, and that's the key to happiness. It's also impossible to lose an argument if you have no real interest in what the other person is arguing: *Other people* might think you lost, but you won't. You might not even realize an argument has taken place. So if I find myself talking to a bunch of American soccer fans about the upcoming Euros, I

A ROSE BY ANY OTHER NAME

might casually employ the term "fútbol," even as I automatically transpose that term into "soccer" within my own mind. I'd make this linguistic concession for their benefit, because it might matter to them for reasons I don't fully understand. I can handle the cognitive dissonance. What those theoretical soccer fanatics would be discussing *is* football, to them. But it's not football to me, nor does it need to be.

▶

(Perhaps you're wondering why, in the previous section about the metric system, I did not make a point of mentioning how American football fields are all 100 yards long, a fact that might seem like a crucial element in my advocacy for the imperial system, particularly since my broader argument is that football is irrevocably ingrained in the American psyche. I certainly could have made that case, and it's always surprising to me that soccer does not use a universal distance for its pitch. It seems like every soccer field should be identical. But this is one of soccer's strengths, in the same way that geometric incongruities make baseball parks more interesting than football stadiums. It's also true that football fields are technically 120 yards, since we can't ignore the end zones, thereby negating the numeric perfection of 100 as the game's defining limitation. Weirdly, the main reason American football needs the imperial system is not for the length of the field but for the width. Football fields are 53 $\frac{1}{3}$ yards across, requiring a unit of measurement that's easily divisible by three. No one knows why football fields aren't 100 by 50. They probably should be. What's more, the concept of a metric football field—100 meters by 50 meters, with two 10-meter end zones—feels ideal to me. The premise of needing 10 meters for a first down does not seem unreasonable and would not skew the action. The only downside is that no team would ever be faced with the dramatic scenario of "fourth and inches," and the concept of "fourth and centimeters" sounds ridiculous. A more subtle downside would be that rushing for 2,000 meters would require a running back to gain the equivalent of 2,187 yards, and that's never been accomplished at the NFL level. Eric Dickerson would still possess the single-season rushing mark, but it would stand at 1,924 meters. Or would the number in meters ultimately be the same as it is in yards? Would the flow of the game intuitively expand to fit its new parameters, in the same way an overcrowded four-lane highway immediately becomes an overcrowded eight-lane highway the morning after construction concludes? Would a traditional five-yard run simply *become* a five-meter run? This is the kind of puzzle American football presents: Since the whole strategic enterprise is based on taking land through force, there are existential questions about how physical space works and how behavior is dictated by potential and necessity. This is part of what makes football interesting, even though no fan would consider such questions while the game is in progress. The lack of conscious consideration is what makes it meaningful. Sports are not art, but both function in the same way: What's most interesting is not what can be explained as "interesting." It's what we find interesting despite our lack of understanding. There is something poetic about a man running in motion before the snap, about the equilibrium of the wishbone formation, about the imaginary realness of the goal line's plane. There is something transfixing about the way kinematic physics operates within three-dimensional space. It's a profundity we can experience without effort, because all we need to do is watch football and forget that it's happening.)

▸

There's this thing I do that I don't understand. Maybe it's just my version of something everyone does. I'm not sure when it started, but I do know it

A ROSE BY ANY OTHER NAME

isn't something I've done my whole life. I remember it first happening in the late nineties, when I lived in Akron. But now it happens all the time, sometimes against my will.

What happens is this: Before I go to sleep, I stroll up to my kitchen and eat a bowl of cereal. I know you're not supposed to eat before bed, but I don't care. Midnight is the correct time to eat Cookie Crisp. I sit alone in the darkness, munching away, ostensibly thinking about nothing at all. But somehow, inside my dormant brain, I start telling myself little plotless stories, and the stories are always about imaginary football teams. It's a disorienting automatic process. It often feels like the story is being created by someone else and I'm hearing it for the first time, though I realize that's impossible.

The stories are inevitably about some unnamed high school or some unnamed college (never a pro team, as that would feel mimetic). It's almost always one character explaining something to another character, told in the past tense. Sometimes it's a head coach talking to his offensive coordinator about how his reliance on RPOs is ruining both of their marriages. Sometimes it's a local journalist interviewing a newly hired coach who just arrived in town, and the journalist needs to explain the unreported reason why the previous coach was fired. The most common premises focus on some eccentric interior conflict: An All-State running back, returning for his senior season, realizes an upstart sophomore has inexplicably surpassed his talent and will steal his job. A high school team is overcome with a rash of illnesses and suspensions, forcing them to play for a conference title with no available quarterback on the roster. A foreign exchange student from Sudan who's never seen football (but exhibits supernatural physical potential) must be trained to play defensive end with no knowledge of what defensive ends are supposed to do. The weirdest stories involve a completely unrelated crime—typically a heist or an assassination—that takes place in the same venue as a collegiate coaching clinic, and the criminal event is conducted while a southern Saban-like coach delivers a monotone lecture about why he still likes to call fade routes at the goal line, despite all the analytical evidence against doing so.

What's vexing about these narratives is that they never resolve themselves. No story ever reaches a conclusion before my cereal bowl hits the sink. Instead, I sidetrack my own daydreams with some arcane technical detail that goes on forever. One of my imaginary coaches will offhandedly mention that he wants to install an outside-zone running scheme, prompting someone else to ask if he plans to use his tight end as an H-back "sniffer" who pulls around the back side to block the trail defender, and then I'll spend ten minutes imagining these two unreal goofballs arguing about the strengths and weaknesses of H-back deployment. I'm sure this must sound insane, because it sounds insane to me. But it happens all the time. It happened yesterday. I cannot count the number of nights I've sat at my kitchen counter and accidentally fantasized about two fictitious men pedantically analyzing the various strengths and weaknesses of the I-formation, the power I, the Maryland Triple I, the wishbone, and the Georgia Tech flexbone. I'm actually pretty sick of listening to myself think about the wishbone. My subconscious just won't accept that it's a dead offense.

This nightly preoccupation might be the third-weirdest* thing about me. It also suggests a certain level of psychosis: I'm creating an alternative reality but also refusing to complete the machinations of that reality, fixating instead on technicalities that stop the story from having any meaning

---

*The weirdest thing about me is my belief that a close friend from college was temporarily abducted by a UFO in 1995, a theory he aggressively rejects and that I increasingly believe. I've tried to convince him to visit a hypnotist in the hope of unlocking the repressed memory, but he won't do it. The second-weirdest thing about me is that I rank my weirdest personality traits chronologically.

A ROSE BY ANY OTHER NAME

or moral. Even my fantasies are consumed by unwinnable arguments, waged against myself for no explicable motive.

But you know what? That's who I am and that's why I'm here.

▶

"I'm not into sports," goes another Hedberg joke. "I like drinking Gatorade, but that's about as far as it goes."

I can't relate to this joke, though sometimes I wish that I could. I wish I loved sports, and particularly football, a lot less than I do. It consumes too much of my memory and too much of my time. From late August until February, my whole life revolves around trying to see football games that carry no personal significance. If I didn't have a family, I'd watch thirty hours of football a week, an easy way to guarantee no new family would ever be created. I constantly worry about all the games I cannot see. I've checked my phone at 4:30 on a Sunday morning to see if the Jacksonville Jaguars were winning a game in Wembley Stadium, even though I could not remember whom they were playing, why the outcome was significant, or if the game was actually scheduled for the following week. If asked about my availability for dinner or drinks, I automatically say, "I think I'm free on Wednesday," as this is the only weeknight I'm confident there won't be any football on television. I dread autumn weddings as much as autumn funerals. You sometimes hear stories about "football widows," a term used to describe women who lose contact with their indolent husbands at the inception of every football season, almost as if the man's couch were his casket. The implication is that the wife deserves sympathy. But what about the husbands who *want* metaphoric death, yet are forced to live, even while ESPN keeps broadcasting inconvenient Mid-American games on random Tuesday evenings? Those are the real victims. I'm actually envious of people who don't give a shit about football, in the same way atheists claim to be jealous of people who believe in an afterlife. I'm envious of men who can meet a new person without secretly wondering if the guy saw Timothée Chalamet on *College GameDay* or remembers Christian Okoye. It's a shameful thing. It's an addiction I keep secret, because I know that I must. I know that if someone I like invites me to a book reading on a Friday night in November, I have to attend. I can't say, "I'd love to hang out, but Colorado State is playing Wyoming, and both teams are 6-2." Such a response would seem pathetic and immature, so I say nothing. I go to the reading and stare straight ahead, wordlessly worrying that it might be blizzarding in Laramie and I'm missing a snow game.

I could stop, I suppose. I have before, temporarily, without even trying. During my freshman year at college, I lost track of everything except music and booze, and I missed the entire 1991 Super Bowl. We were at a party thrown by a guy who didn't have a TV, and no one even noticed. Nobody is forcing me to care about this. Football is a game founded on control, but it can't control *me*. It can only control those who want to be controlled, in exchange for the fantasy that this control is my choice. I can do whatever I want.

But then I remember: This *is* what I want.

Some insanities are acceptable. This one is mine. It's normal for Americans to have an abnormal relationship to football, and I'm too normal to confront my simplicities. I want to be controlled. I like it. I don't care if it doesn't make sense. That's the best part.

I am not an exception.

I work for the exception.

Football is called "football" because that's what we call it. The reasoning is circular. The prolate spheroid is not.

Acknowledgments

The four people most responsible for the publication of *Football* are my agent, Daniel Greenberg; my editors at Penguin Press, Scott Moyers and Mia Council; and my extremely competent fact-checker, Mike Lynch. I also want to thank Bob Ethington, the only person who's had the misfortune of reading the unedited first draft of all thirteen of my books.

I often complain about technology and the modern world. Part of my consciousness is eternally trapped in the past, and this book is proof. There is, however, at least one thing about modernity that I love: text messaging. Texting has become my primary means of communication with anyone who doesn't live inside my house. Part of what I love about texting is the way certain text chains naturally coalesce around specific topics, to the point where almost nothing else is discussed within that exclusive sphere. I'm involved in one group chat where the only time we text is when one of us happens to hear the music of Black Sabbath in a nontraditional setting, such as a Thai restaurant or a petting zoo. I have another text thread with an old coworker that's been sporadically active for twenty years, yet the only things we ever seem to discuss are narrative problems within random episodes of *M*A*S*H*. But, of course, the most critical role texting plays in my life involves sports, particularly as it applies to writing

ACKNOWLEDGMENTS

this book. Many of my ideas were either initiated or shaped through ongoing text conversations that will likely continue until I die. Two of these text chains were especially integral. The first involves Jon Dolan, Brant Rumble, and Michael Weinreb (a thread mostly concerned with college sports and our personal feelings about uniforms and broadcasters). The other involves Michael Weinreb and Ben Heller (a thread mainly about pro sports and how it's covered by media). A third significant text chat is comprised of Jon Blixt, Mike Schauer, Rex Sorgatz, and Dennis Sperle (this one tends to focus on FCS teams, athletes who've recently died, and the Minnesota Vikings, though Dennis and I have a lot of side conversations about the CFB playoff committee). Other interactions warranting mention: Eli Saslow (primarily regarding the Denver Broncos and gambling); John Backer (the nexus of pro football and politics); Erik Ebeling (officiating controversies, the Kansas City Chiefs, raw athleticism); Rick Sparks (the Indianapolis Colts, things Rick hates about the Chicago Bears, and outlet malls that sell football cleats); Steve Marsh (the NFC North, problematic personalities, performance-enhancing drugs); Nick Chase and Eric Peterson (North Dakota, NIL money, the transfer portal); Dr. Chad Hanson and Dr. Dave Beck (players we dislike, the severity of certain injuries, fantasy football, and our own past). I watch all NCAA title games in Damon Brennen's living room, where we also analyze the motivations of Deion Sanders. I talk about the Tennessee Volunteers (and sometimes the LSU Tigers) with Charlie Doty. I talk about the Minnesota Gophers and the NFL's free-kick rule with Mathew Sletten. I talk about Stanford University and the concept of integrity with Mike Maerz.

A few more people and organizations who helped this book in indirect ways: Chris Ryan, NFL Films, Peter Schrager, Seth Wickersham, Bill Simmons, Michael MacCambridge, *The Sporting News,* Pro Football Reference, David Giffels, Wright Thompson, *Sports Illustrated,* Brian Windhorst, Kevin "KJ" Jackson, Greg Milner, Zander Hollander, EA Sports,

ACKNOWLEDGMENTS

Brendan Vaughan, Scott Throlson, Doug Skipper, Dave Hodgson, Roger Thomas, and the DS '93 collective (Robert Huschka, Luke Shockman, Amy Everhart, Mark Pfeifle, Denise Bower, Jon Miller).

Both of my parents are dead. That's sad for lots of reasons, one being that this is probably the first book I've ever published that would make any sense to them at all. I was raised in a home where every football game being broadcast automatically appeared on the family television, even if no one was watching. Knowledge was ingrained through osmosis. Three of my sisters (Laura, Susan, and Teresa) and one of my sisters-in-law (Marianne) never seemed particularly enamored with sports, yet they still understand the culture of football more than most people I encounter in Portland. My fourth sister, Rachel, watched hundreds of games with me when we were kids and would have been an All-State wide receiver if girls' high school football was something that had existed in the 1980s. I can't even begin to estimate how many thousands of tight spirals my two older brothers, Bill and Paul, threw to me between the ages of six and sixteen. Whenever they were working around the homestead, I would go outside and performatively play catch with myself until they noticed I needed to run some post patterns. They took me to games, they told me stories, and they bought me equipment from the hardware store. My brother-in-law Steve was always, always up for action and may have thrown me as many backyard passes as Bill and Paul combined. Steve also explained to me how the NFL Draft worked, years before he married my sister. My brother-in-law David talked to me about sports as if I were an adult when I was still very much a child, an incredible intellectual accelerant that still pays dividends today. My brother-in-law Tom thought football was ridiculous, but he was the first person who ever talked to me about the Beatles and the first person who ever told me I could make a living as a writer. My sister-in-law Nanette joined our family as a Viking fan and is now a Packer fan, a transformation both hilarious and profound.

ACKNOWLEDGMENTS

It's been a long time since I enjoyed writing a book as much as I enjoyed writing *Football*, and that's only partially due to the subject matter. The real reason is that this manuscript was written during the happiest period of my life, a circumstance exclusively tied to my immediate family. My wife, Melissa, my son, Silas, and my daughter, Hope, are the three personalities who give my life meaning. They are the people I think about within every moment of every day, and they control every thought or feeling I have about anything else. So much, in fact, that I just realized I also need to thank our dog, Trixie, because Hope will be very annoyed with me if I don't.

Index

The Academy Awards, 34
AC/DC, 29
Affirmed (horse), 244
Afghanistan, 154
Aikman, Troy, 62
Alabama Crimson Tide, 166–69
Alaska, 77
Ali, Muhammad, 194
Allen, Josh, 18
Allen, Marcus, 125
All the Right Moves (film), 159
Altman, Robert, 151
Alydar (horse), 244
Alzado, Lyle, 236
Ambedkar, B. R., 63–64
American Civil War, 148–50
American exceptionalism, 262–63
American football. *See also specific topics*
    American society and, 253–56, 261–64, 273–74
    Arena League, 232
    Canadian football compared to, 210–18
    danger in, 233–42, 248
    escapism with, 270–73
    future of, 246–52, 249n, 256–58
    GOATs in, 93–98
    history of, 43–44, 49–50, 125n, 260–62, 261n, 269–70
    race in, 176–77, 184–91, 198–203, 236
    soccer and, 264–67
    violence and, 226–27, 231–33
    war compared to, 148–56, 236
American Football League, 75
American Pharaoh (horse), 244
American society
    after 9/11 attacks, 154
    American football and, 253–56, 261–64, 273–74
    American supremacy, 220–21
    baseball in, 14, 16, 41, 55, 69, 216, 243–44
    boxing in, 226–27
    for Canadians, 209–10
    change in, 3–4
    eight-man football in, 77
    entertainment in, 26–27, 243–46, 254
    football coaches in, 158–61
    football in, 2, 11, 17–18, 50, 148–56, 215–16, 225, 234–36
    high school football in, 9–10, 37, 256
    junior high school football in, 8–9

INDEX

American society (cont.)
   masculinity in, 5
   morality in, 227–29
   NFL football in, 4, 34–39, 41,
      46–47, 67
   police violence in, 192, 195–98, 196n
   racism in, 70n, 123, 183–86,
      195–96, 196n
   religion in, 200–201, 236–38
   soccer in, 264–66, 268–69
   sports in, 42, 45, 80–81, 243–45
   Super Bowl in, 254
   television in, 2, 20–21, 26–27, 28–29,
      33–34, 36–37, 217, 217n
   Texas in, 57–58, 62–63, 69–70
   Thanksgiving in, 81–82
   Turkey day games in, 82–83
   youth in, 157–58, 170–74
America's Game (documentary), 41
America's Game (MacCambridge), 41
Among the Thugs (Buford, B.), 264–65
antifragility, 28, 30
Any Given Sunday (film), 159
Arena League, 232
Arizona Cardinals, 30, 56
Arizona State, 84
Army football, 103–4, 155–56
Atari, 136
Atlanta Falcons, 106
Auburn, 133
Australia, 261
Australian Rules football, 36
autobiographies, 7

Ball Four (Bouton), 69
Baltimore Colts, 18–19
Baltimore Ravens, 194, 201n
   Cleveland Browns and, 145–46
Bargatze, Nate, 267
Barkley, Saquon, 125, 177
Barrett, J. T., 202
baseball, 30–31, 36, 125, 263, 266–67

   in American society, 14, 16, 41, 55, 69,
      216, 243–44
   for fans, 7, 21, 26, 139, 192, 269
   Major League Baseball, 29, 35, 133,
      185, 219, 249
   World Series, 29, 35, 243–44
Based on a True Story (Macdonald),
   147–48
BASE jumping, 225
basketball, 16, 45–46, 263
   college, 29, 74, 140n, 177–78, 180
   dunking in, 267
   for fans, 13–14, 21
   NBA, 30, 35, 42, 168, 178–79, 206–7,
      249, 252–53
Bates, Michael, 110
Battle of Gettysburg, 149
Baugh, Sammy, 94
Baylor, 60
the Beatles, 91–92
Beatty, Warren, 218
Beethoven, Ludwig van, 146
Belichick, Bill, 115, 167–70, 167n
Bell, Bert, 115
Bell, Le'Veon, 230, 233
Berg, Peter, 59
Berman, David, 52–53
Biderman, David, 25–26
The Big Bang Theory (TV show), 24
Bissinger, H. G., 58–59
Black athletes. *See* race; racism
Black Athletes (documentary), 182–84,
   189–90
Black Robe Christianity, 80
Blarney Castle, 51
Bledsoe, Drew, 113
Bleier, Rocky, 176
Blur, 265
Body Heat (film), 53
Boise State Broncos, 193
Boldin, Anquan, 188
Bolt, Usain, 102

INDEX

Bonaparte, Napoleon, 149–50
Bonnett, Neil, 225–26
Boone Pickens Stadium, 137
Boston Bandits, 15*n*
Boston Celtics, 168
Boston College, 257–58
Bostrom, Nick, 130–31
Bouton, Jim, 69
Bowden, Bobby, 188
bowling, 14, 30–31
boxing, 226–27, 243–44
Boys Ranch, 56
Bradshaw, Charlie, 172–73
Bradshaw, Terry, 48–49, 110
Brady, Ben, 116
Brady, Tom
   in draft combine, 112–13
   GOATS and, 116–17, 121–22
   Manning and, 48
   for New England Patriots, 96–97, 114–15
   receivers for, 106–7
   reputation of, 103, 113–14
   Rice, J., and, 98–99
Branch, Cliff, 110
Briscoe, Marlin, 186
Brock, Dieter, 218
Brokaw, Tom, 182–83
Brown, Antonio, 230–31, 233
Brown, Jim, 94–96, 98, 125*n*, 194–95
Brown, Paul, 47–49
Brown, Ron, 110
Bryant, Bear, 75, 167–68
Bryant, Kobe, 42
Buffalo Bills
   Cincinnati Bengals and, 125
   Hamlin for, 241–42
   Kansas City Chiefs and, 18
   Kelly, J., for, 48
   in Super Bowl, 88
Buford, Bill, 264–65
Buford, Kate, 123

Burnside, John Thrift Meldrum, 207*n*
Burnside rules, 207, 207*n*
Burrow, Joe, 202–3
Bush, George H. W., 228
Bush, Reggie, 125
Butthole Surfers, 53

Caesars Palace, 141
Calgary Stampeders, 216
Call of Duty (video game), 151
Cameron, Bob, 211
Camp, Walter
   football rules and, 207, 214–15
   legacy of, 43–44, 93, 149–50, 152, 155
Campbell, Dan, 164
Campbell, Earl, 55*n*, 176
Canadian football
   American football compared to, 210–18
   Canada and, 208–14, 261
   Canadian Football League, 75, 207, 210–14, 216–19, 217*n*, 221
   rules of, 206–8, 218–21
The Canadian Football League (O'Brien), 217–18
Candlestick Park, 114
Cannon, Billy, 125
capitalism, sports and, 252–54
Carlisle Indian Industrial School, 94, 103–4, 109, 125*n*
Carlisle Indians, 123
Carolina Panthers, 29–30, 76, 233
Carpenter, Rob, 176
Carruth, Rae, 76
Carter, Michael, 110
Carville, James, 153
Catholicism, 64
CBS, 22, 24, 65–68, 134, 183, 232–33
Cecil, Chuck, 232–33
cerebral sports, 30–31
Chalamet, Timothée, 274
Charles, Josh, 64

INDEX

Cheers (TV show), 24
Chicago Bears, 29–30, 94, 110, 186
children, 127–32. *See also specific topics*
Chomsky, Noam, 37–38
Chronic Traumatic Encephalopathy (CTE), 248
   danger of, 229–33
   science of, 223–24
Cincinnati Bengals, 97, 125
Citizen Kane (film), 92
C. K., Louis, 83
Clapton, Eric, 6
Clark, Caitlin, 177–78, 180
Clark, Dwight, 86–87
Clemson, 150n
Cleveland Browns
   Baltimore Ravens and, 145–46
   Brown, J., for, 94–96
   Brown, P., for, 47–49
   coaches for, 168–69
Coach (TV show), 159
Coca-Cola, 92
Coleco, 132
college basketball, 29, 74, 140n, 177–78, 180
college football
   Brady, T., in, 114
   Cotton Bowl, 88
   fans of, 38–39
   future of, 246–48
   Gator Bowl, 173–74
   Heisman Trophy, 133, 140n, 186, 201n
   high school football and, 74
   history of, 100–101
   at Michigan Stadium, 23
   National Black College Football Championship game, 187
   NCAA national title game, 166–67
   NIL revenue in, 73
   1984 Orange Bowl, 18
   race in, 185

   Southwest Conference in, 89
   2006 Rose Bowl, 18
   video games, 135–39, 135n
colonialism, 213
Colorado State, 154, 274
Columbus, Christopher, 262
comic books, 175–76
concussions. *See* Chronic Traumatic Encephalopathy
Corinthians (bible), 72
Coryell, Don, 47, 162
Cosell, Howard, 10, 175
Cotton Bowl, 88
COVID pandemic, 249
Creed, 82–84
Cribbs, Josh, 187
cricket, 26, 30–31
Cricket, 36
Cromwell, Norman, 186
Csonka, Larry, 176
CTE. *See* Chronic Traumatic Encephalopathy
Cunningham, Randall, 187–89
Curry, Steph, 16

Dallas Cowboys
   as America's Team, 54–55, 66–68, 81–83
   Denver Broncos and, 82
   Detroit Lions and, 81–82
   Gent for, 73
   Hayes for, 109
   Jones for, 74–75
   Landry for, 47
   Pittsburgh Steelers and, 55, 142–44
   reputation of, 68–70, 70n, 82–84
   San Francisco 49ers and, 85–87
   Smith, E., for, 96
   Staubach for, 64–66
   Texas and, 55–56, 62, 88–89
   Washington Redskins and, 65–66
   White for, 84–88

INDEX

danger
   in American football, 233–42, 248
   risk and, 229–33
   in sports, 223–27
Dattilio, Gerry, 219
da Vinci, Leonardo, 122
Davis, Miles, 20
Day, Ryan, 174
Daytona International Speedway, 225–226
Dazed and Confused (film), 159
Death of a Salesman (Miller), 15
Debbie Does Dallas (film), 71–72
Deep Purple, 205–6, 221
DeLillo, Don, 151–52
Dempsey, Tom, 260–61
Denver Broncos, 29–30, 39, 82
Detroit Lions, 81–83, 96
Devil Wears Prada (film), 68
Diamond, Jared, 212–13, 212n
Dickerson, Eric, 74–75, 270
Dickey, Eldridge, 187
Dierdorf, Dan, 97
Diesel, Vin, 26
Disneyland, 127–31
Dorsett, Tony, 85
drowning, 233–34
drugs, 234, 259
Duerson, Dave, 224
Dukakis, Michael, 228
Dunn, Roderick, 76
Dylan, Bob, 54

Earnhardt, Dale, 225–26
Earnhardt, Dale, Jr., 226
EA Sports College Football (video game), 135–39, 135n
East Timor, 38–39
Edelman, Julian, 186
Edmonton Eskimos, 218
Edwards, Harry, 184
Eeghen, Mark van, 176

eight-man football, 77
Eisenhower, Dwight D., 103–4
Elizabeth (queen), 36
Elliott, Phil, 70–71
Elway, John, 95
End Zone (DeLillo), 151–52
England. *See* United Kingdom
Enron, 135–36
Epstein, David, 102
Erving, Julius, 42
escapism, 5, 35, 37–38, 270–73
ESPN, 25, 70n, 73–74, 166, 192–93, 273–74
Ethridge, Tyler, 79–81, 89
Euclid, 122
Europe, 109, 265, 268–69
Everything Everywhere All at Once (film), 34

Facenda, John, 46–47
fantasy football, 139–48
Farmer Boy (Wilder), 165–66
The Fast and the Furious (movie), 26
Favre, Brett, 95
Federal Trade Commission, 116
Ferentz, Kirk, 260
Ferragamo, Vince, 218–19
A Few Good Men (film), 161, 171–72
field goals, 260–61
Fields, Justin, 202
Final Four tournament, 29
flag football, 15
Flavor Flav, 182
Flood, Curt, 192
Florida Gators, 171–72
Florida State, 104, 188
Floyd, George, 192
Flutie, Doug, 218, 258
Foer, Franklin, 265
football. *See specific topics*
Football (Camp), 149–50
football cards, 8, 175–76, 203

INDEX

football coaches
  on all-22 view, 25
  in American society, 158–61
  journalists and, 10
  legendary, 166–70, 167n
  with players, 11
  reputation of, 161–66, 170–74
  training with, 9
A Football Life (documentary), 64
football practice, 16–17
football rules, 43–44
football uniforms, 150n
football video games, 131–39
Fortnite (video game), 131
The Fourth Dimension (Rucker), 214
Fouts, Dan, 47
Fox News, 52
France, 35–36, 266
Franklin, Dennis, 185
Frazier, Tommie, 187
Fredrickson, George M., 149
Fresno State, 125
Friday Night Lights (Bissinger), 58–61, 74–75
Friday Night Lights (film), 59
Friday Night Lights (TV show), 59–60, 62–65, 74–75, 159
Friends (TV show), 15

Gambler (Walters), 141–42
gambling, 139–48, 140n, 142n
GameStop, 136
Gator Bowl, 173–74
Gault, Willie, 110
Gauss, Carl Friedrich, 122
Gent, Peter, 68–71, 70n, 73–74
Georgia Bulldogs, 166–67
Gibbs, Joe, 47
Gillan, Ian, 205–6
Gillis, Shane, 152

Glanville, Jerry, 163
GOATs
  in American football, 93–98
  in history, 92–93
  Moss, R., and, 104–12, 123–24
  in music, 91–92
  in NFL football, 98–103, 111–15, 123–26
  Thorpe, J., as, 103–4, 116–22
The Godfather Part II (film), 136
Goldberg, Zach, 180–81
golf
  baseball and, 30–31
  costs of, 14
  live, 21
  pace of, 26
  simulations of, 16
Graham, Otto, 47–49
Grambling, 182n, 188
Grand Theft Auto (video game), 131
Grange, Red, 94, 103
Grant, Bud, 213
Grant, Ulysses, 149
Gran Turismo (film), 132
Grateful Dead, 21
Great Depression, 258
Green, Darrell, 102
Green Bay Packers, 186, 194
  Detroit Lions and, 83
  in NFL Championship game, 109
  operating costs of, 251n
  Starr for, 47
  in Super Bowl, 216
Gretzky, Wayne, 92
Grey Cup, 212, 212n
Griffin, Archie, 155
Gruden, Jon, 163
Guerrero, Alex, 116–17
Guns, Germs, and Steel (Diamond), 212–13, 212n
Guns N' Roses, 29

◄ 284 ►

INDEX

Hall, Kenneth, 75–76, 79, 89
Hall Trophy, 75–76
Hamlin, Damar, 241–42
Harbaugh, Jim, 193–94
   for Michigan Wolverines, 255
Hard Knocks (TV show), 164
Harris, James, 186
Harris, Kamala, 160
Harris, Paul, 79
Harrison, George, 6
Harry Potter ride, 128–29
Hartman, Sid, 104
Harvard University, 60
Haskins, Dwayne, 202
Hawkins, Trip, 134–35
Hayes, Bob "Bullet," 109–10
Hayes, Woody, 154, 173–74, 173n, 215
Heaven Can Wait (film), 218
Hedberg, Mitch, 259–60, 273
Heffelfinger, William "Pudge," 93, 97
Heisman Trophy, 133, 140n, 186, 201n
Heller, Joseph, 54
Henry, Derrick, 99
"The Heresy of Zone Defense" (Hickey), 42
Hernandez, Aaron, 15n, 229
Hickey, Dave, 42, 45
Higbee, Tyler, 140
Higgins, Tee, 241
high school football
   in American society, 9–10, 37, 256
   college football and, 74
   future of, 248
   Hall Trophy in, 75–76
   in Ohio, 57
   six-man football in, 77–81
   statistics, 76n
   on television, 22–23
   in Texas, 56–59, 61, 75–76
Hill, Tony, 65
Hill, Tyreek, 102

hockey
   participation in, 14
   Stanley Cup, 35
   understanding, 42–43, 43n
Hogeboom, Gary, 87–88
Holieway, Jamelle, 187
Home Field (Texana), 56–57
Hornung, Paul, 186
horse racing, 243–46, 253–54, 256, 258
Houdini, Harry, 94
Houston Lutheran High, 75–76
Houston Oilers, 55n, 65, 218
Houston Texans, 74, 145–46
How Soccer Explains the World (Foer), 265
Hud (film), 78
Hudson, Rock, 172
Huff, Sam, 232–33
The Human Condition (film trilogy), 86
Humane Society, 52
Hunter, Travis, 100
Hurt, William, 53
Hurts, Jalen, 166–67

Idiocracy (film), 83
imperial system, 266–68
India, 36
Indianapolis Colts, 29–30, 39, 112n. *See also* Baltimore Colts
Indonesia, 38–39
I Never Played the Game (Cosell), 10
The Inner Civil War (Fredrickson), 149
Iraq, 154
Islam, 237
Iverson, Allen, 104

Jackson, Bo, 133–35
Jackson, Lamar, 180, 201, 201n
Jackson, Phil, 42
Jackson, Russ, 218
Jacksonville Jaguars, 34–35, 273
Jainism, 237
Japan, 36

INDEX

Jefferson, Justin, 119–20
Jenkins, Sally, 98, 123
Jewett, George, 185
Johnson, Butch, 144
Johnson, Chris, 102
Johnson, J. D. "Boody," 75
Johnson, Jimmy, 88
John Tyler High School, 76
Jokić, Nikola, 42
Jones, Cardale, 202
Jones, Jerry, 74–75, 88
Jones, Paul, 56
Jordan, Homer, 187
Jordan, Michael, 95
journalists. *See* media
Joyce, James, 92
junior high school football, 8–9, 239–41
Justify (horse), 244

Kaepernick, Colin, 191–201
Kansas City Chiefs, 201*n*
    Buffalo Bills and, 18
    Houston Texans and, 145–46
    Mahomes for, 138–39
    Montana for, 95
Kansas Jayhawks, 154
Kapp, Joe, 218
Kelce, Travis, 186
Kelly, Brian, 164–66
Kelly, Chip, 163
Kelly, Jim, 48
Kennedy, John F., 69
Kent State, 186
Kentucky Derby, 244
Kentucky Wildcats, 172–73, 180
Keteyian, Armen, 142
Khan, Genghis, 92
Klosterman, Dan, 10
Kuechly, Luke, 233

Landry, Tom, 47, 53, 69–71, 70*n*, 88
The Last Picture Show (film), 78

"Layla," 6
Leach, Mike, 163
Leaf, Ryan, 82
Letterkenny (TV show), 208
Lewis, Carl, 69
Lincoln, Abraham, 122
Lindley, Ryan, 30
Liske, Pete, 215–16
Lloyd, Odin, 15*n*
Lofton, James, 110
Lombardi, Vince, 47, 162
Los Angeles Chargers. *See* San Diego/
    Los Angeles Chargers
Los Angeles Lakers, 16, 168
Los Angeles Rams, 186
    Arizona Cardinals and, 30
    Brown, R., on, 110
    in NFL playoffs, 65
    in Super Bowl, 218–19
Lott, Ronnie, 5
Louisiana State University, 150*n*,
    164–65, 202–3
Lynch, Marshawn, 125

MacCambridge, Michael, 41
Macdonald, Norm, 147–48
Mackey, John, 229
Madden, John, 163
Madden NFL (video game), 134–36, 176
Mad Max: Fury Road (film), 27–28
Mad Men (TV show), 29
Mahomes, Patrick, 138–39, 198–99
    Allen and, 18
    salary of, 73
Major League Baseball, 29, 35, 133, 185,
    219, 249
Makato West High School, 160
Manning, Arch, 140*n*
Manning, Eli, 225–26
Manning, Peyton, 48, 225–26
Manning Passing Academy, 101
Man O' War (horse), 244

INDEX

Manufacturing Consent (Chomsky), 37–38
Maradona, Diego, 265
Maraniss, David, 123
Marino, Dan, 95, 100–101
Marley, Bob, 240
Marshall, Bobby, 185
Marshall, George Preston, 186
Marshall University, 105, 108
*M*A*S*H* (film), 151
Mattel, 132
Matuszak, John, 69–70
McCaffrey, Christian, 176–77, 181–82, 203
McDaniel, Mike, 159–60
McVay, Sean, 161–62
meaning, 41–50
media
   mediation and, 17–18, 21–22
   sports in, 10–11
memoirs, 8
Mendenhall, Rashard, 181–82
merchandising, 251
Meredith, Don, 70–71
Merron, Jeff, 70n
Messi, Lionel, 265
Metallica, 29
metric system, 266–70
Metro-Dynasties, 59n
Meyer, Urban, 171–72
Miami Dolphins, 18, 31–33
Miami Hurricanes, 88, 153–54, 257–58
Michigan Stadium, 23
Michigan State, 69
Michigan Wolverines, 23, 114, 154–55, 174, 185, 194
   Harbaugh for, 255
Miller, Braxton, 202
Minnesota Vikings, 86
   Atlanta Falcons and, 106
   Moss, R., for, 104–6

   in NFL playoffs, 106
   in Super Bowl, 87, 188
Missouri University, 154
Mitchell, Brian, 187
Monday Night Football, 35, 65, 125, 175–76, 241–44
Montana, Joe, 47, 85–87
   career of, 95–96
   reputation of, 98, 114
   Young and, 105
Montreal Alouettes, 208, 211, 219
Moon, Warren, 188–89, 218
morality
   free will and, 230–32
   moral conflict, 227–29
   philosophy of, 224–25
   sports and, 233–42
Moss, Randy, 104–12, 123–24
Motley, Marion, 185
Mott's, 73
Mountain Dew, 268
Mount Everest, 225, 227
movies, 26–28, 34. *See also specific films*
Muñoz, Anthony, 97
Musburger, Brent, 257
Muscular Christianity, 149–50, 152
music, 29

Nagurski, Bronko, 94
NASCAR, 225–26, 261n
National Black College Football Championship game, 187
Native Americans, 94, 123
Native American Son (Buford, K.), 123
Naval Academy, 64
Navy football, 155–56
NBA basketball. *See* basketball
NBC, 19, 59–60, 62–63, 182–83, 217n, 249n
NCAA athletes, 74, 110. *See also specific athletes*
Nebraska, 77

INDEX

Nebraska Corn Huskers, 18, 160, 218–19
Nehemiah, Renaldo, 110
Nelson, Craig T., 159
Nerf footballs, 8, 66
New England Patriots, 186
   Bledsoe for, 113
   Brady, T., for, 96–97, 114–15
   Miami Dolphins and, 31–33
   Moss, R., for, 106–7
   New York Giants and, 106
Newman, Paul, 173*n*
Newton, Cam, 98
Newton, Isaac, 99
New York Giants, 232–33
   Baltimore Colts and, 18–19
   New England Patriots and, 106
   in Super Bowl, 127–28
The New York Times (newspaper), 52, 119, 181, 183
NFL football. *See also specific topics*
   abroad, 273
   in American society, 4, 34–39, 41, 46–47, 67
   as business, 72–74, 119–20, 152–53, 248–53, 249*n*, 257
   Canadian football compared to, 211–14
   for Canadians, 209–10
   college football and, 248
   CTE for, 224, 230–31
   Dallas Cowboys and, 54
   as distraction, 3–4
   draft combine, 112–13, 133–34
   field goals in, 260–61
   gambling on, 141
   GOATs in, 98–103, 111–15, 123–26
   halftime shows in, 82–83
   history of, 47–48, 93–94, 185
   ideology of, 61
   metric system and, 269–70
   myths about, 4–6
   NBA basketball compared to, 42
NFL draft, 101
NFL Man of the Year, 224
NFL Network, 64, 96, 199–200
NFL Players Association, 133
NFL SuperPro Club, 8
   pace of, 31–32
   player strikes in, 73
   Pro Football Hall of Fame, 200–201, 261–62
   racism in, 179–80, 185–91
   receiving records in, 104–5
   rushing records in, 94–96, 176–77
   semiotics of, 31–33
   7-on-7 football and, 101
   on television, 2, 10–11, 19–26, 29–33, 62–63, 241–42, 253
   Turkey Day games in, 81–83
   understanding, 44–45
   USFL football and, 10
NFL playoffs. *See also* Super Bowl
   AFC championship, 201*n*
   AFC Divisional Playoff, 145–46
   Los Angeles Rams in, 65
   Minnesota Vikings in, 106
   1981 NFC Championship game, 86–87, 114
   1958 NFL Championship game, 18–20
   1967 NFL Championship game, 109
   Philadelphia Eagles in, 85
   Riggins in, 176
   San Francisco 49ers in, 194
   2021 AFC Divisional Playoff game, 18
The NFL Today (TV show), 183
Nicholson, Jack, 161
Nickelback, 82
NIL (Name, Image, and Likeness), 73
9/11 attacks, 82–83, 154
nine-man football, 8–9, 8*n*, 77
Nintendo Entertainment System, 132–33, 136
Noll, Chuck, 48–49

INDEX

Nolte, Nick, 72, 72*n*
North America. *See also specific topics*
   football in, 2, 261
   sports in, 121
   Super Bowl in, 35
   tackle football in, 14–15
North Dakota, 51–52, 58
North Dakota State, 168
North Dallas Forty (film), 67–69, 71–72, 74–75
North Dallas Forty (Gent), 68–75
Notre Dame, 85, 104, 114, 164–65, 186

Oakland Raiders, 70
   defense of, 110–11
   Dickey for, 187
   Jackson, B., for, 133–34
Oasis, 265
O'Brien, Steve, 217–18
O'Connell, Kevin, 161–62
Ohio State Buckeyes, 23, 154–55, 173–74
   Black quarterbacks for, 202–3
   fans of, 57
The Oiler Cannonball (film), 55*n*
Oklahoma Sooners, 38, 89, 154, 162
Oklahoma State, 137
Okoye, Christian, 274
Ole Miss, 150*n*
Olympics
   flag football in, 15
   in Paris, 101–2
   records in, 110
   in Stockholm, 93
   Thorpe, J., in, 99–100
   track and field at, 108–9
   trials for, 110
Orange Bowl, 18
Oregon State, 154
Oregon University, 154
Osborne, Tom, 18, 160

Ottawa Rough Riders/Redblacks, 210
overtime football, 19, 29–30
Owens, Jesse, 102

Pacino, Al, 159
Paisley, Brad, 187–88
Palmer, Carson, 136
Parcells, Bill, 170
Parsons, Micah, 119
Pascal's Wager, 130
Path Lit by Lightning (Maraniss), 123
Payton, Walter, 95, 98, 125
Peanuts (comic strip), 92
Pearson, Drew, 86, 187
Pelé, 265
Pelosi, Nancy, 80
Peltier, Leonard, 98
Penn State, 150*n*, 152, 215–16
Permian High Panthers, 59–60
Petro-Dynasties, 59*n*
Phelan, Gerard, 258
Philadelphia Eagles
   Barkley for, 177
   Cunningham for, 187
   on *Monday Night Football*, 65
   in NFL playoffs, 85
Phil Simms, 127–28
pickleball, 14
Pimlico race track, 245
ping-pong, 14
Pittsburgh Steelers
   Bradshaw, T., for, 48–49
   Dallas Cowboys and, 55, 142–44
Pizarro, Francisco, 213
Plano East Senior High, 76
police violence, 192, 195–98, 196*n*
Pollard, Fritz, 185
Pop Warner football, 109
postmodernism, 7
Pringle, Mike, 208
Procter & Gamble, 250
Pro Football Hall of Fame, 200–201

INDEX

Public Enemy, 182
Purdy, Brock, 73

Quakers, 237

race
  in American football, 176–77, 184–91, 198–203, 236
    Kaepernick and, 191–201
  in sports, 177–84, 182n
racism, 153
  in American society, 70n, 123, 183–86, 195–96, 196n
  in NFL football, 179–80, 185–91
Ragland, Shannon P., 172–73
The Raid (film), 27
Randle El, Antwaan, 188
Ratliff, Harold, 75
Raye, Jimmy, 187
The Real All Americans (Jenkins), 123
Real Sports (TV show), 229
Reid, Eric, 192
religion, 200–201, 236–38
Rewilak, Johan, 265–66
Rice, Grantland, 94
Rice, Jerry, 96, 98–99, 104–5, 111–12
Rice, Tony, 187
Richardson, Anthony, 112n
Richland Springs, 79
Riggins, John, 176
Riley, Pat, 69
risk, 229–33
R. Kelly, 220
Robinson, Jackie, 185
Rockingham Speedway, 226
Rodgers, Johnny, 125
Romo, Tony, 26
Rooney Rule, 153
Rose, Pete, 139
Rose Bowl, 18
Rosenberg, Michael, 154–55
Royal, Darrell, 215

Rucker, Rudy, 214, 214n
rugby, 36, 208n, 263
Russell, Bill, 194–95
Ruth, Babe, 125, 244
Ryan, Bob, 54–56
Ryan, Nolan, 16
Rypien, Mark, 185

Saban, Nick, 166–70
St. Louis Cardinals, 67–68, 97. *See also* Arizona Cardinals
Salvation Army, 82
Sam, Michael, 152–53
Samoa, 191
San Angelo Standard-Times (newspaper), 79
Sanders, Barry, 96, 125
Sanders, Deion, 73, 187
Sanders, Shedeur, 73
San Diego/Los Angeles Chargers, 18, 47, 232
San Francisco 49ers
  Dallas Cowboys and, 85–86
  Kaepernick for, 180–81, 191–92
  Lott for, 5
  McCaffrey for, 176–77
  Nehemiah for, 110
  in NFL playoffs, 194
  Purdy for, 73
  reputation of, 85, 114
  Rice, J., for, 96
  in Super Bowl, 47–48, 194, 198–99
  in Super Bowl XVI, 87–88
Santa Anita racetrack, 245
Saratoga racetrack, 245
Sash, Tyler, 229
Saving Private Ryan (film), 24
Schaap, Dick, 95
Schembechler, Bo, 154
Schweitzer, Albert, 63–64
scuba diving, 225
Seabiscuit (horse), 244

INDEX

Sealy High School, 74–75
seatbelts, 233–34
Seattle Seahawks, 56
Seattle Slew (horse), 244
Seau, Junior, 225
Secretariat (horse), 244
Seinfeld (TV show), 24
7-on-7 football, 101
sexism, 178
Shakespeare, William, 122
Shanahan, Kyle, 161–62
Shaw, Bernard, 228
Sherrod, Rick, 59*n*
"She Watch Channel Zero?!," 182
Shula, Don, 167–68
Simpson, O. J., 4, 73, 125, 215–16
The Simpsons (TV show), 83
simulation theory, 130–31
six-man football, 77–81, 88–89
skateboarding, 225
Skycam cameras, 25
skydiving, 234
Skylab, 67
Slap Shot (film), 173*n*
The Slaughter Rule (film), 159
Smith, Alex, 193–94
Smith, Emmitt, 96
Smith, Robert, 105
Smith, Will, 260
"Smoke on the Water," 205–6, 221
Snyder, Jimmy "the Greek," 183
soccer
    fans of, 21, 30, 268–69
    international appeal of, 13–14, 98, 261, 263–66
    stadium riots, 264–65
    in World Cup, 35–36
softball, 14
Solomon, Freddie, 187
Sony PlayStation, 135–36
South Africa, 261
South America, 265

Southern Methodist University, 110, 150*n*
Spain, 213
Spin (magazine), 135–36
The Sporting News (magazine), 96, 172
sports. *See also specific sports*
    in American society, 42, 45, 80–81, 243–45
    in Australia, 36
    capitalism and, 252–54
    cerebral, 30–31
    during COVID pandemic, 249
    CTE and, 229
    danger in, 223–27
    as entertainment, 27–28
    as escapism, 37–38
    in Europe, 109
    fans, 273–74
    gambling on, 139–48, 140*n*, 142*n*
    meaning from, 41–50
    in media, 10–11
    metric system and, 269–70
    morality and, 233–42
    names of, 261*n*
    in North America, 121
    participation in, 13–14
    race in, 177–84, 182*n*
    racism in, 185
    strikes in, 73, 219, 251
    on television, 30–31
Sports Illustrated (magazine), 86, 110
Spradlin, G. D., 72
Spurrier, Steve, 163
Stabler, Kenny, 187, 229
stadium riots, 264–65
Staley, Brandon, 159–60
Stallworth, John, 49
Stanley Cup, 35
Stapp, Scott, 83–84
Starr, Bart, 47, 215
"The Star Spangled Banner," 197
Star Wars ride, 128–31

INDEX

Staubach, Roger, 62–67, 71–72, 84–87, 89
Stingley, Darryl, 231–32, 238
Stratego (board game), 151
strikes, in sports, 73, 219, 251
Stroud, C. J., 202
Succession (TV show), 29
Summers, Champ, 69
Sun Tzu, 152
Super Bowl
  in American society, 254
  Brady, T., in, 96–97
  Buffalo Bills in, 88
  on CBS, 24
  Chicago Bears in, 110
  Green Bay Packers in, 216
  Los Angeles Rams in, 218–19
  Minnesota Vikings in, 87, 188
  Montana in, 95
  MVPs, 64, 113, 127, 176, 186
  New England Patriots in, 113
  New York Giants in, 127–28
  in North America, 35
  race in, 185
  San Francisco 49ers in, 47–48, 194, 198–99
  Super Bowl I, 22
  Super Bowl X, 143
  Super Bowl XII, 8, 65
  Super Bowl XIII, 55, 142–44
  Super Bowl XVI, 87–88
  Super Bowl XVIII, 125
  Super Bowl XXV, 274
  Super Bowl LVIII, 22
  viewership of, 2
  Williams, D., in, 182, 182*n*
Supreme Court, 146–47
Supermoto cycle racing, 225
Survivor (TV show), 87
Sutherland, Donald, 208–9
Sweat, T'Vondre, 112–13
Swift, Taylor, 120

Swingers (film), 132
Switzer, Barry, 162
Symphony No. 5 (Beethoven), 146

Tablet (magazine), 180–81
tackle football, 14–15
Tagovailoa, Tua, 166–67
Taleb, Nassim Nicholas, 28
Taliaferro, George, 186
Tampa Bay Buccaneers, 97, 113, 133, 182*n*
Tarkenton, Fran, 188
Tatum, Jack, 231–32
Taylor, Lawrence, 98
teachers, 120–21
Tebow, Tim, 172, 200, 215
Tecmo Bowl (video game), 132–35
Ted Lasso (TV show), 159
TED Talks, 170
television
  advertising on, 249–50
  in American society, 2, 20–21, 26–27, 28–29, 33–34, 36–37, 217, 217*n*
  audiences, 24
  high school football on, 22–23
  NFL football on, 2, 10–11, 19–26, 29–33, 62–63, 241–42, 253
  Skycam cameras for, 25
  sports on, 30–31
10-Yard Fight (video game), 132
Tennessee State, 187
Tennessee Titans, 34–35, 56
Tennessee Volunteers, 154
tennis, 14, 21, 30–31, 36, 170
Tetris (video game), 131
Texana, Charles N. Prothro, 56–57
Texas
  in American society, 57–58, 62–63, 69–70
  culture of, 52–53, 59–61, 74
  Dallas Cowboys and, 55–56, 62, 88–89

◀ 292 ▶

INDEX

high school football in, 56–59, 61, 75–76
   Petro-Dynasties in, 59n
   six-man football in, 77–81
Texas A&M, 60, 74–75
Texas Christian University, 60
Texas Longhorns, 18, 89, 140n, 154
Texas Stadium, 65, 76, 82–83
Texas Tech, 74
Texas Western, 180
Thatcher, Margaret, 160
Theismann, Joe, 218
The Thin Thirty (Ragland), 172–73
This American Life (radio show), 52
Thornton, Billy Bob, 59
Thorpe, Charles, 122–23
Thorpe, Jim
   biography of, 93–94, 117–19, 122–23
   career of, 98–100, 102–3, 109, 124–26, 125n
   as GOAT, 103–4, 116–22
Three-Down Problem. *See* Canadian football
Thrower, Willie, 186
Thursday Night Football, 29–30, 39
TikTok, 170
tobacco, 232
Tomlin, Mike, 153
tourism, 51–53
track and field, 14, 108–9, 119
training, 9, 101, 114, 122–23, 164, 248
tribalism, 5
Triple Crown, 244
Trump, Donald, 80, 152–53, 180–81
Turkey Day games, 81–83
Tyson, Mike, 105

UFOs, 272n
Ulysses (Joyce), 92
Unitas, Johnny, 19
United Kingdom, 35–36, 266, 273
United States. *See also* American society

Agricultural Census, 245
American Civil War, 148–50
American exceptionalism, 262–63
   Canada and, 209–10
Capitol building, 80
Federal Trade Commission, 116
government, 80–81
Great Depression in, 258
metric system in, 268
monoculture, 226
Native Americans in, 94, 123
9/11 attacks in, 82–83, 154
racetracks in, 244
Supreme Court, 146–47
teachers in, 120–21
track and field in, 108–9
in Vietnam War, 64, 155, 173n, 176
Universal Studios, 127–29
University of California Los Angeles, 150n
University of Colorado, 73
University of Nevada, 192–93
University of North Carolina, 167n
University of Southern California, 18, 136
University of Texas, 74
University of Texas Press, 56–57
University of Toronto, 207n
USFL football, 10

Varsity Blues (film), 159
Vertigo (film), 24
VHS tape technology, 115
Vick, Michael, 135, 201n
Vietnam War, 64, 155, 173n, 176
The Violent World of Sam Huff (documentary), 232–33
Vitale, Dick, 14n
volleyball, 14
VR headsets, 16–17

Waco High, 75–76
Walker, Herschel, 88, 110

INDEX

Walls, Everson, 85
Wall Street Journal, 25–26
Walsh, Bill, 47–48, 162
Walters, Billy, 141–42
Walz, Tim, 160
War as They Knew It (Rosenberg), 154–55
Washington, Gene, 187
Washington, George, 122, 152, 267
Washington, Kenny, 185
Washington Post (newspaper), 101–2, 181, 196n
Washington Redskins, 65–66, 182, 185–86
Waters, Andre, 224
Watt, J. J., 110
Webster, Mike, 223–24
Wembley Stadium, 273
West Point, 152
West Virginia sports, 108
Wheaties, 94
White, Danny, 84–88
Wikipedia, 51
Wilder, Laura Ingalls, 165–66
Will, George, 7
Williams, Caleb, 38

Williams, Doug, 182, 182n, 188
Williams, Jason, 108
Willis, Bill, 185
wingsuit flying, 225
Winnipeg Blue Bombers, 211
Winslow, Kellen, II, 153–54
Winslow, Kellen, Sr., 153–54
Wintour, Anna, 68
The Wire (TV show), 24
WNBA, 178
World Cup, 35–36
World Football League, 84–85
World Series, 29, 35, 243–44
World Trade Center, 83
wrestling, 14
Wright, Eric, 86–87
Wright, Rayfield, 69
Wyche, Steve, 199–200
Wyoming University, 154, 274

xenophobia, 266

Yale football, 43, 93
Young, Steve, 96, 105, 125
Young, Vince, 18